# One of the Children

Men and Masculinity
*Michael Kimmel, Editor*

# One of the Children

## Gay Black Men in Harlem

William G. Hawkeswood

EDITED BY

Alex W. Costley

UNIVERSITY OF CALIFORNIA PRESS

*Berkeley / Los Angeles / London*

University of California Press
Berkeley and Los Angeles, California

University of California Press
London, England

Copyright © 1996 by The Regents of the University of California

Library of Congress Cataloging-in-Publication Data

Hawkeswood, William G., d. 1992.
    One of the children : gay black men in Harlem / William G.
Hawkeswood ; edited by Alex W. Costley.
        p.   cm. — (Men and masculinity ; 2)
    Includes bibliographical references and index.
    ISBN 0-520-08112-9 (cloth : alk. paper)). —
ISBN 0-520-20212-0 (pbk. : alk. paper)
    1. Afro-American gays—New York (N.Y.)   2. Gay
communities—New York (N.Y.)   3. Harlem (New York, N.Y.)—
Social conditions.   4. AIDS (Disease)—New York (N.Y.)
I. Costley, Alex W.   II. Title.
III. Series: Men and masculinity (Berkeley, Calif.) ; 2.
HQ76.2.U52N55   1996
305.38'9664'097471—dc20                                    94-49565
                                                                CIP

Printed in the United States of America

1   2   3   4   5   6   7   8   9

*To Sashi*

# Contents

# Foreword

William Hawkeswood was one of my favorite graduate students; indeed, he was beloved by everyone in the Anthropology Department at Columbia University. He was always larger than life but also capable of great intimacy and warmth, and he was unfailingly generous with his time, his considerable expertise, and his spirit. When he died in the summer of 1992, his loss was felt deeply by everyone who had known him.

Bill spent his last years writing this book, and one of the sadnesses of his death is that he will not hold it in his hands. I know that he would have been pleased not only to see his work put before the public but to take his place among the social scientists committed to the analysis and understanding of gay life in America. For Bill, this was a particular passion, an expression of his own identity and his intellectual center.

*One of the Children* is more, much more, than a description of gay black men in Harlem. It is an attempt to understand the often uneasy fusion of race and sexuality in a country with a long and tortured history of segregation and bigotry on both counts. Harlem, one of the cultural capitals of African-American society, was the focus of Hawkeswood's ethnography because it is in Harlem that so many gay black men have created lives that bring together their experiences as African-Americans and as gay men. Bill wanted to show that an effervescent, creative, and historically grounded culture has evolved in the heart of the inner city, that it is a source of sustenance for ordinary people and extraordinary artists.

Bill also wanted readers to understand that gay black men participate in, and often secure the foundation of, social and familial networks that provide for the well-being of other men, women, and children in Harlem. So much that has been written about African-American families in the United States relegates men to marginal roles; here we see gay men as integral in the economic and emotional lives of sisters, younger siblings, friends, and neighbors and their households.

Bill lived in Harlem for several years and was thoroughly integrated into the lives of the men described in this book. Few white men have had this opportunity; even fewer have been accepted so readily. He found ways to work around or through the deep and long-standing divisions separating whites and blacks in this city, drawing upon his prior experience doing fieldwork with Rastafarians in New Zealand, the country of his birth. His ability to find a niche in communities seemingly distant from his own was a marvel to behold.

He is missed by his family in New Zealand, whom he loved dearly and of whom he spoke often, and by his colleagues and friends here, who remember him well. Fortunately, the ideas he lived for are represented in these pages.

Katherine Newman
September 1993

# Editor's Note

William Hawkeswood died of an AIDS-related illness in the summer of 1992, one year after defending his dissertation and being awarded his doctoral degree in anthropology at Columbia University. I began my graduate studies there a few months later. I was aware of his research, as were many others, and awaited the publication of his manuscript. In the fall of 1992, I attended a departmental memorial service where classmates, colleagues, and friends honored his unique vitality, intellectual passion, outspoken nature, and scholarly generosity. Through them, I too came to regret his absence. Six months later, I was given the opportunity to do a final edit for publication. I lacked the benefit of his further insight, as did all who contributed to the editorial process, but I hope we have improved and clarified what he wrote. Having seen this manuscript in various stages from dissertation to finished proof, I know it shows improvement throughout. I believe he would have been pleased with the final version, and I trust that this is the book William Hawkeswood would have wanted to see in print.

I hope that *One of the Children* will encourage others to continue the work William Hawkeswood started. By focusing on the lives of gay black men who are, as he noted, "a missing population ... neglected and relegated to marginal positions" in the social science literature on not only black society but also gay identity, he attempts to make up for these glaring deficiencies (p. 3). In his research, Hawkeswood challenges the legacy of representations of men in studies on black society. Glay black men, he argues, defy most of the negative stereo-types, including absent role models and "street corner men," that are found in many classic studies.

Examining the construction and integration of what many see as dual identities, Hawkeswood concludes that gay black men in con-temporary Harlem experience no such ambivalence. Choosing to identify as "black men first," he says, they use gay identity "as a sta-tus marker within black society" (p. 12). Some may disagree with his assertion that gay men in Harlem experience less social stigma than do gay men elsewhere. Hawkeswood does not deny that gay men are invariably seen as different from other men, wherever they may live. But, given the relative social and economic marginalization experi-enced by most residents of Harlem, he firmly believes that apart from organized religion's traditional dogma against homosexuality, gayness does not in itself draw condemnation from others in the community. As Hawkeswood notes early in his concluding chapter, "the fact that these men reside in a black community rather than a gay community is significant, especially when one of the world's most famous 'gay ghettos' is located minutes away and when most of them have the [financial] means to make the move" (p. 184). I have tried to clarify evidence for this argument in the text. While some may contest Hawkeswood's claim, he still challenges us to consider that "for most people in Harlem, issues of survival . . . are more important than concern about people's sexuality" (p. 167). Ultimately, he shows that the social, cultural, and economic contributions of gay black men are vitally important to the social networks in which they exist, to the lives of their kin and relatives, and to black society as a whole.

Hawkeswood wrote with great compassion for his informants. He also, I believe, completed the manuscript with a sense of urgency. He was genuinely surprised by the relatively small number of AIDS cases among his informants and their immediate social networks (especially given the disproportionately large number of African Americans in-fected with HIV in New York City), and he feared that the epidemic would eventually reach these men if AIDS educators failed to make a concerted effort to target gay black men living outside of "main-stream" gay life. In the manuscript, Hawkeswood added several pas-sages about the threatening AIDS epidemic that were not in the original dissertation, and readers may be struck by the detailed recom-mendations for specific AIDS prevention efforts in his concluding re-marks. These comments may seem somewhat out of place, but I saw no need to tailor these remarks, which express real concern for the lives of his informants. I am not alone in thinking that Hawkeswood felt this urgency personally, as he grappled with his own AIDS-related illness while completing his manuscript for publication.

This book represents the very beginning of a scholarly career that ended much too soon. With more time, I believe that Hawkeswood would have not only passionately continued this work but also welcomed intellectual challenges to his ideas, and I feel that it is fair to mention some possible areas of contention. While highlighting the deficiencies of previous research, Hawkeswood employs rather traditional tools to construct an alternative. He seems particularly determined to show readers that gay black men lead "ordinary" lives "typical" of those who neither are gay nor live in Harlem. He often seems torn, however, between two goals, on one hand presenting a traditional ethnographic case study of a "discrete" and "special community," and on the other compiling quantifiable data for an epidemiological profile. Attempting both of these things poses some problems for later analysis. Hawkeswood establishes clear criteria for his research sample, stating that participants had to "live in Harlem, socialize in the gay scene in Harlem, and prefer black men as sex partners" (p. 14). While this undoubtedly does present him with a unique group of black men, it makes it harder to generalize about a gay black experience for men who do not fit the profile he has created. Some difficulties appear in chapter 6 and chapter 7 as Hawkeswood struggles to determine how many men actually share the common experiences and perspectives he identifies, particularly with regard to early socialization and the importance of "the scene" in gay life. Similarly, there appear to be some internal contradictions in his discussion of the importance of the church and organized religion for these men and the degree to which they experience anti-gay bias and harassment in their daily lives. Interestingly, Hawkeswood actually saw an apparent contradiction in his informants' accounts of gay stigma, but he saved the comment for a footnote in chapter 6. However, with some qualification, his basic argument still stands, and we are encouraged to consider the experiences of men who appear to regard homophobia as the lesser of two evils when compared to racism.

Hawkeswood's work challenges existing research on the "social construction" of black and gay identities to explore the intersection of the two. But, while showing how these men negotiate their public and private identities, we too often see presentations of mere visual "style" in his discussions of "performance culture" and "lifestyle" in his discussions of "being gay." Perhaps other questions would have elicited more complex responses. For readers seeking more material on the construction of sexual identity, Richard Parker and John Gagnon's *Conceiving Sexuality: Approaches to Sex Research in a Postmodern World* is a useful anthology, especially for the pieces by Jeffrey Weeks ("History, Desire, and Identities"), Dennis Altman ("Political Identities"), and Roger Lancaster ("That We Should All Turn Queer? Homosexual Stigma in the Making of Manhood and the Breaking of Revolution in Nicaragua"). Hawkeswood shows us, on one level, how black identity is fashioned for public display. For another, more philosophical approach to the issues of "body image" and "body-experience" for black men, Charles Johnson's "A Phenomenology of the Black Body," in Laurence Goldstein's *The Male Body*, may be helpful.

Focusing on social networks, Hawkeswood reveals the ways in which gay black men construct a "family" for themselves. While he concludes that this construction of "family" serves to "enhance a sense of community" (p. 65), we are left to imagine other less symbolic functions of this metaphorical construction: the relationship between material marginality and a very real dependence on alternative social networks, for example. For further insight into gay social networks, Peter M. Nardi's "That's What Friends Are For: Friends as Family in the Gay and Lesbian Community," in Ken Plummer's *Modern Homosexualities*, provides an interesting discussion of gay and lesbian marginality and alternative "families" as a political and social force.

Hawkeswood is right when he observes a lack of "ethnic minorities" in studies on urban gay communities. As he notes in his introduction, research on gay male identity often assumes that the subject is white. Though the following works do not deal with African-American men in particular, nor with identifiable "gay communities," there are some exceptions in recent anthropological research on homosexuality, including Roger Lancaster's *Life is Hard: Machismo, Danger, and the Intimacy of Power in Nicaragua*, Joseph Carrier's *De Los Otros: Intimacy and Homosexuality Among Mexican Men*, Michael Tan's "From Bakla to Gay: Shifting Gender Identities and Sexual Behaviors in the Philippines," in *Conceiving Sexuality*, Huseyin Tapinc's "Masculinity, Femininity, and Turkish Male Homosexuality," in *Modern Homosexualities*, and Richard Parker's *Bodies, Pleasures, and Passions: Sexual Culture in Contemporary Brazil*.

Similarly, Hawkeswood is also right when he notes that literary accounts of the black male experience in America often assume that the subject is heterosexual. In Herb Boyd and Robert Allen's ambitious anthology *Brotherman: The Odyssey of Black Men in America*, for example, the contributions of openly gay authors is relatively scarce. (Out of 157 entries, only 4 are by openly gay or bisexual authors.) Curiously, when the editors praise the diversity of men's caring relationships, homosexual ones seem almost incomprehensible. "What's love got to do with it?" they ask. "Everything! Especially when you realize how many deep caring relationships exist outside of the romantic male-female bond. Some of the most dynamic relationships in a man's life occur between him and his grandparents, his siblings, and his children" (p. xxvi). Hawkeswood's work clearly shows that gay black men have these relationships too, but regrettably their primary romantic relationships are too often ignored in print.

Lamenting the lack of "gay identities" in literature on "black society," it is a shame that William Hawkeswood did not live to see the publication of some recent notable literary efforts documenting gay black experience. The issues Hawkeswood begins to explore in the section "Social Status and Sexuality" in chapter 7 are most compelling, yet much too brief. For another, illuminating analysis on negotiating gay identity and black masculinity, see Don Belton's discussion with poet Essex Hemphill and filmmaker Isaac Julien in *Speak My Name: Black Men on Masculinity and the American Dream*. Two other anthologies are invaluable resources for writings on a variety of issues including social status and homosexuality in black society. In Essex Hemphill and Joseph Beam's *Brother to Brother: New Writing by Black Gay Men*, see especially Issac Julien and Kobena Mercer's "True Confessions: A Discourse on Images of Black Male Sexuality," Ron Simmons's "Some Thoughts on the Challenges Facing Black Gay Intellectuals," and Charles I. Nero's "Toward a Black Gay Aesthetic: Signifying in Contemporary Black Gay Literature." For other perspectives on the complexities of living with a "double consciousness" as gay and African-American men, see Bruce Morrow and Charles Rowell's *Shade: An Anthology of Fiction by Gay Men of African Descent*. And finally, for readers wanting more subjective accounts of black gay men's experiences of the AIDS epidemic, *Sojourner: Black Gay Voices in the Age of AIDS*, edited by B. Michael Hunter and the Other Countries writing collective, is an important resource.

At several points during the editorial process, it was clear that excessive changes would have produced a radically different book, a book that Hawkeswood did not write. As it stands, his work is presented with both its strengths to enlighten readers and its weaknesses to encourage new intellectual challenges. My work as editor was made easier with the help of several people. I wish to thank Katherine Newman and Roger Lancaster for their knowledge and insight. I owe special thanks to Harvey Molotch at the University of California at Santa Barbara for valuable comments and suggestions, to Peter Kosenko and Sheila Berg for their extraordinary copy-editing skills, and to Michelle Bonnice and Rebecca Frazier, production editors at University of California Press, for their patience and encouragement throughout the lengthy and often complicated editorial process.

Alex W. Costley
New York City, 1996

## Recommended Readings

Belton, Don, ed. *Speak My Name: Black Men on Masculinity and the American Dream.* Boston: Beacon Press, 1995.
Boyd, Herb, and Robert L. Allen, eds. *Brotherman: The Odyssey of Black Men in America.* New York: Ballantine, 1995.
Carrier, Joseph. *De Los Otros: Intimacy and Homosexuality Among Mexican Men.* New York: Columbia University Press, 1995.
Goldstein, Laurence, ed. *The Male Body: Features, Destinies, Exposures.* Ann Arbor: The University of Michigan Press, 1994.
Hemphill, Essex, ed., with Joseph Beam. *Brother to Brother: New Writing by Black Gay Men.* Boston: Alyson Publications, 1991.
Lancaster, Roger N. *Life Is Hard: Machismo, Danger, and the Intimacy of Power in Nicaragua.* Berkeley: University of California Press, 1992.
Morrow, Bruce, and Charles H. Rowell, eds. *Shade: An Anthology of Fiction by Gay Men of African Descent.* New York: Avon Books, 1996.
Hunter, B. Michael, ed., with the Other Countries collective. *Sojourner: Black Gay Voices in the Age of AIDS.* New York: Other Countries Press, 1993.
Parker, Richard G. *Bodies, Pleasures, and Passions: Sexual Culture in Contemporary Brazil.* Boston: Beacon Press, 1991.
Parker, Richard G., and John H. Gagnon, eds. *Conceiving Sexuality: Approaches to Sex Research in a Postmodern World.* New York: Routledge, 1995.
Plummer, Ken, ed. *Modern Homosexualities: Fragments of Lesbian and Gay Experience.* New York: Routledge, 1992.

# Acknowledgments

During the four years I was involved with this study, I received encouragement and assistance in many different ways from many different people.

Primarily my gratitude is extended to all of my informants in Harlem. Without their willingness to share their lives with me I would never have been able to experience "core black culture." Most especially, I wish to thank Henry, Tony, Alan, Walter, Darryl, Michael, Kenny, Arthur, Dennis, and Ali. Many other friends and neighbors in Harlem also contributed to my experiences there; thanks to Rufus, Steve, Sam, Neal, Leroy, Bernard, Rita, and Wescott.

I owe much of my understanding of being black to my friends Marshall Swiney, Ron Hutson, Jackie (Bree) Holloman, and the late Kendal Johnson. They introduced me to life on the streets of New York City—Greenwich Village and Harlem in particular.

Other friends proffered support, including references to people and institutions. I thank John Ambel (for editing), Sandy Baker, Rodson Manning, Henry T. Jones Jr., George Bellinger, Jr. (of the Minority Task Force on AIDS), Darryl Stevens (of the Schomburg Center), Derek Martin, and David Patterson.

Colleagues in anthropology encouraged and assisted me in a variety of ways. Thanks to Carole Vance, Arthur Spears, Joe Carrier, Jerry Wright, and Jane Miller.

I received continual financial support from Columbia University and encouragement and assistance from members of the Anthropology Department. I wish to thank especially Alexander Alland, Jr., Libbet Crandon-Malamud, Claire Ceasareo, and the members of the writing seminar: Kate Dudley, James Edell, Sarah Mahler, Bill Peace, and Jean Scandlyn. Special thanks to Joyce Monges and the staff of the department, who contribute much behind the scenes. Most important, thanks are due to my mentor, Katherine Newman. Her enthusiasm, constant encouragement, and editorial assistance enabled me to complete this work.

Thanks are due to my editor at the University of California Press, Stanley Holwitz, his staff, and the anonymous reviewers. Their constructive criticism has been invaluable.

My family and Sashi Meanger, back home in New Zealand, provided sustenance in many ways. May this book suffice as reward.

W. G. H.
August 1992

# Introductory Note

Toward the conclusion of the research for this ethnography, "African-American" began to replace "black" as the descriptor of choice for Americans of African heritage. Debate in the academic and popular black press continues. I have retained black for a variety of reasons: my informants used this term for themselves throughout the research; the obvious dichotomy between black and white has important implications for the residents of Harlem who utilize these terms to separate "us" from "them"; and most of my informants, who were educated in the 1960s and 1970s, regard "being black" as a positive form of self-identification. African-American was used by two of my informants after the research period came to an end. They explained its use to me as an attempt to "Africanize" black identity. People who use African-American opt to promote African roots in a positive light rather than to use the confrontational black. As well, African-American has political implications. Its users, wittingly or unwittingly, are part of a movement to replace race as a central issue in civil rights activism with a claim for ethnic status in the United States—for all intents and purposes a more successful pitch in the search for equality.

I quote extensively from tape recordings of interviews with informants, and I have attempted to reproduce black diction, while retaining a readable script. I hope I have avoided giving scholars such as Lawrence Levine reason to berate me for distorting both black diction and standard English. In discussing his own use of earlier renderings of black dialect, Levine noted,

The language employed in these quotations, of course, is not invariably the language actually spoken by Black Americans but representations of that language recorded by observers and folklorists, the great majority of whom were white and a substantial proportion of whom were southern. The language . . . is a mélange of accuracy and fantasy, of sensitivity and stereotype, of empathy and racism. The distortions, where they exist, were not always conscious; people often hear what they expect to hear, what stereotype and predisposition have prepared them to hear. Thus the variety and subtlety of Negro speech was frequently reduced to what the auditor thought Negroes spoke like. Even when the pronunciation of a given word was precisely the same as that of the collectors, their desire to indicate the exotic qualities of Black speech led them to utilize such misleading and superfluous spellings as *wen* for "when," . . . *wuz* for "was," . . . and so on and on. (1978:xv)

Because I have tried to avoid such parodies of black dialect, the vibrant intonation of black diction is missing from my transcriptions; I hope that this does not destroy the excitement of the spoken word for readers who have heard it.

# 1

## "He's Family": An Introduction

*They my brothers. They all my brothers. Well, some of them be my sisters, you know. The close girlfriends. But we're all one big family. "We are family!" That's how I think of us. That's the way we be treatin' each other. Just like we was one big family.*

—Harry

The gay community in Harlem includes members of all socioeconomic classes, all age groups, and several religions. It is not formally structured or institutionalized, nor is it geographically discrete or stable in membership. People are connected to one other through series of interdependent social networks and through participation in gay social events or institutions. Close gay members of each individual's social network become his "family" and are accorded familial titles. In this manner, everyone is related to someone else by fictive kin relationships. During the two years it took me to complete the research for this book, I was honored to be considered a member of the "family."

Late in the winter of 1985, Rex,[1] a fellow Columbian and a journalism student from Trinidad, invited me and Martin, a black gay friend from Washington, D.C., to join him for drinks in a bar on 125th Street in Harlem. This street is a major shopping and nightlife center. Always crowded and noisy with traffic and people, and colorful

with neon lights, the street conceals the Harlem of popular concep-
tion: not until you step into the surrounding neighborhoods do you
see broken sidewalks, neglected red-brick brownstones, abandoned
tenements, and street corner people. After a four-block walk into the
cold wind, we reached the awning over the narrow entrance to Pete's
Paradise. We had been told little about the bar, except that it was
"pretty rough," that drugs and sex were readily available there, and
that we shouldn't stay too late, because the neighborhood got "real
rough" after midnight.

I remember my first impressions well. The bar seemed cavernous:
long, crowded, and smoke-filled. It had red walls and ceiling and dim
lighting. I was very conscious that people were looking at me, the only
white man in the place. The jukebox roared sixties Motown music,
and some of the clientele were dancing. One young man approached
Rex, and they disappeared toward the back of the bar, leaving Martin
and me alone. We stood with our beers, leaning on the railing along
the wall opposite the bar. We were both a little anxious, until an older
gentleman approached and introduced himself. He was a large man,
dressed in a white sweater and white corduroys, wearing a white
*kufi*.[2] He asked us where we were from and chatted briefly with Martin about D.C. He offered to buy us another beer, but we declined,
noting we had to go home to study.

We left, quickly, and stopped a couple of blocks away in a pizzeria
to regroup. After we had ordered food and played the jukebox, Rex
appeared, apologizing for deserting us in the bar. Some repartee en-
sued concerning his activities during his absence, then we set about
analyzing our experiences at Pete's Paradise. Rex noted that we were
probably perceived by some of the patrons as drug dealers trying to
move in on someone else's territory—a fantasy in his mind only, I
hoped. All in all, we felt very excited about our "adventure," and I
was especially thrilled to have made my first foray into "Harlem,
U.S.A.," a special corner of the United States that I had read and
heard so much about. Yet two and a half years would pass before I
would go back, and then under the formal pretext of conducting fieldwork.

In the meantime I made friends in New York with a black gay choreographer. His social network of black gay artists became an integral
part of my personal social network. And I made friends with another
black man from Brooklyn. I visited him frequently in East New York,
now notorious for its high levels of drug-related crime; over the past

five years it has replaced the South Bronx and Bedford-Stuyvesant as the consummate black ghetto in New York City. Concurrently, I attended courses in urban anthropology at Columbia University, which borders Harlem. One of these, "The Social Anthropology of Contemporary American Society," focused on the urban poor in America. Reading Hannerz, Liebow, Stack, Kornblum, Piven and Cloward, and Clark, among others, aroused my anthropological interest in black society. And all during this time I maintained a residence on the western edge of Harlem, shopping on 125th Street and 7th Avenue, socializing in bars and clubs on St. Nicholas, Seventh, and Lenox avenues, and eventually conducting research between 110th and 160th streets.

I was also working during this time as an interviewer on a large research project studying the AIDS epidemic,[3] and eventually I came to realize that the respondent sample in that study was somewhat skewed: 87 percent of the sample were white gay men; only 6 percent were black (Martin and Dean 1990). New York City, which defines the geographical limits of that study (that is, the five boroughs), is now over 50 percent non-white. Even the gay scene boasts a more visible black population than the sample evidenced. Also, according to statistics published by New York City's Department of Health, AIDS is spreading most rapidly in the black and Hispanic communities within the five boroughs (New York City Department of Health 1989). Given these facts, I became interested in studying the identities of gay black men and the impact of AIDS on their lives and communities.

Gay black men are as yet a missing population in the literature on black society. They are an interesting population not just because they are a newly discovered "tribe," exploited in a recent fashionable trend by the gay media and documentary filmmakers, but because they offer an opportunity for the social scientist to investigate the intersection of two presumably distinct and contradictory identities, both born out of oppression and resistance.

In fact, black men generally have been neglected or relegated to a marginal position in the literature on black society. When they are the focus of ethnographic study, one type of black man—the street corner man—is described. Where black men have been mentioned in the social science literature,[4] in the media,[5] or in fiction,[6] they have been painted as unemployable drifters (Anderson 1978), absentee fathers

(Stack 1974), and substance abusers (MacLeod 1987; Sullivan 1989)—veritable "street corner men" (Liebow 1967). When black men write about themselves, what little that has been published in scattered anthologies of fiction is painfully realistic in its attempts to locate black men in American society.[7] Even in this literature and in the statistical accounts of black life provided by sociologists, psychologists, and census tracts,[8] black men remain marginal to black society.

Most of the sociological literature on black society has been influenced by the Chicago school of sociology. That school sought to present black society as an ordered cultural unit (because it had been, and still is, described as being disordered; see Moynihan 1965, 1986). The search for order and structure in the apparent chaos of urban ghetto life resulted in descriptions of geographically discrete communities in much the same way that anthropologists have traditionally defined and described societies in Africa, the South Pacific, and elsewhere. The resulting ethnographies provide neat maps of social relations within black communities; the populations of the communities are also neatly categorized according to socioeconomic strata and other sociologically definable variables, to further order the structure of ghetto life. From my own experience and research, I find that these kinds of ethnographies do not reflect the variety of social relations in black urban life.

Gerald Suttles's (1968) analysis of a Chicago slum set the stage for sociological and anthropological ethnographic exercises seeking to confirm that the "moral order" Suttles proposed existed.[9] Suttles's work obviously influenced the ethnographic work of R. Lincoln Keiser (1969) and Elijah Anderson (1978). While Keiser's ethnography of a Chicago gang is colorful, it is concerned only with the group's interaction with other gangs. All the men described live on the streets, and other people in the community are omitted. Anderson's ethnography of a black bar deals with black men "regulars," "wineheads," and "hoodlums" who live on the streets of the neighborhood and utilize the bar as the focal point of their social life. We are left with a picture of a highly structured black community, but one in which black men seem irresponsible, unemployable, and unattached to other people. Other types of men in this particular community are ignored.[10] We do not see fathers actively involved in child care or men who hold regular jobs.

Elliott Liebow's (1967) ethnography is a detailed account of the lives of a group of men who hang out on a street corner in Washington, D.C. It describes how they have internalized social roles prescribed for them by the broader community. The ethnography also reveals how

these men have developed a system of "shadow values" which provides social and psychological support for individuals whenever they
fail to perform to their own expectations. The study is an excellent
analysis of these particular black men's lives, but again neglects the
roles of other, nonmarginal black men in the community. Such work
has left social scientists with little information about black men in general or about their roles and relationships in the black community.
They give us the mistaken impression that all black men are street
corner drifters or unemployed and unemployable hustlers who father
children somewhat randomly.

In anthropology, there are several works that attempt to contextual-
ize life in the ghetto. Ulf Hannerz's (1969) description of a black
ghetto in Washington, D.C., addresses the different types of people
who live there. Again we see street corner men, but Hannerz tries to
go beyond them. He sees other men in other "lifestyles" as "mainstreamers" and "swingers," but his description and analysis of those
groups are not detailed. In fact, his work gives the impression that
"mainstreamers" are a minority.[11]

Hannerz's focus is really on the family. Presumably these are the
black "matriarchal families" to which Daniel Patrick Moynihan was
referring in his controversial analysis.[12] Decades of research have
been aimed at correcting Moynihan's distorted view of black families
and contesting his shortsighted predictions on the future of blacks
in America. Elmer Martin and Joanne Martin, among his detractors,
have presented the "strength-resiliency perspective" (Martin and
Martin 1978:103). In their analysis of broad "extended families" and
the interdependence of individual family units within the kin network,
most especially in the urban environment, they found substantial
emotional, financial, and other material support for individuals and
"sub-extended families." Early on, Andrew Billingsley leveled the
most significant criticism of Moynihan's work. He contended that
Moynihan reached "faulty and inverse conclusions" due to lack of
theoretical direction and limited data (Billingsley 1968:200). Billingsley argued that heritage, extended family, and class had to be taken
into account in any meaningful analysis of the black family. These
issues have been dealt with more substantially over the years by other
researchers.[13]

Hannerz focuses on women, presenting all men as sexually
"straight" and sometimes socially pathological. Carol Stack maintains this focus in her excellent ethnography All Our Kin (1974),
which describes the structure of relations between female-headed

households. Her work on the strategies of survival in black kinship networks is probably the most significant contribution to the literature on the strength and adaptability of the black family. Her focus on women led to an analysis of the exchange systems they had developed to link both kin and non-kin in reciprocal networks of sharing and mutual help. However, because she highlights female-headed households where women oversee cash flow and child care, men appear only sporadically. These households socialize young men by mother's instruction, based on her perceptions of what is masculine. Men are present (often relatives, rarely fathers), but they are not consistently involved in family affairs. One gets the impression, once again, that they are drifters or street corner men. Admittedly, Stack's ethnography focuses on women and their roles, but it marginalizes black men by omission.

Bettylou Valentine's (1978) work seeks to redress this shortcoming somewhat. The families in her study depend on sources of income other than welfare alone. Here men are present. They work long hours at several jobs, and they play an important role in the socialization of their children. But they are frequently absent, either working or making themselves scarce in the face of the "man" as social welfare agent, census taker, or social scientist. Nevertheless, families are important and we see hardworking men and women in stable unions struggling to maintain them.

My experiences in East New York, Brooklyn, and Harlem have confirmed this. A two-year period of data collection, the fieldwork for this project, further supported my perception that most black men, and gay black men in particular, are anything but street corner men. This is not to say that street corner men do not exist. They do, even within the gay black population. But they are not such a prominent feature of black society from an insider's point of view. They are marginal members of an intense, historical, expressive culture (Gay and Baber 1987) that has ramifications for American society far beyond the boundaries of the black community (Drake 1987).

Most black men, and gay black men, whom I have encountered, are well educated by American standards, religious, employed, good fathers, and major contributors to their families' incomes and their children's socialization. I am not denying the poor their rightful place in the scheme of things. So much has been written about them, especially in black society, and frequently by and for social policy makers, albeit falling on deaf ears, that to reiterate their story here would be redundant.[14] But because the literature on the poor is so vast, it creates an impression that they are the majority, especially in the black community. However, there is little reliable evidence for this. For example, 78 percent of the sample in this study, which includes college educated and employed people, did not participate in the last census, so how reliable can census-based statistical analyses of black society be? Reynolds Farley and Walter R. Allen's (1987) figures on income, education, and employment are based on nationwide data and do not necessarily represent the uniqueness of Harlem. In fact, even on the nationwide scale, Farley and Allen (1987:293) note that approximately 25 percent of blacks are using food stamps, Medicaid, and publicly subsidized housing. They also note that 86 percent of black men have an income, 73 percent are employed, and only 19 percent are unemployed (ibid.: 225, 330).[15]

Likewise, the social science literature on gay men in America rarely focuses on minority groups. Studies of gay society present descriptions of the gay social scene or psychological analyses of gay identity but do not consider the dynamics of the ethnic and racial composition of the gay population. This tendency has been carried over into the literature on AIDS in gay society, in which ethnic minorities are rarely mentioned (Altman 1986). Black gay men in particular are absent from the growing social science literature on gay society. My background reading and archival research has yielded no anthropological or sociological reports on a gay black community.[16] Even literature within gay studies and on AIDS has scant offerings on this population.[17] Most social science literature describes and analyzes the social setting of gay life but rarely deals with the inhabitants. In anthropology, most of the literature consists of papers on the existence of homosexuality, gays, and transvestites or transsexuals in different cultures and the social construction of sexuality in those cultures.[18]

In the literature on urban gay communities, especially in the United States, ethnic minorities are also missing. Laud Humphreys's (1975) pioneering work on sexual activity does not locate the "scene" of this behavior within the larger community of his informants, nor does it discuss other aspects of the "gay" lives of the individuals involved. However, his book was the first sociological ethnography focusing on homosexual behavior.[19] Other sociological efforts tended to be more descriptive of physical settings than analytical, especially when referring to the gay scene in New York City (Canavan 1984; Delph 1978; Soares 1979).

Within anthropology, a few ethnographic forays have been made into gay society in America. Esther Newton's (1979) work on drag queens provides interesting data on an often neglected and maligned subculture. Her ethnography deals with the "symbolic geography" of male and female styles as enacted in the homosexual concepts of "drag" and "camp" but ignores issues of ethnicity within the population. As my research has confirmed, drag is very popular in the black community, and much of what is called "camp" has been influenced by the strong presence of black men in the world of drag performance.

Kenneth Read's (1980) study of social behavior in a gay bar derives its importance not so much from the "thick description" of his subject matter as from the exercise of symbolic anthropological analysis. It provides a rare insight into the ways gay men experience their daily lives on the West Coast. His ethnography clearly indicates a diversity of lifestyles embraced by those gay men, and his analysis shows how gay lifestyles symbolically mirror those of heterosexuals. Yet, even here, ethnic diversity remains a hidden or unanalyzed dimension of gay life.

One of the few references to black gay men appears in Dennis Altman's (1971) work on the gay liberation movement. He analyzes the oppression that that movement sought to overcome and compares it to the black and women's movements of the same era. Altman also raises the issue of racism and the frequency of its expression in the gay world, indicating how it mirrors racism in mainstream American society. Yet we learn nothing about black gay men per se. In his work on AIDS, Altman (1986) noted again that gay social life in the United States is racially segregated. He also noted that this segregation appeared "odd" given that gays now argue that their "sexual identity is, by itself, the basis for a sense of community" (D. Altman 1986:100–101). Altman does not pursue the issue of race any further,[20] not so much because he believes race is an irrelevant issue in the gay community but because black gay men are an instance of an "invisible minority" within another minority, the gay population.

Gay black men do surface in the contributions of Eric Garber (1983, 1989). He has published interesting papers on the participation of gays in the Harlem Renaissance. In them, he describes literary Harlem of the 1920s and "considers the effect of the intersection of racial and sexual oppressions in creating a distinctive black gay subculture" (Garber 1989:318). While he makes no attempt to delineate this subculture, he does identify gay artists of the period and the literary works of the time in which reference was made to gay characters (for example, Claude McKay's *Home to Harlem*, published in 1928). In literature, gay black culture is legitimated, yet no ethnography exists delineating the gay community or the gay identity of the individuals who make up gay black society.[21]

What identity is and how it is developed and sustained have been the topic of social-scientific analysis for some time. Within anthropology, A. L. Epstein's (1978) work on the sociological aspects of identity has its roots in work by E. H. Erikson (1968) and Fredrik Barth (1969). Barth provided an alternative perspective on identity as a process of group boundary maintenance.[22] "Ethnic ascription" exists, he notes, when a person is classified by his or her "origin and background." Diacritical features of such an identity include "dress, language, house-form, or general style of life," as well as the "standards of morality and excellence by which performance is judged" (Barth 1969:13–14). These characteristics of ethnic identity vary in significance from social group to social group. What is important is that they define an exclusive group that exists in opposition to all others. These people express identity during social interaction with other people by "overt signals or signs" and by their "basic value orientations." Their characteristics are diagnostic for membership and can be manipulated by members of a group to signal membership and exclusion. Such groups need not have territorial counterparts. Barth calls for an analysis of the way that such expression of identity is continued and continually validated.

For Erikson and Epstein, who believed that identity formation is a psychosocial process,[23] sociological aspects of identity become apparent during the study of culture transmission and group boundary maintenance. They include not only manifestations of group boundary maintenance (for example, those expressed as symbols of ethnicity) but also statuses and roles, expressive cultural traits, religious and political beliefs, and moral attitudes. These culturally defined traits are transmitted during socialization and inform the development of identity.

Academic discussions of gay men always include one fundamental aspect of their identity: the central fact of homosexual behavior.[24] Many psychologists believe that an individual's homosexuality is a naturally determined aspect of one's being.[25] Psychology and biology, they assert, are more determinant of sexual orientation than the social environment. Other social scientists, however, believe that "sexual desires are learned and that sexual identities come to be fashioned through an individual's interaction with others" (Halperin 1990:41–42). When sociologists began to study the "gay community," psychologists were pressed to reexamine their views of homosexuality, and sociological factors of gay identity development gained more attention.[26]

In 1971 Barry Dank noted that gay men exposed to knowledge of homosexuality gleaned from social experiences (sociosexual interaction with other homosexuals, attendance at homosexual social institutions, and reading homosexual newspapers) were able to overcome negative "public labeling" (and other mainstream societal restraints) and to develop a psychologically and socially satisfying positive identity (Dank 1979).[27]

Other social scientists have noted the interaction of culture and individual experience in the formation of gay identity. The most constructive approach to the study of the sociological aspects of gay identity formation has come from Humphreys (1979) and Thomas Weinberg (1983). Taking a symbolic-interactionist approach, Weinberg concludes that gay identity is a product of "personal" (intimate) and other levels of social interaction, and Humphreys resolves that, while a degree of voluntarism is involved in the development of a gay identity, there are indeed "highly determinative" cultural factors, such as socioeconomic, ethnic, racial, and religious backgrounds and even the range of available sexual orientations, which limit the personal construction of that identity and levels of participation in gay life.[28] Thus, a variety of sociocultural and psychological variables influence the construction of a social identity.[29]

Although understanding the development of a gay identity is difficult from a sociological point of view alone (Halperin 1990:53),[30] a sociocultural approach that examines the context within which the social construction of gay identity occurs is important for understanding that identity. To quote Kenneth Plummer,

While there is now a vast literature on homosexuality, most of it is firmly in the clinical tradition and usually concerned with the question of primary aetiology. I have demonstrated some of the drawbacks of such an approach by stressing that homosexuality cannot be adequately understood apart from the meanings constructed around it in a predominantly hostile society. (1975:199–200)[31]

Social interactionists, like Plummer,[32] have opened the way for an approach that seeks not only to explore the development of the gay identity and gay culture but also to focus on questions of cultural meaning.

Meaning is more important than actual sexual behavior in the development of a homosexual identity. Actual sexual experiences with other males is neither a necessary nor a sufficient factor in labeling oneself as homosexual, and sexual relations with women do not necessarily lead to a "bisexual" or "heterosexual" self-definition. "Doing" does not necessarily eventuate in "being." (Weinberg 1983:300)

Since a whole variety of cultural factors influence such meaning, they challenge the typologies (homosexual, heterosexual, bisexual) with which we have restricted our comprehension of the diversity of conceptualizations and experiences of human sexuality. By focusing on sexual behavior and socialization—that is, on the social interaction of individuals—we can begin to reconstruct alternative images of sexuality. Collecting data on sexual behavior, reconsidering sexual typologies, and analyzing socialization experiences are necessary steps in obtaining a fuller understanding of the meaning of sexuality for a given population. Revealing the cultural meaning of sexuality for gay black men will not only inform us of the importance of sexuality to them but also yield a greater understanding of their community.

Gay black culture, then, allows for the exploration of a number of issues that confront the social scientist: race, class, regional culture, urban subcultures, gender roles, and sexuality. Usually anthropologists who work on identity focus on or work within one of these issues. The study of gay black culture allows for the investigation of all of these issues and their relationship to identity. The intersection of sexuality, race, and class in particular is important to the presumed double identity of gay black men.

This study adds another dimension to the discourse on gay identity. It focuses on the intersection of racial identity and gay identity as two culturally definable phenomena that come together in gay black men and on how such men express and manipulate each in differing circumstances. Focusing on the gay black man in Harlem, this study demonstrates the importance of the individual's incorporation of sociocultural variables into an identity.

What unfolds here is an analysis of both the gay and the black aspects of the identity of gay black men and how these men negotiate their status in society. My initial assumption that gay black men would "codeswitch" between being gay and being black was challenged by these men. While there may be some ambivalence about identity for black men in mainstream gay society, gay black men in Harlem choose to identify themselves as black men first, using the gay identity as a status marker within black society.

Social-organizational and social-interaction theory[33] underlie my analysis of this gay black male community's relationship with outside, dominant groups:[34] black society, which geographically engulfs it; the gay community in which it is an "invisible minority"; and mainstream American society, whose neglect of both dimensions belies ignorance. Drawing heavily on the theory of the social organization of the family[35] and symbolic approaches to the study of community,[36] I analyze social relations between the members of this population and their kinfolk. The inclusion of fictive kin in the resulting social networks[37] and the maintenance of these networks evolve as important foci of the investigation. It is through such symbolic constructions of community that individual members within the gay community are able to refer to each other by saying, "He's family."[38] Symbolic anthropological approaches to "community" in Harlem help reveal the meaning of this metaphor by which members of the gay black community identify themselves and their interrelatedness.

Gay black men's sense of community and identity depends on their understanding of their sexuality. They regard being gay as a distinctive element of their identity, one that positions them in a unique niche in black society. In addition, it has important implications for these men as they confront the AIDS epidemic.[39] My ethnographic research on gay black culture explores the sociocultural context of gay black men's double identity, being black and gay in America, and of the impact of AIDS in their community.

## Black Gay Men and Gay Black Men

Men who are both black and gay live scattered throughout New York City. To find a community of such men could have been a vast undertaking. But with a little ethnographic foraging, I was able to identify two general groups: those who live scattered throughout the city and who socialize by and large in mainstream gay areas (that is, black gay men); and those who live and socialize within the geographic confines of a black neighborhood (that is, gay black men). My research focuses on the latter group.

Black men are a highly visible component of New York City's large gay population. Their presence in the gay social life of New York City has been long-standing and prominent, especially in such milestone events as the Stonewall riots on Christopher Street[40] and the formation of the Third World Gay Revolution,[41] both in 1969. Today their participation in annual gay pride parades in New York, their involvement in the formation of exclusively black social organizations, and their continued presence in mainstream gay social life, in the bars and discos and gay social clubs of the city, is ever increasing.[42] What is important to note is that most of these men live in the Village, Brooklyn, the Bronx, or nearby New Jersey cities—Jersey City, Hoboken, and Newark in particular.

Today, black gay men are becoming organized in many ways in New York City. Several branches of national gay organizations, such as Men of All Colors Together (MACT), have large numbers of black gay members. Black gay men have also infused many other city-based organizations—for example, Maranatha, a church group; the Lavender Light Black and People of All Colors Lesbian and Gay Gospel Choir; and Friends and Neighbors of Brooklyn. Black gay men have become important social leaders in fundraising organizations such as Men Who Cook and in providing the essential services at the Minority Task Force on AIDS. Black gay men have also established an organization, Gay Men of African Descent (GMAD), that boasts some Harlem members, although most are from Brooklyn, Newark, and other New Jersey cities.

As well, this population has set about creating its own artistic expression. News publications and journals such as *BLK, BGM, B&G, Blacklight, Blackheart*, and *Black/Out* have emerged around the country. Art exhibitions around the city and poetry readings at the Gay and Lesbian Community Center and the Studio Museum in Harlem have promoted their presence in both the gay and the black communities. A writers' collective, Other Countries, has risen to prominence in the literary world in New York, publishing an excellent first anthology (Johnson, Robinson, and Taylor 1988).

However, I decided to label the population in this study "gay black men" because they reside in a black community and their social network members and sexual partners are also black, choices that enable them to affirm their identity as black men—black men who are also gay. Although I met black gay men from all over the metropolitan area—indeed, from all over the country—who used to live and still occasionally socialize in Harlem as well as black gay men who live in Harlem but socialize in Brooklyn, Newark, or New Rochelle, the informants I eventually selected to concentrate on for life history collection had to meet certain criteria: they had to live in Harlem, socialize in the gay scene in Harlem, and prefer black men as sex partners.

## The Study

Because black men have been misrepresented or omitted from earlier ethnographic accounts of black society, I presumed that they had been hard to reach. Therefore, I undertook intensive research of the participant-observer kind in order to gain access to "core black culture" (Gwaltney 1980, 1981). I chose to analyze the social construction of a gay black identity and the social status of gay black men in a black community by focusing on the cultural aspects of identity formation and investigating the social practices and social relations that sustain that identity.

In early 1987, I raised my ideas for a book on gay black culture with three friends. Two of these men, one of whom has since passed away, were especially excited and have been a source of constant encouragement and verification of my findings. The third friend, from out of town, visits Harlem frequently and has many friends there. In the summer of 1987 he took me into the bars and introduced me to his friends.

I had used this method of making initial contact before, especially in complex urban settings. An introduction as a "friend" facilitates the outsider's entrée, especially in a population that is politicized to the extent that it is very distrustful of outsiders of a different color, race, or ethnic group, or those who may even unwittingly represent the "system," the "man," or the governmental power structure.

After initial contacts and explanations were made in bars and clubs in Harlem, I asked my new friends to introduce me to their friends, in and out of the "scene." Thus I was able to "snowball" people's social networks.[43] The idea of random sampling an amorphous and "invisible" population of gay black men within Harlem would otherwise have proven impracticable.

Some informants I met only in the bars. I was introduced to some, others approached me, or I approached them directly. One informant, a hustler, proved an invaluable networker, introducing me to many important contacts and to several of the other hustlers who frequented these places. With his assistance I was able to comprehend the significance of the hustler population in the wider gay community in Harlem. The staff of two of the bars provided support and contacts. They introduced me to their regular patrons, often cliques of men who formed social groups based on different occupations or church affiliations.

Some of my initial contacts in the gay scene provided me with introductions to gay men outside of the scene: in their residential neighborhoods, at their churches, or at other private social functions such as dances, card games, dinner parties, and boat rides. Meeting friends, relatives, and lovers, I was able to break away from the scene—the bars and clubs—and reach into people's homes, daily lives, and social networks. This I hoped would provide a better contextualization of the black lives I was to describe and analyze than had been previously attempted by other social scientists. Many aspects of black people's social lives have not been studied, especially life at home and in the workplace. The persistence of the street in the ethnography of black society represents a superficiality on the part of ethnographers.

One key informant, Cleveland, was initially a little cautious about introducing me to his close gay friends. Yet he and his lover, Randy, escorted me to private functions (dances in particular) and to church and invited me to their homes for meals, where they introduced me to several other informants. From these introductions, I was able to meet additional friends at other dinners and card games. In the gay scene itself, Cleveland introduced me to many of the men who became my key informants.

One of the benefits of accumulating a sample population in this "snowball" manner is the maintenance of contact. I was regularly informed of important social events and was thus able to observe and participate in their social lives and in the dissemination of information among the network's members. I was always able to locate any member of the extended network through other contacts and invariably was able to hear at least what somebody was up to. This became important when verification of information was necessary. It also meant that I was able to stay in touch with members when they took a leave of absence from the social scene or if they left town for any length of time.

By the end of the fieldwork period, the network of informants who had contributed to this study comprised 193 people. Among these were 156 gay black men, 57 of whom completed extensive life history interviews. I call this subsample of 57 men "respondents," and a few of these men became key informants. Thirty-seven non-gay people contributed to the study also: they included family members of my informant group, friends, neighbors, co-workers, and clergymen.

For the duration of the study, all 193 informants lived in Harlem, in an area bounded by Riverside Drive and Third Avenue and 110th and 164th streets. All of them socialize in Harlem, either in the social institutions of the gay scene or in the private homes of friends in their extended social networks. This is not to say that they all socialize exclusively in Harlem, as, like many New York City residents, they have kith and kin spread throughout Manhattan and the other boroughs, even in Westchester County towns and New Jersey. But these gay black men pursue their gay lives in Harlem. As well, all of these men prefer black men as sex partners. Some have experienced sex across race lines, but their preference keeps them active one way or another in Harlem.

My introduction to potential informants by friends also proved to be essential in gaining entrée into many settings. Many social institutions in Harlem have locked doors, through which only the recognizable are permitted entrance. On first visit it was therefore essential to arrive in the company of someone who was already familiar, not only with acceptable procedures of behavior but also with the operators of the institution. This, in fact, was how I gained entrée into the four gay bars, the three jazz clubs, and the bathhouse where I was to conduct much of my participant observation.

To meet people, and to gain their confidence so that I could be admitted into their personal social networks, it was important that I spend time in the social institutions and in the company of community members. Overall, I spent almost two years in the field. The first six months were spent meeting people, explaining my intentions, and defining the community within which I had decided to work. This initial period also allowed me to test the feasibility of the project and some of my ideas and assumptions.

By creating a social network of informants around myself, I was able to observe and participate in the everyday lives of the gay black men I wished to describe. I was invited to dance socials, birthday parties, dinner parties, and card games, and often for meals, at which my research would be the main topic of discussion. I attended drag balls, boat rides, and talent nights at jazz clubs, as well as art exhibitions, shows at the Apollo, and shopping expeditions on 125th Street.

These social experiences enabled me to map the extent of gay life in Harlem. My work was further facilitated by my residence in the area and by my day-to-day interaction with my informants in the stores where they shopped and on the streets where they lived.

This participant observation was bolstered by the collection of life histories. Fifty-seven respondents were guided through a loosely structured interview that lasted between two and six hours. These interviews were taped and transcribed and provided much of the data that are presented and analyzed in the pages that follow. Conversations and more detailed discussions were conducted with a further 136 informants, who provided extra information or corroborated the data already collected. Usually, prior to my introduction to informants, my presence in the community had been explained. At the point of introduction, I was able to discuss any ethical considerations that may have concerned the informants.

While Black society is part of a larger society that supports institutionalized homophobia,[44] I found greater levels of tolerance in Harlem than I had expected.[45] In any event, I did not wish to attract unwarranted attention to this population. I was aware of the fact that the larger black community of which gay black men are an integral part is their hometown. Although it became apparent that most of the members of this community were open about their gayness, I could not presume that all their family members and neighbors knew that they were gay. In fact, a few of my informants were not out to their neighbors, for whatever reason, and some were not out to their family members, who also lived in the area. Discretion in their presence was always uppermost in my mind. In two instances when I met informants on the street in the company of other people, I was ignored. One informant later apologized, noting that he was not out to the family member he was with (his grandmother) and that introducing me might have been problematic.

In the social scene in Harlem, large quantities of illicit substances are consumed, quite openly in some places. This itself could have posed a problem, especially on the two occasions when plainclothes policemen entered one particular bar. In this instance my presence was a blessing: the policemen's attention was directed at me and away from the other clientele. Nonetheless, my mere presence in such a scene could have had serious repercussions for the continuation of the research. Consequently, I offered total anonymity to all of my informants and have pursued this throughout the entire undertaking.

Most important, as a white man, albeit a foreigner, my outsider status was constantly confirmed by my skin color. On one particular occasion, eighteen months into the fieldwork, a patron in one bar complained about my presence, calling me a "white motherfuckin' Jew." The very large gentleman was considerably drunk, and he was consoled by three of my informants, much to my relief. For the first time in many years of anthropological research in many different racial and ethnic communities—in fact, for the first time in my life—I was confronted publicly with the issue of race. However, my informants bid me stay, assuring me that I was very much a part of the "family." Fortunately, none of us have seen the gentleman since he left the bar, a half-hour after the incident.

I was, of course, concerned that any involvement on an intimate level would destroy the confidence I had built with other members of the community. It would also threaten the continuation of the research. However, the fact that these men prefer other black men as sex partners deflected any interest in me as a potential partner.

As a representative of Columbia University, a large institution that does not figure too favorably in the opinions of its neighbors, I found it necessary to conceal my academic affiliation on many occasions. This I felt was an extension of the overall attitude of neighborhood people toward anyone visiting from a position in the white power structure of New York City. Columbia University was definitely felt to be a part of that power structure.[46]

Most of my informants would assure me before I entered a new scene that I would be treated amicably, and this was always true. People in Harlem have been extremely friendly and hospitable, everywhere and on every occasion, despite knowing in advance who I was and what I was doing.

## The Ethnography

The composition of an ethnographic study is influenced by many factors, not the least of which is the ethnographer's own biases. As always, I have endeavored to present my subjects' stories in their own words, utilizing their concepts and perceptions of themselves. This is why I rely so heavily on lengthy quotations from interviews and notes. Extracting words or sentences detracts from the quality of the fuller expression being conveyed by the speaker. Enough is lost in the translation of verbal expression into the written word. This is especially true here, where black diction is such a vibrant, expressive art form.

The structure of this ethnography follows what I hope is a logical progression for the reader as he or she becomes acquainted with gay black men, their society, and their identities. The division of information into the following chapter topics is the result of my impressions of the significance of these topics for my informants.

Chapter 2 describes the informants and the variety of lives led by gay black men in Harlem. Chapter 3 investigates the social networks of these men and describes the symbolic construction of the gay community in Harlem. Chapter 4 describes the social world of gay life in Harlem as the locus for expression of a gay black identity. These three chapters present the impressive nature of gay black life as I encountered and experienced it.

Chapter 5 delineates the aspects of black culture that gay black men have indicated are significant for the construction of their black identity. I rely on the extensive literature that exists in many academic disciplines, including folklore and fiction, to further illustrate what these men mean. Chapter 6 performs the same exercise in relation to gay culture. Itself a relatively recent social construct, much of "gay sensibility" (Bronski 1984) has not yet reached uptown. But the substantial politicization of gay men in Harlem (by virtue of their double identity) attests to the significance of this new culture for these men. Chapter 7 defines the importance of sexuality to the construction of gay black identity, deconstructing in the process the received image of the black male in the literature on sexuality (Hernton 1965) and reconstructing an alternative picture.

Chapter 8 addresses the impact of the AIDS epidemic, currently invading black society disproportionately within the U.S. population. In New York City in the 1980s, the study of a gay population of any race or ethnicity inevitably raises issues surrounding AIDS. This chapter reflects my interest in that impact on the established social networks of these gay black men and how they and the members of their social networks have coped with the disease.[47]

Chapter 9 summarizes the development of a social identity, the gay black identity, as it has been constructed historically by gay black men in Harlem, and how this identity is being negotiated and maintained in contemporary black society.

# 2

# "A Host of Different Men": The Diversity of Gay Black Men in Harlem

All types of men are gay in Harlem—men of different regional origins and socioeconomic backgrounds who support different Christian churches and work a wide variety of jobs. All of these different types of gay men, scattered throughout Harlem, are connected to each other through a series of interdependent social networks, which in turn make up the gay black community. These social networks and this community are made by individuals, whose lives are typified by the examples below.

## Gay Black Men in Harlem

Of the fifty-seven men from whom I collected extensive life histories, twenty-seven were born and raised in Harlem, fifteen had arrived as children and were raised and schooled in Harlem, and the remainder moved to New York City as adults. Those raised and schooled in Harlem had migrated to the city as children with their families. Most came after World War II, between 1945 and 1965. Some had migrated earlier, in a system of "chain migration," again linked to familial migration.[1]

Over a third of my informants have attended college. Not only does this mean that we are dealing with a well-educated population; it also means that many of these men cemented friendships during college that they have carried forward into adult gay life as the core of their current social networks. These college friends are "brothers," "sisters," or "girlfriends" with whom the informants interact on a daily or weekly basis. Some are roommates, some are in business together, some are lovers, and all are part of the "family."

The adult group came to attend college in New York City or to pursue careers. Every one of these men also came because he was gay: to get away from the confines of extended family at home, to move into a significant gay black community where color was not an issue, or to be "where the boys are"—that is, where a gay black man would be surrounded by fellow black men.

Being gay is cited frequently as a motivation for urban migration by adult gay men (Martin and Dean 1990). Although no formal studies have been made of this phenomenon, a large percentage of any city's gay population have immigrated from the hinterland. Gay men do this to avoid family and friends who are homophobic and to participate in the gay social life that most cities offer. New York City is known by gays the world over as a "gay town" and probably has the largest gay population of any city in the world. It has attracted men from all over the United States and from around the world.

So it is with Harlem. In the gay black world, it is well known that Harlem offers a gay lifestyle. While Washington, D.C., Atlanta, Oakland, and St. Louis are also known to have large gay black populations, New York has a double attraction: a large gay social scene as well. Here the issue of race is also important. Gay black men wishing to escape smaller towns, families, and integrated gay social scenes can immerse themselves in gay black culture in only a few places. Harlem is one of these. Whether to avoid a largely white gay scene or because they are interested in other black men, many of these adult immigrants choose to live in a black community. Harlem offers them a gay community within a black community.

While only one of my fifty-seven respondents is a "leader" in the community, some others are prominent figures because they maintain high visibility in the gay scene in Harlem. However, as was explained to me, most gay men born in Harlem or living in Harlem do not "hang out" in the scene there. Like the majority of the gay population in any city, they stay away from the bar, disco, and bathhouse scene because it does not appeal to them for one reason or another. In other words, the gay scene in Harlem leaves one with a false sense of the total gay population there. It excludes, for instance, closeted and bisexual men. However, come a major celebratory event in the lives of gay people, such as the Gay Pride Parade or the Halloween Parade in New York City, some of this silent population will emerge, swelling the ranks, in some cases, by hundreds of thousands of people. In Harlem, dance socials and boat rides evoke a similar response. Attendance is well above the core population of the gay scene, filling the venue to overflow.

Apart from such extraordinary social occasions (described in some detail later), gay men in Harlem lead very ordinary lives. They go to work Monday to Friday, mainly from 9:00 A.M. to 5:00 P.M., and spend their evenings in a bar, shopping, dining out, going to the movies, or at home watching television. On the weekends they perform household chores, go shopping on 125th Street or downtown, visit friends and family, throw dinner parties and card games, go to bars and dances, and attend church on Sunday. These activities draw all the different types of gay men together: men from different socio-economic groups, men born in Harlem, and men who have immigrated from "down South."

## Immigrants in Harlem

Two of my respondents were born in the West Indies. Arnel was born in Barbados and emigrated with his family to Harlem when he was nine. He feels quite comfortable here in the gay scene: "I love Harlem. It's the *only* place! ... It's the black gay capital of the world." Nevertheless, as a West Indian he has to deal with a certain amount of prejudice. He notes verbal discrimination on the streets of Harlem: "These children [fellow gay men] will wear you out. Sometimes I just wanna go home. Actually, as I get older I do go out home more often. These boys just wear you out." "Home" for Arnel is Queens, where his family moved some years ago and where he attended both high school and college.

Clifton was born in Kingston, Jamaica, and emigrated to Harlem in 1978 at the age of twenty-eight. Like many of the informants who came from other parts of the United States, he came to Harlem for a variety of reasons, one of which was to escape the narrow confines of family and anti-gay discrimination in Jamaica: "I was tired of it, y'know. I mean we got no respect at home. Not even from our families. It was hard. So I saved me money and here I am." He too has experienced some difficulty making friends and adjusting to the big city life, but he certainly prefers his gay life here to the life he led in secret in Jamaica.

Sixteen of my respondents were born in the South, including two from Washington, D.C. Seven came from South Carolina, five of whom completed high school there before emigrating. Both of the men from D.C. were schooled in Harlem, as was one of the two from Alabama. The five men from Virginia, North Carolina, Georgia, Florida, and Louisiana had all completed high school before coming north. Most came for familial or economic reasons, some for education. All of them cited being gay as a reason as well: the need to be able to live in a community of gay black men, within an all-black society.

## Brothers from Georgia

As mentioned above, some informants came to Harlem as children with their immediate families or as part of a chain migration of relatives.[2] This process occurs when one or two relatives move north to urban areas, obtain employment, and settle into accommodations. Then they "send for" (usually paying the way of) a sibling, spouse, or parent. In this manner, whole extended families have come north since World War II. A similar mode of migration unites gay family members and gay friends formerly from the South but now living in Harlem. This chain migration connects people to social networks of support and introduces them to role models who enable them to settle into their new lives in the gay community in Harlem.

Quint moved to Harlem in 1981 from Thomasville, Georgia. His older brother, Warren, had come to New York to further his career in banking. He had leased a bank-owned apartment on the block where he worked in Harlem and sent for Quint to join him. Quint had been two years out of high school and had not found steady work. He had made odd forays into Atlanta but ended up drifting around town for weeks at a time with other gay friends. He admits that the "bright lights" and large gay scene of Atlanta had got to him and that the drugs would inevitably get him into trouble. But he needed to get out of Thomasville. There were too many brothers and sisters and cousins and aunts and uncles, and always "church, church, church."

Quint had grown up in a family of five boys and three girls. He and his twin brother were the youngest. His father, a native of Thomasville, was a carpenter, and his mother, who hailed from Tallahassee, across the border in Florida, was a schoolteacher. They had a large home on the edge of town and a large property for the boys to play in. Quint said that when he was "real young," he remembers his grandparents visiting and helping them pick fruit from the peach trees that covered the property. His parents supplemented their incomes by growing and selling fruit and vegetables.

QUINT: Me and my brothers used to complain about bein' slaves. I mean, every time we'd come home from school, we had to work in the fields. And for what? I mean we didn't even get pocket money. It was "go to school," "do your homework," "go pick [peaches]." That's why we used to take off on the weekend. Especially when we got older—in high school.

When they "took off" on the weekends, the boys would borrow an older brother's car and head for Tallahassee or Atlanta. Warren had a close friend from Thomasville who had moved to Atlanta with his family. They would stay at his place if it was too cold to sleep in the car or if they couldn't find someone else to stay with.

QUINT: [Warren] really was the one. He took me to Atlanta the first time. We were real close so, y'know. He knew. He took me to Backstreet [a gay club in Atlanta]. The place was full of men. Dancin' together. Kissin'. And holdin' hands. My eyes were so busy. I guess he saw that. And that's when it all started. Every time he went, I went.

Quint's homosexual experiences had started some years before in elementary school, where he'd been "foolin' around" with some of his classmates. There were two boys he remembers having sex with on a regular basis. They did not conceive of themselves as being "lovers," but the three were known as "tight friends." These friendships, and what was presumed to be going on, alienated Quint from his twin brother. He had his own circle of friends, and he and Quint never hung out together. In high school, Quint starred as an artist and contributed to a large mural that was commissioned for a new auditorium. He was the only student at the school selected to assist the artist in painting the vestibule. Everyone in town read about him in the newspaper. But, he says, everyone at the school already knew who he was. He used to hang out with the basketball team, although he never played, and he even had sex with some of the players.

QUINT: I think I had a reputation as a punk. I wasn't sissy or nothing like that. We had one boy who was a real sissy. He was younger than me. He used to hang out with the girls all the time. . . . I used to feel sorry for him. They gave him a rough time.

Because of this other boy's obvious femininity, he became the primary target for attack. Appearing more masculine in comparison, Quint escaped a lot of the anti-gay abuse that might otherwise have been directed at him. But he did get ragged a little by some of the boys with whom he had sex. Then again, they knew, so Quint says, that "they were on to a good thing" and "they didn't give me too much grief."

Quint believes that it was from this crowd that his older brother, Warren, heard about his likes and dislikes. He never said anything to Quint, but he dropped hints about what he knew, and that made Quint suspect that Warren might also be gay. After several visits to Atlanta they talked about it. Warren liked both men and women sexually, but he enjoyed the company of men socially.

QUINT: You know, it's the same old story. Straight men and women love the gay crowd. Not only for the sex. For the parties. Gay men know how to have a good time. . . . In Atlanta, all the time there'd be crowds of straight boys hanging around us. Looking for some stuff. Looking for drugs. They just wanted a good time. And they knew where to come find it.

It was at this time, with his gayness becoming public knowledge and a desire to experience life in a gay environment away from family, that Quint plotted with Warren to move away. New York City, and Harlem in particular, seemed to be the logical place. Harlem is still regarded as a mecca for black folks moving north. Also, New York boasted a large gay scene.

Quint and Warren have been living together in New York for eight years now. Quint says he's still not sure about Warren. Warren has never had a girlfriend or a boyfriend in New York. Quint says that Warren keeps his sex life to himself, although he always hangs out in the gay bars in Harlem. But the two never go out together anymore. Warren has a group of male friends he runs with, and they have all been having some problems with crack. Quint too went down that road, but after losing one job and having to struggle to get back into the banking world, he has managed to avoid getting into it again. He only hopes that Warren's romance with the drug will soon be over, because he too is about to lose his job. Warren has a good job in New York and even found one at the same bank for Quint.

Quint has felt caught between settling down in a new life and the "bright lights" of New York City. However, a social network of gay friends and the example they set have enabled him to pursue his career goals. After a few months in New York, Quint began attending college. He has since earned an Associate's degree and is currently taking courses part-time to complete his Bachelor's. He has had no luck finding a lover, a permanent partner, but has been pursuing one man for some years: "The guy's a drunk. I mean he's so sweet, and the lovin' is good. But he drinks every night at the bar. And I can't get him to do anything else." In the meantime, Quint has dated several other men. He would like to find someone, a permanent partner or "husband," so that he could move away from his brother and start a life of his own. He prefers black men as sex partners and friends, and likes living in Harlem, but says that he is ready to move away: "I have a good chance to make it. But I need to get away from the drugs. It's too much. Everywhere you go people's doin' it." Meanwhile, Quint is working hard to get promoted at work so that he can make more money, become more independent of his brother, and finish college.

Quint's story is typical of the young adult gay men who migrate to Harlem. Not only is the immigration linked to other family members but the maintenance of ties to family back home is regarded as important. Quint and his brother return home often for holidays and significant family events. Patterns of stable employment and the continuation of education are evident among this migrant group. These activities enhance security (in the new environment) and economic and residential independence.

## Louis and Paul

Louis met Paul in 1983. They dated for two years, but Louis continued to play around, until Paul delivered the ultimatum: we live together or break up. Louis chose to stay, and the two men have purchased a spacious apartment in a brownstone. Several of my informants own their own apartments and cars. Often homes were inherited, but maintenance costs and other payments demand well-paying employment, which most of them retain as well. Paul works two jobs to help with payments on the house and with savings to buy a car, and Louis struggles with night school as he completes his Master's degree. They are active socially in most of the "gay scene" in Harlem, visiting the gay bars there at least two or three nights a week, often staying longer on Fridays and Saturdays. They also support citywide, black gay social clubs that provide a wide variety of social gatherings, from picnics and boat rides to dances and dinners. Louis considers himself very lucky.

LOUIS: I am lucky, you know. Paul is so very good to me. What he has to put up with.... I wouldn't want to be out here alone now. Not with this AIDS shit. It's scary. I mean, I've always got someone to go home to. Give thanks for Paul!

Louis and Paul have been living together for about seven years, just off St. Nicholas Avenue at 150th Street in Harlem. Louis is very proud of himself, his college degrees, and his vocational history. He says he is proud to be both black and gay and that his non-gay friends and family are slowly accepting and understanding his gayness. He is currently working hard to put a younger sister through college, an act that is endearing him even more to his mother. He and Paul also support two less fortunate gay men in their immediate neighborhood as they struggle to complete their high school equivalency diplomas. Louis serves on his co-op board, and both he and Paul support three large, citywide, black gay social organizations (which will be discussed later). As well as maintaining a high profile in the gay scene in Harlem, both Louis and Paul visit their mothers, together, every weekend. This can be an exhausting task as they haven't yet bought a car and their mothers live in New Rochelle and New Jersey, respectively.

## Education and Occupation

All of my respondents attended high school: thirty in Harlem, nine elsewhere in New York City, three in Mount Vernon, one upstate, two in New Jersey, eleven down South, and one in the West Indies. Twenty-one of them have also attended college, seven of them outside of New York City. Four hold graduate degrees, one in law, one in education, one in music, and one in business. Two are currently registered at graduate schools in the city: Louis and Scott are both studying for Master's degrees in fine arts, one in theater and the other in film. While Scott has family support for his degree, Louis is employed at the same time that he is studying. His employers assist with defraying his mounting tuition costs.[3]

Unlike the picture we have of black men in the social-scientific literature, all but one of the men I interviewed for this study have been continuously employed since they left high school or college. One is now retired, and one is on welfare. Willis gave up his job as a Wall Street investment company's receptionist so that he could stay home and take care of his preschool-age son. The remainder of these men work at regular jobs, one or two moonlighting to cover extra expenses incurred by purchasing a car, an apartment, or a home.[4]

By background and occupation, the informant group of 156 men represent a variety of socioeconomic groups. Many of them work in the business world, as temporary office workers, secretaries, receptionists, administrative assistants, office supervisors, accounts clerks, bank clerks, insurance clerks and agents, retail sales clerks, storeroom clerks, and one as a computer programmer. There are three barmen, four teachers and a high school counselor, two tradesmen, two cooks and a catering chef, a nurse, a librarian, two postal clerks, and two transport authority employees. Five men work full-time in the arts: a production assistant at a theater, a film director, a singer, a dancer, and a musician. Ten are self-employed: a lawyer, a travel agent, a tailor, a car-service and laundry operator, two mortuary owners, a hairdresser, a photographer, a carpenter, and a florist. All of these people employ other gay men in their businesses, and the latter four employ gay personnel exclusively. All of them live and work in Harlem, although some do serve clientele from other parts of the city. These men do not fit the stereotypes of being gay—that is, of hairdressers and florists running around and "partying" all night. They are engaged in stable employment. Also, their broad range of occupations reflects the typical class, professional, and income dimensions of any American city. Such permanence of employment is a rare feature in social-scientific descriptions of black men, as is the degree of success associated with these men's careers, especially in business.

## The Twins

Even the Harlem- born and raised informants contradict received wisdom on black men and their lifestyles. Although at least two distinct socioeconomic groups have emerged—that is, the gay men and the "boys" (hustlers)—neither of these groups fits patterns already described for black men in the literature.[5] Some of the "boys" do fall into the "street corner man" category, many of those only temporarily, yet they still aspire to the same goals in life as gay men who are employed, housed, and educated. While socioeconomic background is often influential in determining later class membership, in the gay community itself, class is not a major issue. The brotherhood of the gay community in Harlem stretches across class lines (see "Cleveland's Buddies" and "Miss Donny" below).

Carter has been hairdressing for almost thirty years. He used to work at home, serving a clientele composed of family and friends, but five years ago he opened his own salon, employing three other gay men as stylists. They brought with them their clients, who come from all over Manhattan, Brooklyn, and New Jersey. The venture has proved so successful that Carter intends to open another salon next year. Now he rarely works in the salon itself, spending his time managing the business and negotiating future property and mortgage deals from home.

CARTER: I didn't realize how easy it would be to expand the business. I would have done it years ago.... I owe a lot of it [his success] to my employees. They're marvelous. They work long hours and love their work.... They're very popular with all the young boys. With these new cuts. Especially Margie [a drag queen]. She's really a man. Sometimes I wonder if some of those young men, especially those tough little ones, you know, from across the street [in the projects], I wonder if they know she's a man.

Carter's twin brother, Adrian, has helped him financially. He is also gay, and they live together in the apartment where they were raised, above the restaurant where Adrian is a cook. Their mother worked in the same restaurant for forty years. Adrian says it was "natural" for him to follow in her footsteps. He brings home an endless supply of food, and they are allowed to use the restaurant kitchen to prepare food for the large, and popular, dinner parties the pair frequently throw. Cleveland says, "You know I can cook. I use my Mama's recipes an' all. But those boys can turn it out. They can really cook."

Cleveland's judgment of Carter and Adrian as "good gay friends" rests as much on these men's catering abilities as it does on the fact that they have been stably employed for many years and can operate a household successfully. Raised in a single-parent, female-headed household, these twin brothers have been regularly employed, now owning their own businesses and home, and maintain a large social network of friends and family.

## Living Arrangements

Some of the gay men interviewed for this project live with family members: some with other single gay or non-gay brothers, some with sisters, and some with parents or grandparents. However, many of the men live by themselves.

Cleveland lives alone—"not that I want for company when I needs it"—as do twenty of the respondents. Twenty-nine have one roommate, nine of whom are lovers. Five have two roommates, two have three roommates, and one has five—his lover and four children. Twenty-five say they are the head of their household. Five share such responsibilities and seven say they do not: their lovers or other family members run the household. Forty-eight rent their apartments in Harlem from other gay, black, or, most commonly, "Arab" landlords. (Not one of my informants has a "white" landlord.) Seven men own their own apartments, and three own houses (two inherited whole brownstones from their parents, and one, who lives in a rented apartment in Harlem, also owns a house in Jamaica, Queens, which he rents out).

The fact that these black men are responsible for other family members, as heads of households or as home owners, contrasts with much of the information we have on black men in the social-scientific literature.[6] And many of these respondents have non-gay brothers or other male family members who have similar lifestyles.

## The "Boys"

A distinct group of men within the gay black population are hustlers or "boys." These are men who sometimes sell or exchange their sexual favors exclusively within the gay black community for "cash dollars," shelter, food, or other consumer items.[7] Forty-one hustlers were associated with this research project. Thirty-four of these became informants, all of whom classified themselves as gay.

The "boys" ranged in age from twenty-one to forty-two. Fourteen of them came from single-parent homes, many of which were welfare-dependent. Thirteen came from two-parent households, mainly in the projects. In these cases either both parents worked (often two jobs) or the family was welfare-dependent. However, some of the "boys" came from two-parent, stable families and chose their vocation.[8] These men had no need financially to enter into a life of hustling. Their experiences as hustlers were not the result of economic deprivation or child abuse, as most of the reports on gay hustlers would have us believe.[9]

One of the hustlers had been orphaned as a child, and six had no contact with any kin and did not know whether their parents or siblings were still alive. They had had contact with both parents earlier in life. Two of these men were homeless for the duration of the project. Sometimes they stayed in men's shelters in Harlem. Although sixteen of the "boys" had dropped out of high school, thirteen had finished, four had some college education, and one had completed a college degree. Twenty-three had spent some time in jail, and most had been or were currently addicted to an illicit substance. Fourteen had formerly used intravenous drugs, but all of these men now smoked reefer, crack, ice, or bazooka. Occasionally some hashish, cocaine, opium, or dust would come their way, but more expensive items, including prescription pills, would be sold for cash to purchase larger quantities of cheaper drugs.

Several of the "boys" were intermittently employed in regular jobs. Johnson worked as an office clerk for six months; Andy was employed as a building superintendent for one year; Jasper worked throughout the research period as a waiter; Lewis worked at a carwash; Mario occasionally modeled; and Malik was a mechanic. Calvin had trained with a stonemason.

CALVIN: I worked for a few years with a stonemason. He was training me to carve. Headstones, mainly. He had a big lot in the Bronx and we'd go there every day and work. I started with some cleaning work and then he started to show me how to use the tools and shit. But even then I was gay. You know, I'd spend the evenings at the bar and I'd pick up men. They started offering me money to have sex. I didn't ask for it. Not at the beginning. Then they'd tell me I was good. Some of them would give me more money. I was making just as much there as at the job. So I soon got tired of goin' to work every day. It was more fun to hang out down here at night. That's how it got started.

It is important to note here that many hustlers became involved in money for sex at the invitation of their prospective partners. Several of them told me that they became hustlers because they were offered money rather than having gone out to seek it. Most of them will still have sex with other men without payment, especially if they really like the person involved. Many of them will not ask for money directly and will take what they are offered.

Some hustlers made money within the drug industry (mainly as runners or vendors), and some hustled other goods. Mikey sold books and furniture in the bars, and André could always find good cuts of meat. In fact, most of these men had other jobs besides hustling sex, which merely supplemented their income. Although not paid much in "cash dollars," they often received payment in kind: meals, accommodations, drinks and cigarettes, maybe a night out, a weekend holiday, or a new pair of sneakers.

Others hustle to support a drug habit. Tracey comes from a middle-class family of three boys and one girl. His father has a high-ranking job in a city department, and his mother operates her own business. The family recently purchased a house in New Rochelle, where his sister and her husband have also purchased a home.

About five years ago, Tracey was attending Hunter College. (He attended parochial schools in Queens, near where his grandmother lives. In fact, he lived with her during his high school years.) But he became disillusioned with college and began spending his days hanging out in midtown gay bars. He watched as other young black and Hispanic men tricked the older businessmen clientele. Although he met a couple of men who wanted to keep him, he preferred sex with the black men in the Harlem scene. Gradually he became more and more involved with gay life in Harlem.

At the same time he began to use cocaine and its derivative, crack. The ensuing addiction cost him all the money he could muster. Eventually his parents, sister, and grandmother refused to have him live at their homes because of his stealing, and so he has been at the mercy of his friends in the gay scene for somewhere to stay. Twice he has been through rehabilitation programs, but he was back into his drug habit for the duration of this research. Tracey is a very attractive man who always draws comments and trade from a crowded bar, but he is slowly losing weight and taking less care with his appearance—the telltale signs of going under to crack. Several men in Harlem have taken him in. Currently, he is staying with Cleveland.

CLEVELAND: I won't leave him in the house alone. He calls me at night, comes by, showers and sleeps, and leaves in the mornin' when I does. I like the boy, but he's gotta get himself back on line. He's been to school. He's a well-spoken, educated boy. He can get himself a good job. Not like most of the others you'll be seein' in here.

All of these men featured in the social networks of my other, non-hustler, gay black men. They were involved in the financial, social, and emotional support systems that constitute the gay community in Harlem. Many were the recipients of money, food, and shelter, but many also contributed: as companions, sexual partners, by running errands, or doing household chores.

Most of the "boys" had grown up on the streets where other informants lived and thus easily became part of the "family" once their sexual orientation was known. This long association with other gay men meant that they were taken care of within the support capabilities of the social networks to which they belonged. They were regarded by non-hustler gay men as "brothers" and treated accordingly. Most of the "boys" protected their relationships with other gay men simply because they were "family"—someone to turn to when in trouble or without a place to stay.

Cutting across this social network organization was a set of hustler cliques, each a group of young men clustered around a leader, an older hustler who acted as their teacher and protector. These smaller groups of close friends also acted like families in terms of support and sharing resources. Herbie has such a clique around him.

## Herbie and His "Family"

Herbie was the first of the "boys" to befriend me. He offered me assistance and "protection" and pointed out that two or three of the other senior hustlers were not to be trusted. Later I found out that these men contested his leadership and seniority in the bars. Several younger men hang out with Herbie, who is thirty-six, and run errands for him or any of the bar patrons that need cigarettes or food. Herbie oversees the "boys" behavior inside the bars and on the sidewalk immediately outside. He recommends the younger "boys" to older prospective clients. For this service he would receive a beer, money, or at least the understanding that an obligation had been established for the particular patron to "lend" him cigarette money or carfare.

Herbie lives with his lover, René, a drag queen. According to René, their relationship, over ten years old, was fraught with problems: Herbie's drug use, physical violence, and theft. René say she puts up with it because she loves him. "He gets away with all that shit, 'cause I love him." They rarely go out together, but René takes good care of Herbie, feeds him, and houses him.

Herbie also has a "wife," the mother of five of his children. She lives north of the city, in Yonkers, and holds down two jobs in order to keep the children. Occasionally Herbie goes uptown to visit for a few days. He takes some money and toys for the children, but after a while he has a falling-out with Helen and is dispatched back to René. Herbie's eldest son, at twenty, is beginning to appear in the gay scene. Herbie has said that he would do anything to prevent his son getting caught up in the life but admits that ultimately it's his son's own choice.

Herbie is one of half a dozen senior "boys" who lead a small network of younger hustlers. Each of these leaders is linked to the broader gay community through lovers or friends in the social networks of non-hustler gay men whom they have known since childhood or school days. A few of them have children from earlier liaisons with women, but all now engage exclusively in same-sex behavior.

Herbie says he was "always gay." He began hustling to help pay for his drug-habit expenses. But there are many other reasons why these men sell sex: long periods of underemployment or unemployment, lack of career training or motivation, lack of education, and poverty. Sex is usually only one of a range of commodities that they sell.

## Darrell the Boxer

Darrell was the fourth son born into a Black Muslim family of eleven children. He has not heard from his father in twenty years and assumes he is dead. Darrell was raised by his mother and a maternal grandmother. Now he lives with his grandmother but seldom sees her because his hours are irregular.

Darrell has a son and a daughter who live on 127th Street with their mother. Whenever he can he takes some money there for the children, but their mother will not allow him to see them. Darrell had had a short but successful career as a boxer, winning thirty-two of thirty-three public bouts. But drugs undid his success. To support his habit he worked in the drug business, selling marijuana and pills. At twenty-eight, he became a full-time gay hustler to make more money. His poor education left him feeling that he was unemployable in the mainstream job market and that the occupations of selling drugs and sex, which he enjoyed, were his lot. However, his income from hustling has declined, especially since he is older and has a reputation for engaging in unsafe sexual practices. He has also developed a reputation as a thief. According to Leonard, who is thirty-six, "He don't care. Poor boy gonna die. And everywhere he goes he ends up stealing. Him and [Carlos]. He looks and acts and wears clothing that make him look like he's twenty-two. Twenty-five max. Yet to talk with them, they're your contemporaries."

Darrell usually arrives at one of the bars about two or three in the afternoon. He'll have a drink with one of the "bargirls" who work the day shift behind the bar or get one of the older gentlemen who drink in the bars during the daytime to buy him a drink or something to eat. He runs errands for patrons, buys coffee or lunch for the bar staff, and picks up "smoke" (marijuana) for those who need it. When his cohort of hustlers arrives around 5:00 or 6:00 P.M., he starts getting high himself. He goes in and out of the bar, running errands all evening, and stays in the vicinity of the bars until closing at 4:00 A.M.

## "A Nice Guy"

Some of the "boys" have no need for the money but have entered the trade voluntarily because they like the business. Many such men stop hustling once employed, and many have quit altogether because of AIDS. However, even these men often end up as drug abusers.

Freddy is an exception. He was born to a teenage mother who was in school at the time of his birth. She has since moved to California, and Freddy has not heard from her in almost twenty years. To this day he does not know who his father is. He has always shared a home with his maternal grandmother, who "works and goes to church." She takes good care of him, and although he is tired of living at home, he realizes that life there is better than it would be on the street, the only viable alternative that he is aware of.

At twenty-three he is one of the youngest of the "boys" in the scene. He only goes to one bar and rarely stays out late. Born and raised in the projects near 145th Street, he has known little other than his life in Harlem. Regarded as one of the best-mannered, most well dressed, and cleanest of the "boys" in the scene in Harlem, he has no trouble obtaining tricks. He has no particular rate for his sexual favors and will accept payment in kind. He refuses to become employed within the drug world and thus dependent on its easy money, to which so many of his peers have succumbed. While he studies to improve his job chances, he is quite content to hustle.

FREDDY: I don't need to be doin' this shit. It's dangerous. And I just don' mean the AIDS. Some of these motherfuckers will rip you off. They'll be tryin' to get over on you. Sayin' they have no money after you done serviced them. And then there's the other brothers. If they see you takin' their business, they'll be waitin' to cut you. It has its dangers. But I enjoy it. I like to be here with these men. They're friendly. For the most part. They look after me.... I could look for work. You know, but the best way to get a job roun' here is by word of mouth. So they know I be lookin'. So someday somethin'll come up.... Well, I could stay home, but I'd rather be out with these guys than sittin' up there watchin' TV and shit.

Odd bouts with using drugs and a lack of steady employment have made Freddy somewhat withdrawn and introspective. He has a select group of friends within the non-hustling gay black population with whom he will sit in the bar. He spends most of his evenings with Paul and Donny, who calls him "Baby." Both of these men say that Freddy is "a nice guy," speaks well, and does not get into the drug scene too much. In an effort to help him out, Paul and Donny will take him out to eat rather than give him cash, and Paul and his lover, Louis, are paying for Freddy's tuition so that he can obtain his high school equivalency diploma.

While the cliques of hustlers function as social mini-networks satisfying the immediate survival needs of this small group of men, their connection to the gay population in Harlem is via the larger social networks that make up the community. That they are temporary "husbands," "brothers," "cousins," or "children" of the other gay men in the "family" symbolically underlines the fact that these men are a part of the gay community in a very real sense of the word. Their "family" membership underscores years of friendship and companionship with the non-hustler gay men in the very neighborhoods where they all grew up and still live as adults.

In the gay community, the "boys" are regarded by other gay men also as part of the "family." They are just different gay men: men who may have come from poorer circumstances, who may lack the education or other skills to obtain regular employment, who may have a substance abuse problem, who may have fallen on bad times, or who have simply decided to hustle as a vocation. Nevertheless, they are "brothers" in the gay community and are treated as such.

## Kinfolk

Family is a very important factor in the lives of black people. There is much social-scientific literature to attest to this. However, much of the data on families of gay black men in Harlem contrasts with the information that social science has produced for black urban families.[10]

Twenty-eight of my fifty-seven respondents were raised by both their parents, and one was raised by his mother and her brother. Donny noted once that he couldn't understand all the "brouhaha" about single-parent families in Harlem, when he and all his friends were raised by both parents: "My daddy only died recently. But most of us have both parents still alive. You'll see.... When I was in high school, I remember all the fathers taking part in a father and son softball tournament over in Riverside Park. And everybody's daddy came along." Twenty-seven were raised for at least a few years by their mothers alone, and one by his maternal grandmother. Forty-five have mothers still alive, with whom they interact frequently. Twenty-three fathers also figure prominently in the current social networks of these informants. Seventy-seven percent were raised with between one and four siblings, and only two were raised alone. Maternal grandmothers, maternal aunts and uncles, and paternal aunts figure prominently in their social networks as well.

The levels of frequent interaction with older kin reflect the power and importance of family ties to these residents of Harlem. Even more important, and in contrast to the current discourse on black men, is their involvement with their own children. Nine of my respondents are parents, five of whom raise their children. One raises his three sons and one daughter with his lover, and another raises his daughter and son with his ex-wife. Six of these informants are legally divorced, and one is married but separated from his wife. All the rest have never married.

## Church

Religion has played a significant role in the lives of all of these men. They were all raised "in the church," and forty still maintain close ties to a church or faith. Forty were raised Baptist, seven Catholic, six Methodist, three Episcopalian, and one Seventh Day Adventist.

On a bright and humid Sunday in March, Cleveland, Randy, and I attended morning service at a large Baptist church. This was not their regular church, but because it attracted "white tourists" (by the bus load), Cleveland decided I would feel more comfortable than if I commenced my religious experiences in Harlem in his small neighborhood chapel.

We sat at the rear of the church, so "all those church girls won't be watchin' us." The two-and-a-half-hour service was a lively, loud, and colorful event. The bright sunlight streamed into the church through several huge stained-glass windows. The Gothic structure appeared to be floodlit. Behind Reverend Doctor Tucker and his beautifully carved wooden "throne" stood a bank of forty singers dressed in purple and gold-trimmed gowns. They were surrounded by large pots of freshly cut purple, white, and yellow flowers. In the male half of this choir were three of my respondents. One of them performed a solo during the service. Another of my respondents played the organ. The enthusiasm of the choir members and the organist suffused the whole church. They led the congregation in its punctuation of Dr. Tucker's sermon and interjected shouts and invocations into prayers and hymns. During one of the choir's longest and loudest performances, when several of the singers made waving gestures with their outstretched arms, ushers guided collection plates along the pews of the seated congregation.

Months later, I was able to visit the "dressing room" in the vestry before another Sunday service. The men's room was a flurry of activity as the choir members preened themselves for their performance. Several of the more gregarious of the men were "cutting up." There were also some flirtatious glances and a lot of "brotherly affection." This was particularly noticeable between those men I knew to be "in the life." As Leslie says, "Backstage we're all family. But you know it, child, some of us are more family than others, if you know what I mean. They all carry on, even the straight ones. But as long as it's kept in the family nobody's gonna say nothing."

This cloistered gay "family" within the church provides many gay men in Harlem with a social life that is an alternative to the bar and club scene. Gay friendships are formed in the church and carry over into the social lives of these men: they go out together to restaurants or to the movies, attend dinner parties and picnics together, and are active members in each other's social networks of support.

Suffice it to say, the Christian churches' teachings against homosexuality have proved problematic for many gay men and have no doubt played a role in the significant level of lapsed or relaxed participation of gay black men. Seventeen of my informants no longer associate with a church or a religion. Seven current Baptists and two current Catholics do not attend church. One current Methodist and one current Baptist were both formerly Catholics, and two Buddhists were formerly a Methodist and a Baptist. The latter still sings in a Baptist choir on Sundays.

Most of those informants who no longer attend church, or who have changed church or religion, will cite church teachings as a reason for their absence or conversion. As it was explained to me by those who remain, the preachers know that many of their flock are gay. They accept and benefit from the gay men's extraordinary participation; in some cases the only men who participate regularly as choristers, organists, and ushers are gay. Even some preachers are gay. But to keep the coffers replete, the preachers must address their congregation in the most religiously conservative manner possible. In the larger churches, most of the congregation is older, conservative, and from out of town (New Jersey or Westchester County). These non-gay parishioners want to hear the biblical teachings as they know them, and if this means that the preacher must rail against homosexuality now and then, so be it. The gay men who remain with the churches do so in part for the opportunity to socialize and for the prestige that can be gleaned from choir or other church participation, and not just in the black community. It looks good at the workplace too. In turn, the high degree of acceptance the churches show to gay men stems from their participation. Most church participants are women. Their involvement with the gay men at church has resulted in many long-standing friendships. Thus, the preacher and the church get male participants; the women have nonthreatening male companionship; and the gay men find a socially acceptable role in the black community. The importance of church affiliation stems from the fact that the church maintains a central role in black urban life and represents for many black people a tie to their roots in the South and to southern church life. This is especially evident in the lives of the newer arrivals in Harlem.

## The Organist

Wilbert, who holds a graduate degree in music, attends church three or four times a week. He plays organ on Sundays, for three or four hours, to a packed church. Three nights a week he leads choir practice. This can be somewhat grueling after a long day teaching piano to young adults in his uptown studio apartment: "Running between the apartment, church, and the bar exhausted me utterly. But that's life.... Now I have to admit, this new husband is a little demanding. I've had to cut down on my social life to accommodate him. Mind you, I still have to go up by the church every day."

Wilbert recalls that his life has always revolved around a church. His father used to be a preacher in Birmingham, before he retired, and demanded of Wilbert and his two brothers a devotion that Wilbert says has "run out long ago, child, especially where they [his two brothers] was concerned. They gone off and got lost. One in Chicago and one in Atlanta. I don't know where they be. I just hope the Lord is still with them and is guidin' them and protectin' them."

Wilbert was raised very close to home and had no real friends, except his two older brothers, until he went to college in Atlanta. He said he went a little "wild" with "all those big ol' Georgia boys" and would frequently refuse to go home on the holidays, excusing himself on the grounds of too much schoolwork so that he could stay in Atlanta and "have me some fun!" He had one "main lover" in Atlanta. This man would visit him on campus, often bringing some friends, who in turn would find "some fun" with Wilbert's wide circle of gay friends. Wilbert recalls that on two occasions he returned to Birmingham without his parents knowing and performed in drag queen competitions "right under their noses." However, all through college he maintained "the faith"—that is, remained true to his religious convictions and attended church regularly. When he came to "this wicked town, this Sodom and Gomorrah," New York City, to attend graduate school, he sought "refuge" in the church and eventually volunteered his services to the preacher. Such church connections are a significant issue for many of the immigrant population. Displaced and alienated in their new home, they find a local church to help establish friends and security or, more frequently, are introduced to one by their hometown preachers, who are part of a nationwide network of churches.

At first, Wilbert made some close friends in the church, but a group of them got into trouble for having sex in the vestry, so he distanced himself from them. Now he maintains close ties with only two members of the choir, and all three hang out together in Harlem. Most important, all three have "kept the faith" and use the church as the real focus of their social lives. Church is a haven for Wilbert, especially because he is far away from his family and their church down South. The church has also provided him with the social network of support that he needs to get by in the city. "All my best friends in New York," Wilbert says, "I met in the church."

Another factor that emerges from my interviews is an obvious dichotomy between the South and the North. The different cultures and traditions of these regions are exemplified by different types of men: the respondents who are faithful churchgoers as opposed to the "nonbelievers." The churchgoers tend to be Southerners or city residents who maintain close ties with their southern kin. The church participants and the faithful are always defined by the nonbelievers as "church girls." This distinction between urban and secular northern culture and rural and religious southern culture also came up when informants discussed the Reverend Dr. Martin Luther King and his lack of support in the urban ghettos during the civil rights movement heyday of the 1960s. King's contemporary, Malcolm X, drew more support on the streets of Harlem because he was not of the church. While King was thought of as a good man, Malcolm X's confrontational attitude appealed more to the sensibility of streetwise urban

New Yorkers.[11] Malcolm X also attracted many Harlemites to the Nation of Islam in the 1960s. Two of my informants were raised in Muslim families. Several others support the "brothers" and have even considered joining the Black Muslims.

## A Buddhist

Garvey is another gay man in Harlem who has changed his religious affiliation because of the Christian churches' attitudes toward homosexuality. Raised African Methodist in Virginia by his maternal grandmother, he said he and his younger brother, orphaned at age seven and three, were strictly disciplined by the "ol' lady." She oversaw their homework sessions at night and dragged them to church meetings and "church folk's homes" all weekend. They would sit in church for hours at a time. Garvey says he understands why his younger straight brother disappeared as soon as he was able, not returning for three years, until age nineteen, with two children in tow. "If it wasn't for the good-lookin' preacher," Garvey said. "I woulda run away a long time before." Although he hedged when discussing "the preacher," his later accounts about his early sexual experiences did involve some stories about this man, who still figures prominently "in [his] fantasies."

GARVEY: At least for me, honey, I could sit all day and listen to that wonderful man. He was so gorgeous. And he wasn't married. You shoulda seen all those old church women tryin' to marry off their daughters to the preacher. They didn't know. They didn't know him at all.

When Garvey eventually got to college in Florida and experienced what appeared to be the openly gay scene in Tallahassee, he realized that Christianity conflicted too much with his newfound gay lifestyle.

GARVEY: [I] wandered for a few years, until I met Miss [Zachary]. That was here in New York. And she [introduced me to Buddhism]. Ever since then I've been chanting. And it feels great. My ex-roommate...was Buddhist too.... Several of my friends are Buddhist.... If it's all right for Miss Tina [Turner], then it's all right for me.

Garvey's need for continued spirituality and its frequent expression in his life is typical of all of my informants, whether they have remained with an institutionalized religion or not. The added bonus of a gay friendship network within the church has further cemented the affiliation of those who have remained.

The importance of social institutions such as the gay bars, and even the black church, to the formation and maintenance of the social networks of gay men in Harlem will be discussed in the next two chapters. In and away from this social scene, gay men lead very ordinary everyday lives: they go to work, keep house, and spend their leisure time with the members of their personal social networks.

## "An Ordinary Week": Gregory

Gregory is a typical gay man in Harlem. He is known to be a hard worker. At six feet, clean shaven, and well mannered, he is an imposing figure in the scene. He dresses conservatively in slacks and shirts and sometimes a tie (never jeans and sneakers, the standard uniform for bar patrons). His quiet nature has led many to note that he is a "gentleman."

Gregory and his brother and sisters were raised in Harlem by their parents, a Metropolitan Transportation Authority worker and a nurse's aid at Harlem Hospital. All completed high school, and Gregory's brother died serving with the Marines in Vietnam. Their parents are now deceased, but Gregory and his sisters believe that their excellent upbringing enabled them always to have work and somewhere to stay. Both of Gregory's sisters live with their families in the Bronx, and he visits with them once a month or so. But most of his day-to-day existence revolves around his job and his small social network of gay friends. Gregory enjoys playing cards two nights a week with two different groups of friends. Most of his company includes older gentlemen, friends from the "early days," when he first "came out" to gay society in Harlem.

Gregory works as a florist in Harlem, for an older gay gentleman who owns two stores. He manages the small store he works at and employs two younger "gay boys" who help in the shop and deliver for him. Occasionally he goes to the market in downtown Brooklyn, with the owner, to buy flowers, but mostly they rely on the delivery services of an acquaintance from "the Brooklyn scene," who does the buying for them. Gregory works from 9:00 A.M. until 6:00 P.M., six days a week. His store is closed on Sundays.

On Sundays, Gregory rises early, dresses up, and heads for morning service at Canaan Baptist on 116th Street.

GREGORY: That's the Lord's day o' rest. My mama taught me that, and I thank the Lord for it. One day I'm not dealing with all this mess on the street. And I don't have to worry about it. Because one of the kids lives over the store. So I know I don't have to worry about it.

Gregory has been attending church there all his life. It was where he was baptized and where he wants his funeral to be held. He knows many of the people who also attend church there, as they are the folks he grew up with. He has lived in that neighborhood for most of his life. After several years of living with roommates in another neighborhood, he found a nice one-bedroom apartment on 119th Street, on a block where he has many friends. He now lives within walking distance of his work, his church, his best friends, and the two bars where he drinks most often.

After church on Sundays, Gregory dines at the home of his friends, Brian or Walter. At one time he preferred to eat at Franklin's, before his passing, because Franklin could cook "like nobody else." In fact, Franklin's passing had really left a gap in Gregory's life in recent months. He was a close friend, with whom he had attended church and played cards. But Gregory has several other friends who keep him company after church and later on Sunday afternoon and evening at the bar. After Franklin's death, Gregory stopped smoking and drinking.

Gregory now "swills" soda and spends a lot of time photographing his friends as they "party." Actually, he is keen to record people and places important to him.

GREGORY: I'd better get them [the bars] before they all close. It really came home to me when they closed the Baby Grand. That was our main spot. I mean, we were there every day. It was such a nice place. And always a nice crowd. Well behaved. Well mannered. And they put on some great shows. ... I have pictures of some of us in there. Some old pictures taken on people's birthdays and things.[12]

Gregory photographs most of the gatherings at the bars. Throughout my stay in Harlem, he took photographs on birthdays, at talent contests, on Christmas and New Year's Eve, and even on regular nights. In fact, in one bar, the staff are used to him coming behind the bar to take pictures of patrons sitting along the counter. Some days later, Gregory will show his photos proudly up and down the bar and take orders for copies.

Most of the conversation at the bar on Sunday evening revolves around events during the past week, absent friends, forthcoming events, chores to be performed, and analyses of restaurants, the services of tradesmen, doctors, and clergymen, and the health of friends and relatives. Peoples' personal affairs are discussed in some detail, opinions offered, and even sometimes invited. News of best buys are always a favorite topic. Debates over the best cuts of meat, the cheapest good-quality clothes or tailoring, and furniture sales are long-winded and quite heated. Sundays are always a good time to learn what is happening in the neighborhood, in terms of comings and goings, because everybody drops by at some time during the afternoon or evening. If some major event such as a dance social or a boat ride has taken place during the weekend, or if someone has hosted a party, a birthday celebration, or a "rent party,"[13] gossip about the success of the event or who had attended with whom and what food was served and what music was played always evolves into discussions of great length. Sunday evenings are when most of my informants catch up with friends, analyze the past week, and make plans for the forthcoming week.

Before leaving, Gregory always makes plans to go to the movies, to visit someone for dinner or cards, or to make a hospital or family visit during the next few days. He likes to let his close friends know his plans so that they know where to contact him if they need him. If someone has not "featured" at the bar, Gregory leaves a message with the barman to let the individual know that he has been asking after him. Elaine and Colin (the bar staff) are always reliable in that respect, and if someone is missing, nine times out of ten one of them knows where the person is. As communication centers for this small bar community, these bartenders are invaluable to the maintenance of connections between members of different social networks.

Sometimes on a Sunday evening Gregory walks one of his older friends home before retiring. Sometimes he invites someone home to have a drink or watch a movie. Sundays are good nights for him to "carry on" because Mondays are slow at work, and he often leaves the store in the hands of his assistants and sneaks back home to take care of household chores, do some necessary shopping, or sleep some more before returning to the store in the afternoon.

Mondays are quiet for Gregory. After he locks up the store, he heads over to one of the two bars he frequents during the week to catch up with friends he may have missed during the weekend. He also meets up with his boss at one bar, and they briefly discuss the day's business. If news of the illness of some of his older friends reaches him, he will plan to visit them or run errands for them if they cannot get around very well. Sometimes Gregory has photographs to show, or tickets to distribute, or flowers to deliver. On Mondays he likes to go home early and cook, often several different dishes, which he freezes for use during the week. Gregory loves to cook and bake but finds it a tedious chore for himself.

On Tuesdays Gregory arrives at work early. Fresh flowers are delivered that morning, and this means he will be busy. The flowers must be sorted and stored, the outside displays must be changed, and orders start coming in for the rest of the week. His assistants also know Tuesday is a major cleaning day, when Gregory helps them take the store apart: cleaning the refrigerators is the biggest task. During the day he will also perform some light bookkeeping chores. On Tuesday evening Gregory passes by the bars again, usually to meet up with his card partners, and moves on to the chosen apartment for a few games. Usually dinner is provided by the host, and the guests bring drinks. These games are taken most seriously, and scores for partners are kept for a week, or a whole month, leading to a climactic finale that involves much drinking and eating. On Tuesdays and Thursdays Gregory plays with the same three friends, usually a few games of 500, but they end the evening with "something light" like "bid-wiss," to wind down or cool off any tempers. Usually such evenings are over by 10:00 or 11:00, as all of the players are working men. Gregory also joins more casual games on other evenings, especially during the weekends. If there are no major social events to attend, or if a particular evening at a bar is especially quiet, a group of friends may get together at someone's apartment to play cards.

Wednesdays are usually busy at work for Gregory. A big order day, especially for the nearby hospitals, keeps him and his assistants busy until closing time.

GREGORY: That's a night I'll have a drink! I really need a drink on Wednesday. But you won't catch me out too late. No sir, I'll be home in bed early.... I go to work. Like most people I work all week. So you won't catch me runnin' around. Not during the week. I'm just an ordinary guy. An ordinary guy who has an ordinary week.

Thursdays see more deliveries, in and out of the store, more cleaning, and more accounting. It is also the day that Gregory "officially" meets with his boss to go over the books and to lay plans for the next week's purchases and sales. As well, Thursday evening is another card evening, the night that Gregory usually hosts the game. He may even miss the bars in order to get home and cook. He has usually cooked most of the food earlier in the week but always likes to have a fresh cake baked for the guys. He also tidies the house and plants vases of flowers everywhere. Sometimes he prepares tapes of music to play so that he does not have to be changing records all evening. Gregory prefers classical music, especially Schubert, a taste he acquired from a lover he lived with briefly when he was in his early twenties. (That was the only time that Gregory has actually lived with another man, but he does not miss it. The period was full of conflict, and Gregory prefers to forget about it. He has since had two or three long affairs with older men but prefers to live alone, visiting or staying over as the occasion or desire requires.)

Currently, Gregory has no lover. He does, however, have a small group of friends he takes care of. He takes them flowers and bakes them cakes. He visits them on the weekend and runs errands during the week. Most of these friends are in their sixties and seventies, and many are mainly housebound.

GREGORY: They're older, you know. They don't go out so much. If they do I'll be there with them. You know, we might go down to the bar in the afternoon and have a drink, but mostly they stays home. Anyhow, I like to visit with them. We sit and gossip, and carry on, and all. They tell me all about themselves and their lives. It can be really interesting. Sometimes. But they don't have anyone else. Most of them. They're alone. So I don't mind lookin' out for them.... Someday, someone'll do it for me, I hope. You just gotta look after your own kind. That's what I say. And they got nobody else.

Fridays and Saturdays are busier days for Gregory. He gets to the store very early to accept new deliveries and start filling orders. He has two hospitals nearby and several churches for which he has standing orders on Fridays and Saturdays. As well, weddings and parties in the immediate neighborhood keep him busy. He is often very weary on those evenings but finds time to spend at the bars, catching up with friends and planning his Saturday and Sunday social life.

For the most part, Gregory's week is similar to that of most people in Manhattan: going to work Monday to Friday, and often on Saturdays, and playing a little harder during the weekend. Although he no longer goes out dancing like he used to, or drinks and smokes like before, Gregory still finds the long evenings of standing and talking in the bar somewhat tiring. Yet he enjoys the company of his circle of friends and never wearies of hearing somebody's news. Now in his forties, he stays closer to home and rarely has "a long night of it." When he attends parties or dances, it is usually in the company of his close friends from the bars or his fellow cardplayers. He has been saving money and hopes to be able to buy out his boss when he retires in the near future. He would like to keep one of the stores at least and thinks he would be able to operate it successfully. He has been working for his boss for over twenty years and knows the business well.

Although some of the individuals in this community are a little different, even eccentric, for the most part gay black men in Harlem do lead very ordinary lives. In fact, Gregory's weekly routine is similar to that of many Harlemites. Some of his friends have slightly different lifestyles. They live with lovers or work at unusual or a combination of different jobs. However, their routines of work and leisure are typical of other folks in Harlem, and their goals and aspirations are typical of most Americans.

## Ephraim's Week

Ephraim is a handsome young man in his thirties with a mustache and thick sideburns. He wears very fashionable clothing and every week sports a different hairdo. When out in the scene, he attracts around himself a group of other young men. He lives his life immersed in the gay scene, spending time mostly with other gay friends, and tries his best to help those closest to him.

Ephraim is one of Gregory's close friends. He used to work with Gregory at the store some years ago, before he got his current job as a production assistant at a local theater. He meets with Gregory most nights of the week at one of the bars in the neighborhood and plays cards with him once or twice a week. He says he would consider going in with Gregory if he took over the business. His current job pays regularly but not that well. But he has managed to save some money and has invested the money that he inherited when his parents died and left him their apartment.

He rarely sees his brother and sisters, who are all married and live on Long Island. Occasionally his brother comes to town, especially if he is having some marital problems, and stays with Ephraim. He shares an interest in other men, like Ephraim, but has never had an ongoing relationship with another man.

Ephraim has been in a relationship with his lover for eleven years. They do not live together, because Dudley prefers to stay with his elderly mother. He is an only child and his mother has no one else to take care of her. Ephraim spends much of his time with Dudley and his mother, sleeping over during the week. Dudley is on welfare but occasionally gets some acting work. He was a drag performer when they met, but such work seems harder to come by now. Occasionally he will perform if one of his drag friends puts together a show. Ephraim helps out with expenses in Dudley's household and also manages to keep his own apartment running.

He has two roommates, also gay men, who both work downtown in well-paying office jobs. Each of the three men has his own room in the large apartment, which is filled with potted plants. Ephraim grows ferns and orchids, and both his roommates take an active interest in maintaining the household. The three roommates do not socialize together, but occasionally they will have a meal together. The presence of the other two men in Ephraim's life is a constant source of strife in his relationship with Dudley. Dudley found out that Ephraim had slept with both his roommates, and that almost split them up. Ephraim notes that it just happened, as such things do between men, but that his love and caring for Dudley have always remained constant. He says he proves this by spending almost all of his leisure time with Dudley and his mother and by contributing financially to their household.

Ephraim's work keeps him busy in the theater on Thursday, Friday, and Saturday evenings, and sometimes on other evenings as well. He makes social calls on the bars in Harlem after his work is over, around 10:00 P.M. or midnight. He rarely does drugs and prefers to smoke marijuana at home with Dudley, but he will always have a cocktail or two while out. He meets with Gregory, Roman, and Harry most nights and stays up drinking until 2:00 or 3:00 A.M.

During the week, he sleeps late at Dudley's and spends most of his days shopping, running errands for Dudley or his mother, and "taking care of business." He usually goes to the theater for rehearsal or performance preparations around 3:00 or 4:00 P.M. When he does not have to be at the theater, he spends time making tapes on his expensive recording equipment at his apartment. Much of this recording gear he acquired when he was a disc jockey at an old disco in SoHo in the late 1970s. The club catered to a large black clientele on

Wednesdays, Fridays, and Sundays and an almost exclusively gay black clientele on Saturdays. Most of the big black clubs at that time had gay night on Saturdays, unlike the white clubs, which had gay night on Sundays. Most such nights were private—that is, for members and their guests only.

During this time Ephraim made enough contacts in the gay "underworld" to maintain a sideline business making tapes for clubs and bars all over the city. Among his clients now are two large discos in Chelsea and about twenty bars on the West Side, in Chelsea, and in the East Village. These reel-to-reel tapes take several hours to put together and have to be updated regularly. They are used as background music in most places on quieter nights during the week. One bar on the West Side uses his tapes as music for the dance floor. Sometimes on a Friday night Ephraim visits the club and spins a few albums on its equipment. He does not get paid for these visits, but the work helps him maintain a feel for the job and for what people like to dance to.

Ephraim's week passes quietly. Monday to Friday he awakens at Dudley's, goes shopping or hangs out with Dudley, takes care of his plants or makes tapes in the afternoon, and works at the theater in the evenings. On the weekends he spends his day sleeping, usually at his own home, works at the theater in the evenings, and spends the night hours in and around the gay scene in Harlem. Some nights during the week and on the weekends he meets with Gregory and other friends to play cards. Ephraim and Dudley occasionally attend community dance socials, talent contests, and drag balls together, but most often Ephraim socializes with his gay friends in the gay bars scattered around Harlem. He spends a lot of time in the gay scene and has many gay friends in his social network, but he keeps his social life and private life (with Dudley) quite separate. He likes to have nights out "with the boys and girls."

## Summary

All kinds of men are gay and black in Harlem. Many have been born and raised in Harlem; several are from families who have resided in Harlem for five generations or more (ever since blacks moved uptown). Some have migrated to New York from southern states, yet they maintain links with the South and the southern black culture that Harlem is known for. Most of these men are religious, and many are loyal members of their churches. Most of them are employed: some own their own businesses, others get by working part-time jobs or hustling to add to other income. Some are raising children—their own or those of siblings or cousins. Their daily lives are similar to the lives of the other folks in their neighborhoods. The major difference is that they are gay.

All of these different types of black men—the Southerners, the college-educated, the caterers, the florist, the organist—are part of an exclusive gay community. Irrespective of what they do, or where and how they live, if they are gay and black, they belong to the "family." This "family," to which we now turn, symbolizes the entire gay black community, made up as it is of a series of interconnected social networks.

# 3

## "One Big Family": Community and the Social Networks of Gay Black Men

The gay black community in Harlem is made up of people of all socioeconomic classes, all age groups, and several religions. It is not formally structured or institutionalized, nor is it geographically discrete or stable in membership. People are connected to each other through a series of interdependent social networks and through participation in gay social events or institutions (see chap. 4).

The interrelated social networks of gay men in Harlem may each comprise between twenty and sixty members, including gay and nongay friends, lifelong neighborhood contacts, business acquaintances, church affiliates, and kinship members. People of all ages and both genders are represented in each social network. They all come together to socialize, celebrate family events, and provide financial and emotional support in times of need.

However, each informant named a close circle of gay friends as the most frequently contacted people within his social network. Most of these people were seen or talked to daily, or at least several times a week. Such close gay members of each individual's social network become his "family" and are accorded familial titles. In this manner, everyone is related to someone else, by fictive kin relationships. These gay men socially construct such a "family" as a metaphor for the entire gay black community.

## Social Networks

In Harlem, I have found social networks of family and friends that comprise all sorts of people, both men and women, of all ages, each contributing in different ways. The heterogeneity of these networks extends Stack's (1974) model beyond welfare-dependent women to include all people in the black community.

Because I focus here on gay black men, the social networks I map are male-centered. Men appear to contribute disproportionately, each network having a core of gay black men engaged in reciprocal exchange of money and good deeds. However, these networks also contain men and women, kin and non-kin, gay and non-gay members.

All of the informants in this study socialize almost exclusively in Harlem.[1] They patronize gay bars and clubs, especially later at night and on the weekends. They also go to "mixed" bars, to cabarets and jazz clubs, to the movies or the Apollo, or, most often, visit friends, gay and non-gay, in their homes, to eat, drink, and play cards.

Most of my informants have large social networks that include at least twenty or more people with whom they interact several times a week. Almost all of these people also live in Harlem, some hanging out in the same "scene" or going to the same church. Many are friends from the same block or building where they grew up. The men met most of their gay friends in their social networks through school or college, or in the social institutions of the gay scene. Some met friends in church.

These social networks have very little formal structure in their membership or in the types of activities they inspire. Attempts to organize these gay men into structured social and political clubs have not been successful, yet they do support Harlem-wide, and citywide, black gay organizations.

The personal networks of the different gay men I interviewed are indeed typical of the networks of most urban dwellers. They comprise both family members and friends, on two levels: close gay friends as an inner core group, and a larger group including kin and other friends surrounding the core.[2] This is not typical of many mainstream (white) gay men in New York City, who by and large live apart from their consanguineous kin in other cities or states.[3] However, although many gay black men are immigrants to the city, their networks often include a wide range of consanguineous kin who are "close" and in frequent contact. Louis compares his black kin to the kin of white people.

LOUIS: Part of the problem is that they are cut off too. I mean if I need something and I can't quite make it then I know my Mama's gonna help me. Or my brother. Or even one of my cousins. But when white folks have children, they lose touch with all the rest of their families. You know, they have to make it on their own. Not us. We got fierce family for that.

The social networks of these black men are usually established early in life and encompass not only close kin, odd distant kin members, fictive kin, neighbors, and former school friends but also friends made in the course of social and work lives.

In Harlem, each network includes gay and non-gay relatives, friends, neighbors, and most notably gay men of different socioeconomic classes.

CLEVELAND: These boys are alright. They don't have the background, you know, to do no better. But they alright. Mostly they honest and they do anything for you. I'd rather have them as friends than half those pretentious sissies.

Because the social networks cut across class lines, they differ from the type of network Stack (1974) has described. One result of this is that more financial resources are available here in each network because so many members are employed in well-paying jobs. Rather than an adaptive response to survival problems, these networks appear to be a common cultural phenomenon in black society, embracing all types of people in differing socioeconomic groups.

These men have maintained some sort of contact over the years even with friends who have moved away.

LIONEL: I ain't seen Bee for some years, since his lover took him over to the Bronx. But his mother lives on my block, so I always hear what theys up to. You do that now. Now this epidemic thing is here. You just like to know where everyone is, y'know.

Two years ago, Willis heard that Frankie, a good friend from high school and disco days, had passed away from a drug overdose. He hadn't seen Frankie either in several years, but when Willis heard about his death, he visited Frankie's mother to extend his condolences.

WILLIS: Man, when I walked up inside there, it was like goin' back to school. All the old gang was there. D—— and W—— and R——. They was all there.

I just started to cry. We talked and talked. All about the old days. Now that's not that long ago, mind you. But you know, back in the early seventies, when disco was just startin'. We used to all go out together and hang out at the Loft and the Flamingo and shit. We had big fun. Man, I miss them days. They all gone now. I often wonder where all those crazy people went. All those wild people from those days. Most of them probably gone too. Too much drugs. And too much sex.

Thus the social networks that most of these men have developed throughout Harlem provide not only a variety of social events to attend, such as birthday parties and card games, but also the financial and emotional support that are so much a necessity of life in New York City. Those whose incomes are not substantial or who have nearby friends, neighbors, and especially family members whose incomes are insignificant are all tied together in a network of mutual support.[4]

Several of the men in this community are single parents raising between one and four children. In networks comprising their lovers, other single gay parents, sometimes male and female non-gay kin, and always other single gay men, these fathers are able to maintain their full-time employment and their apartments and raise and educate their children. These black men are employed, educated (40 percent had attended college), rent or own their own homes (and 20 percent own cars), were raised largely by both of their own parents or one parent and a kin member of the opposite sex, and maintain close and regular ties to their churches.

## Willis and Son

Since he gave up work, Willis struggles from welfare check to welfare check. He says he misses the regular wages, which he earned while employed on Wall Street. Now on welfare in order to stay home and take care of his son, he misses the freedom that his salary gave him to pay for odd luxury items that made life worthwhile. Now he carefully budgets his money to cover rent and food. But unexpected expenses do arise, such as when his son gets ill or needs new shoes or a winter jacket.

Willis's paternal grandmother and an older, single brother live nearby, and they will baby-sit for him or, if their budgets permit, "lend" him ten or twenty dollars: "They knows I take care of my kid. They can see I'm not wastin' my money." His mother and sister live in the Bronx, and he visits with them now and then, baby-sitting for them, having meals with them, and generally keeping in touch, "'cause you never know when you need them."

Willis also has two girlfriends from school days, both single parents living in Harlem, for whom he also baby-sits. One of them works, and she pays him a few dollars for baby-sitting during the week. On weekends they all take turns "covering" for each other so that they can have some free time. Willis's ex-lover also lends a hand financially when he can. He's a student in college. Willis also has two single male friends, one gay and one non-gay, who take him and his son out to the movies or the beach, which Willis says helps him out mentally: "They give me a break. A chance to get out of the neighborhood. Away from all this madness."

Willis says that raising a child is a full-time occupation, and sometimes he gets sick of it. But he knows that in the future he will have someone there for him. Men in Willis's life have been irregular features, and his two attempts to settle down with women have ended disastrously. His son's mother is currently wandering the streets on crack. Willis says she is pregnant again, and he would like to adopt the child to give his son a real brother. Baby-sitting and sharing meals and the little cash that comes their way are the main activities that tie Willis and his gay friends and kin together.

## Byron's Family

Byron is likewise tied into a network of friends for financial and emotional support. He, his eldest son, his family members, and his single gay friends, who lend him financial and emotional support, are all employed. The ease with which money flows into Byron's family, as well as the extraordinary child-care support Byron receives from kin and non-kin, is typical of most of the social networks I mapped.

Byron has been raising his four children by himself for over ten years now. His eldest son works with him in his newly established catering business. Byron works five nights a week as a chef in a restaurant in Harlem and has begun to cater for private parties in the neighborhood. His son helps prepare and serve the food. The other three children are still in high school. He has them in after-school programs at the YMCA in Harlem, where one son is in a drama club and the other two children are involved in sports.

An unmarried brother who lives in the neighborhood often stops by in the evenings to take care of the children. He is a schoolteacher and helps them with their homework. Byron hopes that the three children in school will all attend college. Byron's mother also lives close by and lends a hand taking care of the children. She played a significant role in their upbringing, cooking and making clothes for them, and taking them to church when they were younger.

Byron's two best friends, Edward and Nate, who are also gay, often look after the children and take them to concerts and the park. The children like their "uncles," who, they say, spoil them. Although Byron has always been financially independent, he says that he could not have maintained a decent family life for the children without the support of his family and friends.

## Cleveland's Buddies

Unencumbered single gay men are also involved in social networks for support or to lend assistance. Some help raise their sisters' children,[5] often living with them, and even help finance the education of nieces and nephews, younger siblings, or other gay men. Most single gay men help other gay men who need financial or emotional support in times of difficulty, such as illness or temporary unemployment.

Cleveland's social network includes mostly gay men. Except for a brother and sister, and her husband, who live in the Bronx and whom he sees once every few months, everyone with whom he interacts, even friends from work, is gay. He lives by himself but has a lover, Randy, and together they entertain gay friends at Cleveland's home. They have gay friends over for dinner after church on Sundays, and sometimes during the week they will invite friends over to watch a movie or play cards.

Through the bar scene, which plays an important role in Cleveland's social life, he has met most of the men in this study at one time or another. He maintains close ties with Shawn and his lover,

Lee, who often accompany him and Randy to dance socials and church dinners and picnics. Cleveland's closest friend is Orville, whom he had met at church. They meet two or three times a week at each other's homes for dinner. Orville "ain't usin'" the bar scene, so Cleveland makes a special effort to keep in touch with "the old soldier." At a bar or at a dance social, Cleveland regularly sees Carl, whom he knows from South Carolina; Hamilton, a dancer; his Zodiac soul mates Roman and Nate, whom he met at the bars; and others whom he met at church. His network also includes friends from his immediate neighborhood, a group that includes two or three hustlers. He often provides these men with shelter and, in return, has them do household tasks. All of these men have dinner at Cleveland's quite regularly and accompany him and Randy to other social events such as drag shows, talent contests, and dances. When Roly asked Cleveland to bring some friends to his birthday bash at a rented community hall, Cleveland called on six friends from this group to accompany him and actually ended up with a troupe of ten.

Cleveland is a financially independent man. He is well known in the community as one of its wealthier members. He owns property in New York and down South and is a substantial investor. "He's a financial wizard," says Hamilton, who depends frequently on his best friend for financial aid ("up to $3,000 a year").

Hamilton is a dancer and choreographer who has had some major successes in his career. As he becomes older, he dances less with the companies he once freelanced with and has been trying to establish his own company. But in New York City the competition is tough not only in the dance world but also in the area of black arts. Twenty years ago, he remembers, money was readily available for black artists, but today there are "too many with their hands out" and not enough continuous support. He has known Cleveland for many years, ever since the latter first came to Harlem.

Occasionally Cleveland will write a check for Hamilton, to pay his electric bill or his rent. Most of the time, but not always, Hamilton pays him back. Sometimes, when Cleveland suspects that Hamilton is down about something, he'll slip him a few dollars to buy a drink or something to smoke. Often Hamilton will pass some of this money on to Andy, a gay friend from the neighborhood who has fallen on hard times after losing his job as a building superintendent. Andy now hustles in the gay bars in Harlem, mainly to get somewhere to sleep so that he does not have to go back to the shelters. He also gets donations from Cleveland directly, and this is why Hamilton does not mind sharing Cleveland's gifts with him.

Hamilton's parents still live in Harlem, and he visits them occasionally but feels he cannot rely on them for support at his age, forty-three, and because his three sisters depend on their help to raise their children. Hamilton is particularly close to one of these sisters, and he sometimes houses her and her son to help her through a "rough patch."

Cleveland also helps Carl, since he was raised by Carl's parents down South. Carl works nights as a postal worker and lives with his ex-wife and their two children, whom he helps to raise. Unfortunately, a serious problem with drugs eats up his paychecks and his wife frequently throws him out of the house. "That's when uncle [Cleveland] becomes real important," he says. Carl will stay a few days with Cleveland, until he can persuade his wife to let him come back. He is close to his children, as is Cleveland, who often sends money to the wife to buy clothes for them. Cleveland says that he looks after Carl not only because he comes from the same town in South Carolina but because, no matter what, he always turns up at work. "He makes an honest effort. I only wish he'd get off them drugs."

## "Miss Donny"

Some men in this gay community in Harlem do come from "broken homes," from single-parent families, or from families that are welfare-dependent. Some of these men who are openly gay, even in the yards of their projects, and who are frequently out of work will hustle their sexual favors. Some of them depend on their social networks of gay friends for "coins" to buy drinks, cigarettes, or meals. Some seek shelter, but most are housed with kin or other gay men.

Donny is a "gay godmother," as he calls himself. He buys meals for many of the unemployed hustlers, who address him as "Miss Donny." He always offers them drinks and cigarettes in the bar and has admitted treating them to hotel rooms occasionally, always denying any sexual content in the relationships. He does have his own home and a lover. Donny's generosity is also known to extend to his close gay friends: he has paid Barry's rent on many occasions, as the latter's low-paying job does not suffice. Donny says he does not mind helping his friends make ends meet, because they are the best friends in the world: "We don't want for nothing. Wilson and I have a nice home. Mother's set up nice. So why not share it?" Donny works as an insurance agent, travels all over the country frequently, and makes a lot of money (between $50,000 and $75,000 per year). He holidays every year in the Caribbean, where Aruba is his favorite island. One year he took Colin, the barman, down "to the islands" on an all-expenses-paid holiday.

## Louis's Kith and Kin

Louis maintains close, at least weekly, contact with his mother and his three sisters. He is supporting his youngest sister through college. He attends all the birthday celebrations of his nieces and nephews and never forgets a baptism or a graduation. He is also in daily contact with three of his neighbors, who know he and Paul are lovers. One of them is an elderly lady, and sometimes he will pick things up for her at the store. He also keeps in contact with an elderly couple down on 140th Street, where he grew up. They are the grandparents of one of his elementary school friends, whom he also sees periodically.

Living in the neighborhood where he grew up, Louis is constantly running into old schoolmates. A couple of girls he attended high school with live nearby with their husbands and children. Sometimes he and Paul go to their homes for dinner or to play cards, and sometimes they attend neighborhood socials together. Louis also socializes with gay friends he has met at college and thereafter. Sherman, one of the respondents in this study, is an old gay friend of Louis's from high school. During college years at gay bars and discos, Louis made friends with Demond, Shawn, Harry, and Jerome, all of whom he socializes with at least once a week in the gay bars or at card games. All of these gay friends, as well as his non-gay friends and family members, know one another and share different social events with each other. More recently, Louis has befriended Quint, Darrell, Quincy, and Freddy, who are younger gay men. They socialize with Louis and Paul at least once a week, usually in the bars. In fact, Louis and Paul are helping Freddy complete his high school equivalency diploma.

Much of the socializing with their gay friends occurs in the gay bars in Harlem and at jazz clubs, talent shows (where Louis sings), and dance socials. Again, this network of friends exemplifies the heterogeneity of the membership of the social networks of gay black men in general. Louis's loyalty, and financial and other assistance, extends beyond his immediate family to his lover's family, neighbor, former gay and non-gay school friends, and to his many friends in the gay community. Within the network of his gay friends are men from a variety of socioeconomic groups.

## Community Organization

Because each individual constructs around himself a social network of different members, no two networks are exactly alike and the opportunities for leaders to emerge in the community are rare. Moreover, since the community lacks political organization, no structured leadership positions have evolved.

Some people, like Cleveland and Louis, are well-known members of the gay community in Harlem because of their regular attendance at social events and presence in social institutions. Their charismatic personalities may also be a drawing card, but generally it is their other qualities—such as artistic talent or occupation—that attract a wide circle of friends to them and give them some social clout. For example, Louis, Francis (a popular entertainer), Colin (a barman), or Thurman (a millionaire socialite in Harlem at large) can easily whip up a large group of people for a benefit concert or to support a talent show participant. Likewise, they have no difficulty selling tickets for dances or boat rides, as people flock to them to be in their social set.

However, the large citywide gay black social clubs (really select members-only committees) that exist for the organization of social events do provide individuals with the opportunity to become especially respected members of the community, if not leaders. Membership on these committees is by invitation only, and invitees are carefully screened. To be a member of one of these organizing committees attracts a lot of prestige not only within the gay community in

Harlem but also among black gay people throughout the metropolitan area.

Clarence is one such select member. He engages a large following out of my informant network for his club's social events. He is a quiet, unassuming man, but his social position does give him some clout. He has been known to have people barred from clubs, and his support for a benefit or charity or a local political candidate can influence the way people act or vote. Clarence's social network in the gay community in Harlem is quite extensive and stretches across most social classes and a number of geographically distinct neighborhoods.

The gay black community has no organizational or institutional base save for the gay social clubs, bars, and special social events (see chap. 4). Rather, it is built on the social networks of its members, who are linked together in fictive or real kin relationships into the symbolic "family" that includes all gay men in Harlem.

## Fictive Kin

All of my informants' social networks include friends as well as consanguineous kin. These friends may be from the same town down South or long standing neighbors who live in the same building. More often than not, single gay men become "family" members of the extended kin networks of established gay friends.

CLIFTON: When I arrived here [from Jamaica] Adrian and Carter just took me in. They had me over to dinner a couple of times, and before I knew it, their cousins and aunts were asking me to parties and dinners. They've been so good to me. Just like real brothers.

Absorbing strangers into the kin group exemplifies the black concept of family, which extends to include all other black folks. This model, applied within the gay community, includes all gay friends and especially those new in town.

HAYWARD: A—— and his friends have taken me all over the city. They've shown me where to shop and where to look for men. Honey, I couldn't'a made it in New York without them. His mother even took me to her church. Now she has me goin' to Atlantic City with her and her sisters.

It is in this context that the use of kin terms for close gay friends becomes apparent. Most of my informants referred to friends or neighbors by kinship terms. Carl often calls Cleveland "uncle" because Cleveland was a close friend of Carl's parents in their hometown in South Carolina and because he acts as a role model for Carl within the gay world. Such "fictive kin" terms and the relationships they stand for have been claimed as a distinctly black cultural trait.[6] However, fictive kin are also found in other urban communities and in many other, non-black cultures.[7] Gay society provides a good example.[8] The gay expressions "family" for members of the gay community, "sisters" for close gay friends, and "mother" and "daughter" for especially close friends are used by gay men the world over.[9] However, gay men in Harlem probably use these terms for close friends because the model for an extended "family" of fictive kin is already established in black culture.[10]

Gay black men also use familial labels such as "mother" for non-gay friends: an older aunt or female neighbor, for example, who has played a role in the individual's socialization. "Uncle" designates an older man, sometimes also gay, who had been a role model when the individual was younger. In fact, most older friends are affectionately addressed as "uncle" or "aunt."

BARRY: Aunt A———. She's not my real aunt. Not really. She just a neighborhood girlfriend of my mother's. But I like her so much when I was a kid. We'd always be up in her house. She was like a second mother to me.

This practice shows how the social construction of gay black culture lies at the intersection of both gay and black cultures. Among groups of gay men in the community, for example, the black expression "cousin" is used to define some fictive kin relationship between gay and non-gay male aquaintances who have come from the same building, block, or school in Harlem or who share the same political or religious orientation. Thus the metaphor of "family" is extended beyond the boundaries of the gay community to link the gay population to the larger "family" network that encompasses the entire black community.

## Community as "Family"

Personal social networks are the backbone of the gay community in Harlem. It is through these networks that notices about social events, community news, and gossip travel and that support is mustered in times of need. Dance socials and boat rides organized by the major citywide black gay social clubs are advertised through the networks. News of illness or death is disseminated through them. Invitations to dinner parties, card games, talent contests, birthday parties, or fundraisers are issued through personal contacts in the networks. At any of these types of gatherings, or at any of the social institutions important to gay men in Harlem, such as the bars and jazz clubs, these personal gay social networks come together, allowing people to renew acquaintances and to locate others in the wider social scene that forms the gay community.

The ways in which gay men in Harlem construct this community make them feel they belong to a group of people who share the same aspirations, sense of security, friendships, and sexual preferences as themselves.[11] Gay black men in Harlem refer to their community, this collection of interrelated social networks, as their "family." This conceptualization enhances the emotional meaning of their membership in the group, or gay community, and is expressed verbally by the members in the use of kinship terms for each other. "Mother," "sister," "brother," "aunt," "uncle," "cousin," "husband," and "children" are all commonly used to indicate the status of an individual in the gay community or the fictive kinship relationship between the speaker and another person. The sense of belonging to such a family invokes a loyalty to other members of the gay population. This loyalty is comparable to the loyalty expressed toward real kin and kinship groups in Harlem.

One of the times this loyalty is most evident is at a funeral. On a wet Friday morning, Louis called me: "Miss Francis gone, honey!" When Francis passed away, some confusion reigned as to how to dress him for his "final performance." Francis had been singing in drag around the country for thirty-five years and had a wide following with gay black men and other non-gay supporters of drag in many cities. This was evidenced by the large number of people who attended the funeral who had flown, bused, or driven to New York to pay their respects.

The wake the evening before the funeral filled the small funeral director's chapel and overflowed onto the street. Much attention was drawn to this huge crowd of men, some most obviously in drag. At the same time, the Baptist church next door was holding a revival. Busloads of southern women dressed in white and bearing huge hats mixed with the drag queens on the sidewalk. Some of these ladies entered the funeral home to see the "famous jazz singer."

The wake continued with food and drinks at Francis's apartment, all through the night until the 10:00 funeral service the next morning. The small Baptist church was filled to overflowing. Approximately four hundred people attended, demonstrating the strength of the "family." The service stretched over three hours to accommodate all the tributes from friends, neighbors, family members, and fellow drag performers from Chicago, Detroit, Atlanta, and Birmingham. A prominent Baptist preacher from a large church uptown came to lead the service. Almost all of the 156 informants from this study were in attendance, even though many had difficulty getting time off from work. "I ain't gonna miss this show for nothing," Louis told me. "[Paul's] got the [video] camera and we're gonna record this one. I know these girls are gonna carry on. Just their drag. It's gonna be fierce."

Both Louis and Paul left work to attend. They secured seats inside the church for me and a few others. The most dramatic moment came when, a half-hour into the service, an older man in drag entered the church and, fanning himself, slowly approached the open casket. As the choir sang, he draped himself across the casket and wailed, "Sister, sister, if only I could talk to ya, one more time!"

## Summary

Gay men in Harlem are linked together in social networks of friendship and support. Regular employment and the redistribution of large sums of money between men in these networks are features of urban gay black social networks that we do not see in earlier models of social networks of female-centered households. In fact, the contribution of men to other men, and to women and children, in the social networks I found in Harlem is quite substantial, crossing class lines and even reaching beyond the gay community.

The members of these social networks are interrelated (through membership) and interdependent (socially, financially, and emotionally), leading to the formation of a community. Enhancing this sense of community, and a loyalty to its membership, is the symbolic construction of "family" as a metaphor for that community. This family finds its expression in the classification of members into kinship statuses and in the relationships of interdependency between members.

It is at major social events and in the social institutions of gay life in Harlem that the symbolic construction of gay community in Harlem is most evident. Social network members meet their "sisters" and "mothers" at bars and clubs, at dinner parties, and in church, thereby reaffirming their membership in the social network, their family, and the gay black community. In fact, the bars and jazz clubs are where gay black culture finds its most open public expression.

# 4

# "Close to Home":
# The Organization of the
# Gay Scene in Harlem

In Harlem, a discrete gay society exists, although it is integrated to some degree with the surrounding city, especially economically, and its members do participate in mainstream black and gay social activities. Yet it has all the attributes of any other subculture in the city: its own residential membership, its own social institutions, its own calendar of social and cultural events, its own folklore and cultural heroes. The community is even in the process of establishing its own historical archives. But the chief feature of the community is the "scene," a variety of public places where gay men meet and spend their leisure time.

The social lives of gay men in Harlem are played out in this public arena that is physically integrated with the neighborhood in which they live. Unlike the gay scenes in most urban settings, in Harlem the gay scene is located "close to home." This proximity to family and lifelong, non-gay friends and neighbors has special significance for these gay men. Many of them do not conceal their gay identity and lead openly gay lives alongside their families. Their gay lifestyle is integrated into their daily lives in Harlem: in the gay scene in downtown Harlem and in the churches, libraries, theaters, jazz clubs, and other social organizations of mainstream Harlem society. The focal points for the expression of gay culture in Harlem, however, are the exclusively gay social institutions: the gay bars, the gay bathhouse, the jazz clubs, which feature gay artists and gay talent contests, the dances, the boat rides, the drag balls, the private parties, and the card games. Of these, the most important are the gay bars.

## The Gay Bars

Gay bars in Harlem are places to go to find and enjoy the company of other gay black men, to meet and make new friends, to give and receive news, to talk and gossip, to relax, to drink or "smoke" (reefer), to find out where the parties are, or to "score." Because many gay men live alone, boredom and loneliness are the two most frequently expressed motivations for patrons coming to the bars during the week. The desire to relax and to find a sex partner are also common reasons.

On weekends, most of the patrons use the bar as a place to gather with friends before going to dinner, a party, the theater, or the movies, or before heading downtown to a disco, to other gay bars, or out "cruising." Often friends meet after going out for dinner or attending the theater,[1] after a dance social or a boat ride, after work or school, after shopping, or after church on Sundays. Essentially, the attraction for men who frequent the bar scene is the company of like spirits: the presence of other gay black men.

In the gay bars in Harlem, the atmosphere is even more electric than in the cruise bars downtown on Christopher Street. They are louder, brighter, full of movement and laughter. Yet as one gets familiar with them, they become more sociable, warmer, more human, "more real," as Donny would say.

## Mickey's Place

Mickey's Place, a small bar uptown on Sugar Hill, looks like any other storefront: an awning across the sidewalk, a locked door three steps down from the pavement, and a large window across the front.

By midnight one Friday in January the small bar area was crowded: full of gesticulating men in heavy coats, continuous conversation, and the soft crooning of Billie Holiday on the jukebox in the back room. A row of older regulars occupied the barstools and chatted with Murphy, the barman, and one of the bargirls.[2] Each one of these patrons gathered around them a circle of friends, usually younger gay men. The gossip and repartee were ceaseless. Frequently a seated patron called out to an acquaintance seated farther down the bar and bellowed some reference to "girlfriend's" hairdo or "garments." The language deteriorated to name-calling, and the insults intensified until someone's mother was (jokingly) insulted. Such "contests" resulted in rounds of drinks being purchased, much laughter, and a reshuffle of the standing population.

At Mickey's Place there is seating at the bar for only about a dozen people and not too much room behind them for groups to assemble. But at the back of the bar area a small portico gives way to a large, dark, smoke-filled back room, where small groups of friends sit around tables, waited on by the barman, "conversatin'" quietly and smoking reefer. A gentle atmosphere prevails in the back room, even though the babble of the front bar is clearly discernible.

Occasionally someone will get up and move from the back room into the bar area. Sometimes someone will venture into the back room from the bar, only to beat a hasty retreat on realizing that no one is visible in the unlit room. Ambrose did so one night. He had been drinking downtown on 125th Street for some hours before "twirling on into" Mickey's Place around midnight. He "served" the "girls" at the bar some great "data" and proceeded into the darkness through the portico. Two or three steps in, he accidentally tripped over a table and ended up in the lap of a much younger man, Cameron. Cecil's voice was easily identified as he screamed for "ha ta git offa ma man!" In the half light shining through the portico, one could see young Cameron's embarrassment. Ambrose is not so tall, but he is a little rotund. And, of course, he made a great fuss in the few moments he enjoyed Cameron's lap. The entire back room launched into hysteria, so that one gained the impression hundreds of people were sitting right there in the dark.

Gilbert joined Harry, Wallace, and Roger, who had preceded him uptown by cab. Gilbert, who works for the Housing and Urban Development Department downtown, heads straight for the bars after work every night. He knows he can while away the time, seeing his friends as they come by and catch up on the "tea." Gilbert has a younger roommate to help defray the high rent he has to pay in his new apartment, but they do not get along all that well. Gilbert had hoped that a roommate would be company for him so that he could stay home more often, not spend so much money, and not be tempted to sleep around.

GILBERT: That temptation is strong. Jesus, keep me near the cross! Some of these boys are so cute. I love to play with them. Y'know, joke around with them in the bar. And I would love to take some of them home. But now you think twice about it. You know. You don't want to touch them really. You don't know where they been. And there ain't much left around that's my age. They all settled down. Or dead and gone.

Gilbert had a lover through much of his twenties, but the man left him for one of Gilbert's close friends. He runs into them often and "gets upset by it." Since their breakup ten years ago, Gilbert has been hanging out in the bars in Harlem and spending time with friends. He rarely meets anyone whom he would really like to date but does have a couple of young men he takes home for sex.[3]

GILBERT: I been seein' Roger and Wendell for years. They all right. I know them well. They're always in there [the bar]. I guess we're friends. I do spend a lot of time with them. And they good too. They do things for me. Go to the store, and help me fix things at home. So I don't mind them comin' home now and then. Just sometimes, y'know. Every now and then.

Harry and Wallace were friends from school days, had been raised in the same neighborhood, and had been "running buddies" (hanging out together) ever since. Wallace, at thirty-six, was still in search of the right man but had succumbed to the comfort of good friends in the bar circuit. He and Gilbert spend many evenings together commiserating over lost loves and bemoaning the lack of "real men" (potential lovers) about town.

Harry was a lot more adventurous. He was well connected in the underworld and a favorite with all the hustlers. He often provided the dope on a night out and could be seen almost always surrounded by a group of eager friends, like Wallace, Barry, or Roman, and always by some of the hustlers: Larry, Herbie, and Darnell had all been school friends or acquaintances of his, with whom he still kept in touch. In the often dangerous streets of Harlem at night, these hustlers formed a network of protection around many of my informants. In the scene, if any of the other gay men got into arguments or fights on the street, a group of hustlers always appeared to help out.

HARRY: These boys can make the difference between surviving out here and not. If I didn't know them, I wouldn't be alive now. I'm sure of that. The times they've helped me out, y'know. So I do them a favor once in a while. Buy them a drink. Share a joint. Occasionally I'd take them home. Y'know. Feed them. Wash them up. Let them get a good night's sleep. They're family, y'know. They've been around these streets with me. They grew up with me. They're like brothers to me. And they do take care of me.

Harry has a well-paying job as an office supervisor for a supermarket chain which enables him to maintain the hectic social schedule he pursues in and around Harlem. He attends all the social functions that attract a gay crowd and supports gay friends in talent contests and drag shows. He loves to dance and "used to do all those big old discos downtown. But they're all gone now. So I just stay close to home." His roommate is a dancer, and he helps support him as he struggles to establish his own dance company.

Wallace, who works for the Metropolitan Transportation Authority, shares an apartment with a co-worker who is also gay. His roommate has a lover in Jersey, so he spends his weekends there. Wallace doesn't mind, because it leaves the place quiet for him, and it means he can come and go at all hours of the day and night.

Usually Wallace and Harry leave Mickey's Place around six or seven on a Saturday morning, take in breakfast at M&G's (a restaurant on 125th Street), and go on home as the sun rises. Most of the evening at Mickey's Place is spent talking about people's pasts and gossiping about different people who wander in and out of the back room. Sometimes plans are laid for forthcoming dances. On this particular evening, Harry decided that he would go uptown to purchase the tickets, and everyone would reimburse him later. So at midnight he left.

Roger then took center stage. Wallace and Gilbert started teasing him about getting too old to hustle and too well known to be exciting or trusted. Gilbert remarked, "Ain't none of us want you for a husband, honey." The exchange was resolved when Roger said that he'd rather marry a woman than either of them, because "I knows what you like. I done had you already." Then he got up and visited another table. Such insults, almost ritual in gay repartee, appear to be confined to very close friends within the gay population.[4]

The laughter attracted Barry, Gilbert's best friend and former roommate. Some dispute over rent had split the two up years ago, but, when their respective lovers left them, they turned to each other for support. "I always complain about him, I know," Gilbert remarked. "He is hopeless with his money. I guess he needs someone to take care of him. But he's a good pal. I wouldn't want anything to happen to him." In these bars, the night passes away filled with stories of past sexual conquests, gossip about prominent black entertainers, and name-dropping. During this particular evening, Earl dropped by the table and talked about his piano playing for Aretha Franklin, and Francis told about the time he sang a medley with Ruth Brown at the Baby Grand Club. Fenton passed by, handing out flyers advertising his fashion show the following Thursday evening at a studio in midtown. At thirty-six, his career as a fashion designer was just beginning to take off in the fashion world, and this was to be his first big media-covered event. Door charges, and the fact that the event was downtown, would probably discourage most of this uptown crowd from supporting him. But all would eagerly await news of his success.

Harry returned to Mickey's Place about 2:00 A.M. and distributed the tickets. He brought Carson with him. They had met on the street, and because Carson was so high, Harry thought it best to bring him inside. Harry later told me, "That child's a mess. She's always out there cruising those straight boys. They'll hurt her. We'll be reading about her in the news."[5] When interviewed, Gilbert concurred: "Oh, it ain't the first time. She been through it all before. I remember the time she got arrested." Apparently, Carson had been accidentally caught up in a street fight between two men and had ended up in a jail cell overnight, until he had calmed down enough for the police to understand his protest. Although he knew one of the men intimately and had been walking with him when he was attacked, Carson refuses to acknowledge him anymore, and he no longer ventures into the same neighborhood. He opines that it is dangerous to love "such boys."

CARSON: You best off not even dealin' with them. You know you're in trouble from the minute you meet them. They won't let you go. Nowhere. They follow you everywhere. Now, I don't mind someone being all jealous over me. That's kinda nice. But if you want to finish it up, you are in trouble deep."[6]

Around 4:00 A.M. Gilbert announced that he was hungry, and almost everyone else at the table agreed. Harry stepped out to call a cab to take them down to 125th Street and get breakfast before calling it a night. The farewell procedure lasted some thirty minutes as they said goodnight to friends at other tables in the back room and then to friends seated at the bar. Francis, who was dressed in drag, made the biggest fuss, jokingly calling out to the few hustlers seated around the bar, and to other unknown clientele, that they were leaving unattended, and did anyone fancy this one or that. His deep, booming voice, coupled with the sexual innuendo, caused much laughter. However, no one took him up on the offer as he escorted his friends out the door and into the freezing morning.

These comings and goings highlight the bar as the focus of gay social life in Harlem.[7] Of course, they are also key institutions in the socialization process of becoming gay. All of my informants noted the importance of the gay bar to them as they came out, not only as a safe haven away from family and mainstream society but also as a place where one could learn about being gay. The bars are integrated, stable institutions that operate almost as "living rooms" for this community.[8] The bar becomes a second home for this family of gay men.

## Pete's Paradise

Other proof of the importance of the gay bar to the social life of gay men in Harlem is revealed on special occasions. The bars attract large crowds on Friday, Saturday, and Sunday evenings, as friends gather to socialize. But on a major holiday eve, these bars are packed tight with patrons from all over Harlem. Many are men who rarely venture into the scene. Of course, all of the regular clientele appear. As Louis notes, "I spend Christmas with my folks. But New Year's is mine. I always spend New Year's Eve with my girlfriends. I'm usually at [Pete's Paradise]."

By 9:00 P.M. on New Year's Eve, 1987, one of the most popular gay bars in Harlem was already crowded.[9] After being buzzed through the door,[10] patrons were confronted with a huge Christmas tree, covered in lights, and the jukebox blaring Bing Crosby's version of "White Christmas." The interior of the bar, with red walls and ceiling, a red and black linoleum floor, and mirrors everywhere, was brighter than usual and felt very warm. The radiators were working. The room was crowded, and much energy was being expended whenever a good dance tune came on the jukebox. In fact, people danced rarely in this bar, but on this New Year's Eve everyone was "getting down."

Donny and Barry jived to an early hit of Tina Turner's, and when

Michael Jackson burst forth, a line of guys, all the way to the back of
the bar, began moonwalking.[11] Nicholas and Emmett led the field,
and some of the hustlers joined in. This appeared to be the best evening in the bar for some time. A few weeks before, the bar staff had
been held up twice and all the patrons were stripped of their cash
and jewelry. It has taken a while for the small community who frequented the establishment to return, but New Year's Eve brought
everybody out.

There also seemed to be many people from the neighborhood who
rarely socialized in the scene. Roman, a Southerner who has been living in Harlem for almost thirty years, had gathered a group of friends
around him. He was soon joined by Cleveland, Louis, and Paul. The
group swelled as the evening pressed toward midnight, and the gossiping and singing became quite boisterous. Elaine poured everyone
an extra shot, which helped to encourage the celebration. She was
the favorite bartender of all of my informants who drank at this
tavern and always knew the latest news about any of her "fans," as
she called the clientele. She was reliable when it came to leaving messages for others; in fact, without her as a communications base, the
entire social networks of several of these men would have collapsed.
Because of the scattered nature of the gay social networks in Harlem,
the staff in any bar become the actual heart of communication between friends. Messages are phoned in or dropped off, and parcels or
gifts are left behind the bar. Certain of the bar staff always know where
the regulars can be found at any time. Thus these individuals are nodal
points of communication for many social networks, and Elaine is
the most popular. Her information is always reliable, and she can be
trusted to convey messages accurately. As Cleveland noted, she is
well tipped for her service. On her birthday in August, when she provided bottles of champagne for her favorite patrons, the crew served
up plates of food along the bar.

Before midnight on New Year's Eve, Elaine was at it again. She
lined up a dozen champagne glasses along her portion of the bar and
filled them with an expensive bubbly. These were passed to selected
fans, in preparation for the New Year's toast. By midnight it was getting difficult to move in the bar. It was freezing cold outside, so the
bar seemed even more crowded, with the clientele bulked up in heavy
coats. Lester and Gerard, two older gentlemen, wore floor-length fur
coats. Darnell remarked to me that they were known on the street as
"the fur queens" because they were forever wearing their fur coats to
church, to the bars, and even to brunch on Sundays.

Binga arrived "feeling it." He was the "African Queen" in the community. At social gatherings he always came swathed in African cloth and chunky brooches and beads made of wood, brass, or silver. This particular evening he complemented his khaki harem pants, black woolen jacket, and black boots with a long strip of gold, green, and purple Asante cloth draped over his left shoulder. And a similarly colored kufi. Not given to socializing, Binga bought his cocktail and stood back, leaning on the "meat rack",[12] observing the colorful parade. Louis, as usual, passed comment about Binga's use of makeup: "Girlfriend won't quit with Miss Revlon!"

Those lucky enough to have seats were able to remove their coats and drape them over the backs of their stools. This further cluttered the narrow area behind the bar. But all the pushing and crowding was conducted with a grand air of congeniality. A new year was about to dawn, and it could not be worse than the last. Friends had passed, friends were ill, bars had closed, and "fag bashing" was on the rise. And this was to be a presidential election year (1988). That can make a difference in America.[13] A sense of excitement and the possibility of change always heightens the air of expectancy that a New Year's Eve brings. Suddenly, Thurman, the head barman, screamed "Happy New Year!" at the top of his voice, and the crowd began singing "Auld Lang Syne."

Spending an important event like New Year's Eve in a gay bar is a significant statement about the importance of the gay family to each of the men present. It also stresses the importance of the institutionalized settings of the gay social scene to the members of this particular community.

## Other Bars and Clubs

Many gay men socialize in non-gay neighborhood bars and jazz clubs scattered up and down the avenues of Harlem. Some of these clubs have been in existence a very long time and have been referred to in the literature of the great writers of the Harlem Renaissance.[14] Garber (1989) has also drawn attention to descriptions of such clubs in the works of Blair Niles and Wallace Thurman.

Gay men patronize these bars and clubs for a variety of reasons besides those cited above: non-gay clubs suit them when in mixed company, when drinking or visiting with non-gay kin, or when a favorite

singer or jazz band is performing. Sometimes they visit a neighborhood bar because a friend works there or simply because it is close to
home.

During my sojourn in Harlem, three such clubs were especially
popular with my informants. One, a small, dark, neighborhood
"lounge" on Lenox Avenue, was the haunt of drag queens, who on
more than one occasion scored unsuspecting tricks (that is, they met
men for sex without the men realizing that the queens were not
women). Another was a large piano bar, which was popular with jazz
aficionados and hosted guest musicians and singers, charging a cover
for backroom performances by artists such as Ruth Brown and Art
Blakey. Once a month this club hosted a talent contest in which some
of my informants participated, and it frequently turned its stage over
to groups of gay performers. Well-known drag queens from Chicago
or Atlanta drew large crowds. These events would be advertised in the
*Amsterdam News* and on flyers posted in the street. The third club,
which I will call Mary's Lounge, was a small neighborhood tavern
that served live jazz on the weekends to a noisy, packed-in clientele.

## Mary's Lounge

After attending a poetry reading by black gay men at the
Studio Museum on 125th Street, Cato and some friends "bumped
on up" into Mary's Lounge. It was a freezing cold Friday night in
autumn, and the windows of the bar were all steamed up. Stepping
up from the street, they entered the crowded room. Cato recognized
a few of the men seated at the near end of the bar. He also knew
the barman, Colin, who extended his hand in welcome as Cato approached the counter to buy drinks. They briefly discussed the drag
ball that Colin was helping to organize. He described his new outfit
for the ball, which a fashion-designer friend had especially created for
this year's pageant and drag contest. And he admonished, "You'd better be there. I'm counting on all the support I can get. I want that trip
to Aruba, baby!"

Meanwhile, Cato's "friend" had located the only empty table and
secured some vacant chairs. Cato and his other friends "perched" on
the seats, crammed in among the dozen or so tables that covered the
carpeted half of the bar. Along the other side, the leather-topped bar
counter stretched to the rear of the room. All the available barstools

were occupied, and clients stood two and three deep behind them. To the left of the entrance, a small podium housed a three-piece jazz band: a lead guitarist who sang, a keyboard player who smiled while conversing with the two or three couples attempting to dance in the entranceway, and a white drummer. Each song was greeted with enthusiastic applause and much shouting. Most of the tables were occupied by couples, men and women drinking cocktails and conversing. Many of these people appeared to be familiar with each other.

Cato, like many other gay men in Harlem, uses the bars as a meeting place for friends before or after an event such as the poetry reading or as a place to make friends. Perhaps the most important use for the bars is as a meeting place for potential sex partners or lovers "lookin' for a husband." Cato says he cannot afford to keep anyone and would prefer an older man who is financially independent, who needs a good "wife" to cook and keep house, and who may even keep him. Mary's Lounge is where he has the most success. The bar is known as a place where the older gay crowd hangs out. Cocktails are a little more expensive here, so Cato believes that the older men who drink here will have some money. Ideally they will have enough left over to spend on him. But on this particular evening Cato wanted to wind down after his performance, listen to some music, and catch up with his friends.

Tobias was standing at the bar engaged in conversation with a few friends. He looked over their shoulders and cruised Cato. Eventually he came over and introduced himself to Cato and his friends. Cato spent a couple hours discussing with Tobias and his friends his new apartment and his forthcoming collection of poetry, the first solo publication he has produced. He has long been recognized as one of the black gay community's best young poets, which makes his parents and brothers proud. One brother has attended one of the many public readings in which Cato has participated, both in Harlem and downtown in the mainstream gay community. He finds that working full-time as a health-care consultant is too time-consuming, even though the money is more than satisfactory, because he would rather devote more time to his writing. Cato has written plays in the past, although none have been performed, and would like to pursue playwriting as a career.

At only one other table sat a group of men alone, and these were gay men Cato knew from another nearby bar. One of them, Moses, came over and chatted briefly with Cato. He was entertaining friends from out of town and was awaiting members of his "gang" to join him. His "gang" consists of fellow "church girls," a group of gay male friends who have known each other for many years and who attend church together every Sunday at A.M.E. Zion. They often gather at a gay bar after church and await a rival group from Abyssinian Baptist, a block away. This large group of men, usually numbering between ten and twenty on any Sunday, spends the afternoon and early evening drinking cocktails and debating the relevant merits of each others' faiths. As the drinking wears on, the debating becomes more argumentative, and everybody else in the bar, including the hustlers, knows it is best to give the "girls" a wide berth, unless one is also drunk or able to withstand the loud and vitriolic abuse that is usually hurled among the debaters. On other nights of the week, when they avoid religious debate, the church girls can be convivial company. Using the bar as a meeting place after church, the church girls are able to keep in touch with friends from other churches and inform each other of church events such as picnics and conventions. Sometimes they plan to attend church reunions or revivals in the South where they or their parents had been born.

Moses had been raised in the church in Alabama and Harlem. His father had been a deacon at A.M.E. Zion, and he and his brother are among the church's strongest financial supporters. At fifty-three, he owns his own mortuary business and home and is well known in the gay community as a generous patron of the needy. He has a small select group of "boys" whom he helps support on a continuing basis, and he has a steady flow of visitors at the bar who sell him groceries, furniture, and clothing.[15] On most Sundays he hosts an after-church dinner at his brownstone, before leading the "girls" downtown to the bar on 125th Street.

This particular evening his visitors from out of town were acquaintances he had met at churches he had visited or been associated with in Washington, D.C., and Cleveland, Ohio. He has a network of church friends, mainly gay church members, across the country and frequently hosts them or holidays with them. This evening he intended to take this group of four on a tour of the gay bars in Harlem and had enlisted his best friends, Sidney and Cecil, to serve as chaperones.

Moses and the church girls are a relatively well established group of older men.[16] They are an example of the different types of men and the different socioeconomic groups that frequent the gay scene in Harlem. Through the gay social scene they come into contact with similarly diverse gay men. And through contacts made in the bars they extend their social networks to include gay men who may come to depend on their financial aid. "I met all o' these sissies in here," Moses commented. "It's where I met all o' my friends. If it weren't for the bars I dunno where I'd go. I wouldna have the friends I has now."

Such gatherings at the bars, especially on a weekend evening, were a typical night out for those of my informants who "worked" the bar scene. These outings often lasted until dawn.[17] During the night, one could keep in touch with one's friends, gather quite a group around oneself, and set up a party at someone's apartment. Thus the bars, gay or mixed, become the focus of the social lives of gay men who frequent the scene.

## Card Games

Playing cards is a major source of entertainment in Harlem and an important focus of gay social life in Harlem. Card games provide an avenue of entertainment and participation in gay life for those gay men who do not frequent the scene. For those men who do visit the gay bars and clubs, the card games provide an alternative venue for socializing with friends.

Although some card games are casually organized during a night out, others are planned, and some are permanent dates on the calendar. While in a bar, a casual invitation to play cards is usually welcomed. It is a chance to stop barhopping yet continue partying, get something to eat, catch up on news of and from friends, and "carry on" all night.

Paul and Louis host a card game once every two weeks, on a Wednesday evening. Paul prefers bidwiss, but the group also plays Uno and 500. Louis informed me that when he first met Paul the cardplayers would meet every week, but after they moved in together, he decided that having that crowd around every week was too much.

LOUIS: I know he likes his cards. But it was too much. You get them eating you out of house and home. I mean I don't mind playing, but I used to go out and let them fend for themselves. They're growed up men. They can get their own food and shit. They used to have me runnin' around servin' drinks and shit, and all the time I'd be emptying ashtrays and cooking. I got fed up with it all. So I told Paul to carry on, but just don't expect me to run around after them all the time. I mean none of them invited us for dinner. Not then anyway. Now he has the same three or four each week, and they're our best friends, so I don't mind. And it's not like it's every week. So I don't mind as much.

Wilbur, Brian, and Sherman, a former school friend of Louis, are Paul's regular partners. The four have become tight friends. All drink after work at the same bar in Harlem and accompany one another, with their respective lovers or boyfriends, to major gay social events in the community. They play cards every week, every second Wednesday at Henry's and every other Sunday at Wilbur's. These regular card games provide this group of friends with a way of maintaining their close friendship away from the gay scene. During the games, the players discuss their private and business lives and seek and proffer advice.

## Ambrose's Card Party

It was after midnight by the time the group of friends reached Ambrose's large and beautifully decorated apartment on 138th Street. Ambrose had inherited it from his mother who had passed away fifteen years ago. He had lived with her all his life and had been very close to her. He keeps the house much the way it was when his mother was alive. His maternal grandparents had been "society folks" when they purchased the home in the 1920s. His grandmother, "a real church woman," had a reputation as a "fierce hostess" and, as a friend of Ethel Waters, A'Lelia Walker, the Powells, and the James Weldon Johnsons, was a favorite of the formal party set in Harlem during the Renaissance years. Ambrose has collected a substantial number of photographs, both of his family and of Harlem and Harlemites during those years. These he proudly displays in small wooden frames around the walls of his "parlor," a large living room furnished with heavy Victorian armchairs and art deco fixtures, lamps, and flower stands. Heavy velvet curtains and large vases of garden flowers create an atmosphere right out of Van der Zee's photographs. Recently renovated carpeting and wallpaper maintain this 1920s look.

Three card tables were assembled in the parlor by the "boys." Harry busied himself at the bar in the dining room, while Adrian and

Wallace helped unpack the vast tubs of fried chicken that Ambrose had purchased on the way home. Ambrose was busy in the refrigerator, hauling out trays of sweet potato pudding, macaroni and cheese, and potato salad.

Music blaring, drinks all around, and plates passed, the party got under way. Ambrose slipped upstairs to "climb into something more comfortable," and Harry began to organize the card tables. The twelve players were just the right number for three tables of bidwiss, Uno, or 500. Harry and Wallace began a game of Uno with Mitch and Adrian, while another team set up a bidwiss game. Roger and Sal vied for Ambrose's attention. Their flattering pursuit of him all evening long was the source of much entertaining repartee, especially among Ambrose's "girlfriends"—Barry, Adrian, and Clifton—who were no doubt a little jealous. Such repartee continued at each table, and even between the tables, as the victors of different hands of cards were cursed out by the losers or gossipy snipes were made about friends at another table. Clifton was especially skillful at "reading" Ambrose for the undue attention he was gleaning from Sal. Often Ambrose stood up and sashayed around the tables with his head held high and cigarette holder stretched aloft, rather than verbally acknowledge Clifton's latest retort. Such "carry on" drew quips and shrieks from everyone else as they scattered to cover the cards in their hands. The shouting and laughter, combined with the loud music, must have kept the neighbors awake for blocks around.

This particular evening, the games lasted two or three hours, until Clifton and Adrian decided they needed their rest. At that point, more food was served, Ambrose and Sal retired, and Harry took charge of the cleanup. A few players left, but others continued to play cards until dawn. Such long nights of play were frequent for many of my informants, whether they belonged to the bar scene or not. After many major social events, groups of friends would wind down playing cards, or, as on the boat rides, such games were an integral part of the day's proceedings.

## Major Social Events

Many gay men in Harlem have occupations and networks of kin and friends that keep them out of the neighborhood or

offer alternate sources of entertainment. They may visit a gay bar or
a jazz club on occasion, or join a regular card game. However, they
remain connected to their gay "brothers" in other ways. Their main
link to the gay scene in Harlem is most likely to be one of the major
social events of the gay calendar in Harlem. In other words, dance
socials, the annual drag ball, or one of the several summertime
boat rides will attract even those gay men who do not frequent the
bars.

Large social events are organized by citywide black gay clubs. The
clubs themselves have small "memberships." For example, the Good
Times Club has a membership of about fifteen gay men. They serve as
an organizing committee for dances and other social events. One is
invited, after strict scrutiny, to join such a committee.[18] Most of the
committee members are Harlem residents. More recently, three gay
women have been inducted into the Good Times Club as associate
members. All of these members are prominent citizens in the community, professional or business persons. When a social event is advertised by flyer or word of mouth, much clamoring ensues as the gay
population vies for tickets, on sale from the committee members only.

## The Dance

In a large, rented ballroom, I attended my first of many
dances. I had been invited by Cleveland and Randy, in a small party
they had put together to help fill one of Clarence's tables. Our party
included two other couples: Timothy and Kent, and Shawn and Lee.
Clarence has been a club member for many years and is a respected
elder in the community. He and his lover hosted about eight tables
of ten to twenty people at this particular dance. A cash bar proffered
a full range of liquors, beers, and punch, but Clarence and his lover
covered their guests' tables with platters of fried chicken, potato
salad, macaroni and cheese, banana pudding, and fresh fruit. These
large tables surrounded a dance floor on which over a hundred people performed at any one time. Music was spun by "Mr. Blues," a
master disc jockey. He and his two assistants played a wide range of
music, mostly R&B, house,[19] and some Caribbean salsa. Occasionally
they would mix in a slow tune, or a cha-cha or rhumba, which would
bring out the "serious dancers." Male couples and female couples,

most of whom arrived together or in groups of couples, danced the evening away, until the disc jockey turned down the lights and concluded with an extended fox-trot at around 2:30 A.M.

The guests at this and similar functions were always well dressed, some in suits and evening gowns, some in more recent styles and bright colors. Everyone could dance different ballroom steps. The atmosphere was congenial, and most of the people appeared to know one another. Many of them were unfamiliar to me at the beginning because they were not active in the scene in Harlem. But most lived in Harlem, or were originally from Harlem and now living in New Jersey or Brooklyn.

Orville, who recently moved to Brooklyn after retiring, has been attending the Good Times Club dances for twenty years. He also attends the Unity Club socials, which he says are similar but have an even more mixed crowd in terms of age and residence. The Unity Club committee has members from Queens, Long Island, and New Jersey, as well as Brooklyn and Harlem. Orville feels more comfortable at the Good Times Club functions because they are attended by a larger number of older men and women, friends he has known from around Harlem during the fifty years he has lived there. For men like himself who do not spend time in the scene and who do not like the bars, these dance socials are the best way to make friends and meet potential boyfriends. He noted that sex is always available in the parks and the bathhouse, but if one wants to meet someone special, the dance social is the place to be. Nowadays he attends regularly because the dances provide him with an opportunity to meet up with friends from all over the city. He regrets moving out to Brooklyn six months ago because he is so far away from his friends. But now he is living close to a niece and nephew who take care of him. He has a small apartment in Brownsville and finds life in Brooklyn more peaceful and less expensive. Besides attending the dances and other social functions these large clubs host, he visits friends in Harlem during the week and frequently attends church in Harlem, staying on for dinner at different friends' homes.

These dances have been a fixture in gay life in Harlem for forty or fifty years, according to my informants. Not only are they regarded as formal occasions, in the sense that it is time to dress up and behave properly, but they offer a chance to meet with friends in a congenial setting away from the cruising or sexually oriented social institutions of the gay scene.

## The Boat Ride

One of Orville's favorite outings is the annual boat ride organized by the Trouser League. This is the oldest of the citywide black gay social clubs and the most popular because it hosts the best-attended events and has a wide range of activities—dances, raffles, and picnics, as well as the boat rides.

Louis is a friend of the president of the league and is able to obtain a large number of tickets. Thus he can assemble a large group of friends for his table. On one ride he organized a group of twenty of us, including three friends from Washington, D.C. For weeks beforehand, Louis planned a menu and organized the rest of us to bring different dishes. For all of those attending, this outing proved expensive. Tickets were $15 to $20 a head, food and liquor had to be supplied, new clothes bought, and the whole show coordinated: this involved telephone calls, car rentals, and the purchase of special furniture and other party supplies, which then had to be delivered, initially to Henry's, then to the boat.

The night before, Louis and I went shopping for new outfits. By then the weather patterns were set and we knew what clothes would be the most comfortable for the all-day journey. As well as bringing sumptuous displays of food on elegant tableware, guests need to be properly attired in casual but fashionable clothes. An unwritten competition exists between tables as to who can outdo their neighbors for types and presentation of food, cocktails, and fashions.

Louis and Paul rented a car on the Friday evening and began loading it with the three tables for the food and cards. At 6:00 A.M. on Saturday, Louis dropped Paul off at the boat so that he could stand in line to get on board early and choose a good place to put the tables. He set the tables up at a prominent position, on the second of three floors, at the entranceway between an enclosed disco and the rear deck. A cool breeze at this location helped keep everyone fresh on the humid August afternoon. Two large tables bore the Virginia ham, ribs, fried chicken, potato salad, cold cuts, rolls, macaroni and cheese, cole slaw, baked potatoes, candied yams, stuffed turkey, and every conceivable kind of liquor. A third table was placed nearby, around which Paul, Barry, Brian, and Wilbur commenced playing cards. They attracted a large group of onlookers, who replaced the original players when they wanted to take a break. Alcohol and reefer soothed the expanding group as others on board came to join the party. All day people strolled around the decks, visiting friends or taking in the sun and breeze on the uncovered top deck. Some spent most of the time on board dancing at two discos on different floors. Meanwhile, the boat sailed up the Hudson River to Poughkeepsie before turning around and heading back to midtown Manhattan. The constant drinking and eating, from the 9:00 A.M. departure until the 6:00 P.M. return, proved a little too much for some, who lay back in their deck chairs and went to sleep.

On the return to land, Louis's guests reassembled at a bar in Harlem, viewed Polaroid photos that had been taken, and told stories of what had happened. Some of my informants in the bar who had adamantly refused to be trapped on a dayliner cruise with a whole lot of "sissies" were among the most eager to know who had said and done what on the trip, who had taken whom, and who had disembarked with whom. The description of the day's events and much analysis occupied the travelers until midnight or so, when Louis decided the car should be unpacked and everyone needed to go home, shower, and get some rest.

The significance of these social occasions can only be measured by witnessing the affirmation of gay black men's friendship networks and their pride in who and what they are. Word of mouth through the social networks of gay men ensures that this social institution is well supported. While many bemoan the long day and hard work involved, and, of course, the small fortune it costs, twelve months later they are eagerly planning the next trip.

## The Drag Ball

The annual black-tie drag ball was originally inspired by the female impersonator Phil Black over fifty years ago (Garber 1989:331).[20] His name still appears on the invitations and tickets. Writing about these balls as they took place in the 1920s, Garber notes,

Drag balls, part of the American homosexual underground for decades, had developed from clandestine private events into lavish formal affairs attended by thousands. The Harlem balls in particular were anticipated with great excitement by both Blacks and Whites. The largest were annual events at the regal Rockland Palace, which held up to 6,000 people. Only slightly smaller were the ones given irregularly at the dazzling Savoy Ballroom, with its crystal chandeliers and elegant marble staircase. The organizers would obtain a police permit making the ball, and its participants, legal for the evening. The highlight of the event was the beauty contest, in which the fashionably dressed drags would vie for the title Queen of the Ball. (1983:12)

The drag balls still are magnificent affairs, drawing between six hundred and two thousand attendees. Both men and women participate in drag. At each ball, a competition is held. Drag queens parade on a walkway, as if in a fashion show, wearing magnificent gowns and posing before a panel of gay and non-gay judges. A Queen of the Ball is chosen, and her prizes include travel (usually to the Caribbean) and "cash dollars." Again a feast is presented, and copious quantities of alcohol are consumed. For weeks afterward, costumes and people and partners are discussed, until each year's ball becomes legendary in the folklore of the gay scene.

Harlem, like many other cities with large black populations in the United States, has a long history of drag performances, "costume balls," and famous female impersonators. Several prominent drag queens visit Harlem from time to time, performing at jazz clubs and piano bars. One of Chicago's most successful queens, "Rochelle," performed regularly at the Baby Grand on 125th Street, supported by a cast of local queens led by the infamous "Miss Ruth Brown." While there is some intermingling between the transvestite and transsexual drag populations and the gay population in Harlem at balls or talent shows, normally the two groups socialize apart. Usually the drag queens work the bars and streets and frequent non-gay bars to score "tricks." "Honey," Francis explained, "we need real [non-gay] men."[21] Two or three "lounges" on Lenox and Seventh avenues are favorite haunts of these queens.

Many drag queens, however, do not hang out in the bars. Most drag queens I met lived in relationships with other men and worked regular jobs. Two queens I came to know worked as doctor's receptionists, one in a hospital, the other in private practice. They described themselves as "transsexuals," and one of them held a nurse's aide certificate. By far the majority of drag queens in Harlem are transvestites who will dress in drag on the weekends or on special occasions such as the drag ball. The remainder of the time they dress and act as ordinary men.

Apart from appearances at the occasional social event, men in drag are rarely seen at social functions with gay men. Half a dozen drag queens frequented the gay bars during the period of this research, but most were drinking on their way to or from tricking in the neighborhood. Drag queens in Harlem, as elsewhere, have their own social institutions, which are separate from the "gay scene."

## Private Parties

Another event favored by gay men which has a long history in Harlem is the "rent party" (see n.13, chap. 2). These events no longer excite the social imagination as they once did (Garber 1989:321). Today rent parties are more intimate. The invitees are well known to the host and are usually gay friends and family members. For security reasons alone, these parties are not open to the public or advertised in bars and clubs as they once were.

But private parties are the favored social event in Harlem for many gay men. These events may be a holdover from earlier days when gay social life was closeted, or at least not exercised in public. They may also be the result of earlier, more rigid class divisions in Harlem society, which we do not see so obviously today. Now parties are enjoying a renewed vigor as a result of the AIDS epidemic, which has encouraged many people to stay away from the bar scene and the drug abuse and indiscriminate sex associated with it.

In fact, according to these informants, most gay men in Harlem do not socialize in the public scene. They attend private rent, birthday, or anniversary parties, and it is here that they make friends, expand their social networks, and meet potential lovers. Admittedly, introductions into this somewhat private world are more difficult to get. Contacts are established in the home neighborhood, at school or college, in the bars, the bathhouse, downtown clubs, or the parks. Once a newcomer is initiated into the private party scene, invitations abound, helping to fill his social calendar on most weekend evenings.

Some parties are very small private affairs, others large catered events thrown in rented accommodations such as a community center hall or the common rooms in an apartment complex or the projects. Invitations to such parties are rarely printed. Usually they are issued personally and extend to any guests the invitee wishes to bring along. Thus a host can expect twenty or thirty personal invitees to result in two or three times that number of actual attendees. Frequently, I would be included in such group invitations and end up being a member of a party of ten or twelve people. Although food and drinks were usually supplied, guests would always take along some alcohol.

The importance of these parties lies not so much in the reasons for the particular celebration as in the fact that for most gay men in Harlem they are the primary forms of their gay social life. If most men do not frequent the public social scene, then we can assume that these parties become the focal point of the social lives of whole networks of friends.

## Roly's Birthday Bash

After his birthday bash at a community center, Roly told me that he had ended up with twice as much alcohol as he had started with. His sixtieth birthday was a huge affair with a disco and live music, catered dinner, and two bars. He invited seventy-five people, gay men and lesbians, and catered for two hundred. Over 250 showed up. There was enough food and drink to go around, and the party lasted until 3:00 A.M. Although it must have cost hundreds of dollars, Roly explained that one reaches sixty only once and that this would be his last preretirement party.

Cleveland informed me that Roly has held such affairs several times in the past and that was why this particular party was so well attended. After this event, many of the guests reassembled at one of three or four gay bars in the neighborhood and continued to party until dawn. Again, many gay men at this and other parties make or renew friendships, reestablish contact with the community and its grapevine, and forge or reinforce links to the gay scene by after-party barhopping.

## The Changing Scene

By now (1990) Harlem has only three or four exclusively gay bars. Many have closed because of slack attendance or from pressure exerted by neighboring businesses. AIDS, drugs, especially crack, and the encroaching gentrification of 125th Street and "SoHar" are also cited as possible causes.[22]

Colin remembers when there were at least a dozen bars scattered up and down Lenox, St. Nicholas, Seventh, and Eighth avenues. The Big Apple and the Apollo Bar were very popular in the 1960s and early 1970s. He also recalls that at that time gay people in Harlem were enjoying some freedom, although the police would raid the bars and parks quite frequently.

COLIN: I think we get harassed more now that people know about us. This gay liberation has been good and bad. I know we've won some official respect, but these young kids on the street get over [get the better of] the gay kids all the time. Mind you, its usually nothing more than a bit of verbal abuse. You don't get the kids gettin' bashed up like down in the Village.

Two of the current bars have been situated in their present locations for some years, although under changing management and different names. Colin doubts that they will ever be closed. However, many gay people drink in or follow the jazz sessions at other bars in Harlem, so that there may be several other bars that cater to a mixed crowd at any given time.

Whether the vagaries of time or commercial whim change the setting, gay life in Harlem will persist. I am assured by my informants that although some places do go out of business from time to time, other locales emerge as gay institutions. At the time of writing, two or three other bars were becoming venues for gay socializing: one up on Amsterdam Avenue and two others between 140th and 149th streets.

## Summary

Harlem's gay social life is organized around a variety of gay and mixed social institutions and a calendar of gay social events and private gatherings including card games, dances, boat rides, and private parties. Significantly, the social institutions of the gay scene in Harlem are located within the residential area of most of their clientele. They are, as Cicero says, "close to home."[23] This is an important factor in the conscious construction of identity for these gay black men, as they see black culture as central to their existence.

# 5

## "Different from Other Colors": Black Culture and Black Identity

For the gay black men who make up the informant group for this study, opting to remain in a black community and to pursue social and sexual contacts with other black people is an expression of being black.[1] They perceive learning to be black as a conscious, active process, contrary to the common portrait of passive socialization one gets from the literature on black society.[2] In Harlem, individuals actively seek out information on being black, rather than just experiencing blackness in their daily lives. Growing up in a black environment, they are exposed to many of the elements of black culture.

Here I want to allow a population to speak for themselves about those aspects of socialization, black culture, and black experience that they deem important to black identity. What is immediately evident is that individual actors identify primarily as black, often when they have the opportunity to identify otherwise, for example, as gay or as American. Being black, then, is more than just an issue of skin color. It is a cultural identity constructed from experiences in the black family, in the black church, and out of black history and folklore, and it finds its expression in the social performance of black identity.

## Harlem and Black Culture

Being raised in a black community is of primary importance in constructing a black identity: familial and other cultural contacts are maintained, and lifelong friendships with other black people are established. But Harlem is also a center of black cultural innovation, a historical capital of urban blackness.

LIONEL: Growing up in Harlem? Just like anywhere else, I guess. I mean, I know its different, really, I'm proud that I'm from here. The whole world knows what Harlem is. I mean all the black people in the world know this is where it's at. So, yeah, I feel proud that this is my home.

HARRY: The most important thing to me is that all my friends are black. All my lovers have been black. That's what I like. So, that's why I live here. 'Cause all my friends live here. And they're all black. So, we just live our black lives right here.

Its history as *the* black town, *the* black ghetto, is reinforced by its being a city in its own right, a city that caters to the needs of all of its residents.

FRANCIS: Now you know I like my black boys. You know that. And, child, there's some fierce trade to be had right here in Harlem.... Honey, there ain't nothing like a Harlem boy.... You see, Harlem is the heart of black life in this country, and that's where you come to find real black men. That's why I live here. I been to Chicago. I been to Detroit. There ain't nothin' like Harlem.

Most especially, Harlem is perceived as a place to be black.

COLIN: I truly believe that that's why so many people came north. All these magazines and books about jobs and a better life. We know that ain't true. But what is true is that Harlem was a black town. It was a place where they could come and be black. They didn't have to deal with white folks. In their small towns or in their schools an' their churches. At work. Here in Harlem they could live black lives. I don't think they consider that angle. All these stories have a human angle. And sometimes we just do things because we're human. Not because we want more money, or better living conditions, or a better education. You can get all that better in the South than here anyhow. Harlem was special because it was black. Like the young folks is saying about Brooklyn. They all runnin' off and livin' in Brooklyn. Sayin' it's the biggest black city outside o' Africa. Same reason. Not because they got better jobs there. They still work in Manhattan. Not because the rents are cheaper. 'Cause they ain't. They goin' there because it's so black.

Black people today still believe Harlem is the core of black culture.

MARTIN: The way those children walk wears me out. All that energy. Sometimes I feel like telling those boys to put the energy into me. Come round my place and burn up some energy. But that's them. That's Harlem boys. They carry on. In the street. They don't care who sees them do what. They tough.... These children in Harlem started all that stuff. You can see all these street styles in D.C. or Atlanta, or Chicago, or Philly, but this here is where it's from. That's what I like about Harlem. It's original. It all starts here.... Mind you, a lot of what these children on the street are doing comes from the gay [black] children. You see these boys and their haircuts, and their spandex, and bicycle caps. That all came from the gay children. Now a couple of years ago, they'd be callin' you "sissy" if you carried on like that. 'Specially in the street. But now it's OK. You see, what I'm sayin' is that all this fashion and stuff comes from the gay children. Even the white children are copying it now. So it's a source for all this creativity. Harlem is the source. I guess that's what really makes it famous.... To live in Harlem is to be at the source of black life. That's what I like about it. You're either creating it or taking part in it.

Harlem as a center of core black culture includes many artists—painters and sculptors, novelists and playwrights, musicians and dancers—although its image from the outside is of the ghetto: bombed-out buildings and projects, drugs and home boys. The white world of mainstream America believes the latter image to be Harlem's only truth. And the image of Harlem as a fearful, run-down, chaotic place full of impoverished people has been carried worldwide by the media. In Tokyo or Amsterdam, Mombasa or Sydney, the image of Harlem is that of the consummate black urban ghetto. Yet Harlem has over 300,000 residents, most of whom work, own or rent their homes, go to school, and live very typical urban lives.

## Socialization

Obviously, growing up in Harlem does not provide the only source of information on being black. Gay men have constructed their identities as black men from what they have heard from family and friends, read in newspapers, magazines, and books, seen in movies and on television, learned at school and in college, and most especially from what they have observed in the community around them.

One of the significant reminders of being black comes from close and continuous contact with others. Of course, this experience of being confronted with difference occurs every day on the street, especially in New York City.

CARL: I never knew I was black until I came to New York. I mean at home we just was. You know. I mean all of us was the same. Sure we was told, "Don't you be goin' over there. The white folks don't like us goin' over there." But you didn't really know you was different 'cause you didn't see it. Or feel it. Y'know. But in New York. You learn shit like that. I mean you are forced to deal with so many other peoples. So you become aware that you're different too. I mean you can see it easy enough. People here all look different. And they're all mixed up together, y'know. So you see the differences.

But the most important source of information about being black comes from the family.

STANLEY: Really you learn those things when you comin' up. In family. I learned from my sisters and my grandmother. She was the one. I learnt all the stuff about down South, all the stuff about slaves, and whites. I learnt all that from my grandmother. 'Cause she was the only one that knew. We never saw no white folks. My first white man was a schoolteacher. Now he was fine. So, you know, I had no trouble listening to him!

The next most important source of information are friends in the neighborhood. Interaction with other black people "on the street" exposes the individual to the expressive elements of black culture: clothing and other fashion styles, black English, nonverbal communication skills, music, and dance.

STANLEY: The children on the street was where we got it from. I mean they be the ones that be teachin' you how to behave. They beat it into you. I didn't realize that until I was much older. How much we conform. We all wear the same shit and wear the same [hair]dos. I remember when we all had the same shoes. The whole class at high school was wearing exactly the same pair of shoes. I didn't see it then. But now the kids in the same sneakers, the same coats, the girls in the same earrings. They all conform. And they do it to the beat of the street.

LOUIS: You learn a lot of that stuff [being black] on the street. I remember the first time I saw the children coming up with their Afros. That was the biggest black thing ever. It must have really pissed off the white folks. They couldn't do that one if they tried. But it was exciting. To see something really black. And urban black. Something that was us, here in the city. . . . You learn how to walk, how to talk, how to act, how to dress. You learn all that on the street.

It is important to note that Louis raises the issue of black American culture as racially and culturally distinct from white. The construction of one culture in opposition to another has important ramifications for black people, one of which is providing a psychological cushion against discrimination. Since they often see themselves being treated as second-class citizens in American society, by declaring pride in being black, African-Americans are claiming a culture that is their own.

Some sense of pride in being black is also instilled through formal education. Most of my informants were exposed to black history and the lives of famous blacks while in high school or college.

GARVEY: I didn't really understand about it [being black] until I was at school and we read about famous people. You know, prominent black men and women who'd done things. I'm not just talking about Langston Hughes and Zora Neale Hurston. Or Adam Clayton Powell or Malcolm X. But a whole lotta other folks. Like Carter G. Woodson and Garrett Morgan. And Ida B. Wells. And A. Philip Randolph, Matthew Henson, James Weldon Johnson. And so on. We read DuBois, Washington, Frederick Douglass. I remember one teacher telling us about the famous African kings like Shaka and Haile Selassie. I guess that was all quite forward thinking then. In the sixties. But that education gave me a real sense of being something. That's what's wrong with the children today. They don't know that stuff. Or if they do, it don't matter too much to them. But then, in the sixties, with all that shit going on, we really took pride in knowing about these people. It gave us a sense of who we were. Blacks weren't all bad. Blacks could be famous. It makes you feel better. Makes you feel proud of your race. Proud to be black. Black is beautiful!

For many of my informants, school provided the first setting where they learned about famous men who were both black and gay.

BYRON: I remember reading some of that stuff in school. Not too much. We read [Langston] Hughes and Countee Cullen. We heard about them. I knew who they were. 'Cause at that time ev'rything that was black was cool. You know, the teachers would really push the black stuff. But it was in college that I really enjoyed them. Especially [James] Baldwin. I guess I could understand him then. And [Ralph] Ellison and [Richard] Wright. I loved Ellison's work. And [Maya] Angelou and [Audre] Lorde. That's when I found out about Hughes and Baldwin and Cullen and them being gay. That was wild. I felt really proud of them then.

The fact that some of these famous blacks were also gay proved a bonus for many of my informants. They were able to identify with many of their culture heroes on two levels: as black men and as gay men. One informant even cited Hughes and Baldwin when he came out to his mother. He noted how he thought it helped her to understand his situation and realize that it is all right to be gay if famous black men were gay.

Finding out about black history—that blacks had an important past filled with significant individuals—often sent these men in search of further information about their black forebears.

NATE: I used to go to the library [Schomburg] after school, or after dinner, 'cause I couldn't study at home. Not with all the people comin' and goin'.

So I used to go there and study. I had work to do, but I used to look up all this stuff about the [Harlem] Renaissance. I was fascinated with these writers. I suppose because I wanted to be one. I read about Wallace Thurman and Walter White. And Claude McKay. Then I'd read the other writers too. I used to read Richard Wright's works. I think I read everything he ever wrote. I read W. E. B. DuBois and James Weldon Johnson. I wasn't too interested in the poets. They didn't seem to say that much. Not that much about life in Harlem or down South. Not like the novelists did. I even read *Nigger Heaven* [by Carl Van Vechten]. I used to look up the old papers like the *Age* and the *Crisis*. It was such an informative time for me. I was hearing about all these people and books and I'd do follow-up at the library. I think I knew more than what my teachers did. Especially about the Harlem Renaissance. That was my favorite period. And that was before it became popular.

Often an appreciation of the past was gleaned from family members or sought from friends and neighbors. Leonard learned about his heritage from several sources. From his grandmother he learned about his southern roots.

LEONARD: She told me all about the South. And workin' on the farms. But that was when she was small. 'Cause my grandfather was from up here somewhere. I think he was born in Connecticut. Yeah, he was. And he was a preacher. And he worked in some church in South Carolina. And that's where he met my grandmother. So, when they got married, he brought her up here to New York. To Rochester. 'Cause that's where the church sent him. So she told me about life in Rochester. And in South Carolina. I guess her folks were poor farmers. They had their own farm. But their son, her brother, was killed in some sort of accident. I think he may have been lynched or something. But the family never talks about that. They just say "he met with an accident." So she was their only child. Now, when they died she inherited the farm. One of my cousins lives on it now. He and his wife. But they work in Charleston. They just live on the land. So I used to ask her about my heritage. She was the source of all I know about my own family.... She took us with her. Every year for about eight years I guess. We just stayed on the farm. But we had to work. She had an old man that used to look after the animals and the trees. But we had to pick the fruit, every year. We had a lot of fun though. It wasn't all hard work. And we were near the sea, so we spent a lot of time at the beach. I remember those long, slow, hot summers. You don't get those anymore. Not once you older.

From his older friends Leonard continues to learn about his black heritage.

LEONARD: Oh, C——. Yeah, I really hear about the old times here in Harlem from him. I mean he's a great source of information, because he knew all those painters and writers from the twenties [Harlem Renaissance]. He could tell some great stories about the parties and who was carrying on with who. I want to record what he says, but he doesn't want to. He told me that we black folks keep our history to ourselves. We don't write it down like the white people. We just pass it on by word of mouth. I don't agree with him, really. I think we'll keep better records if it's kept written down. Then they can't say we made it up. I think they will respect us more too if we write it down.... C—— told me about Wallace Thurman, who he knew very well. And Richard Bruce Nugent. They traveled together to England. So they were quite close. He said they were all tramps. They had so many men and when they were traveling, they were more tired from all the sex than from the acting and dancing.... He mentioned a couple of bars where they'd hang out. Now this is in the thirties, before the war. Before that they didn't have gay bars. Not like we remember them, but most of these gay men would cruise straight men in the straight bars, right here in Harlem. But they had a lot of parties too. That's where they'd really hang out. Going to parties. Like the rent parties. And of course there were the parks. Even then Mt. Morris was famous. I was really quite shocked to hear that men my grandfather's age were carrying on like we do. I guess every generation has. It's just you can't imagine your grandfather doin' it.... Every time I visit C—— I hear something new. So I come home and write it down.

From both of these sources Leonard has learned not only about his family's past and the history of Harlem but also what it is to be black.

Television and the movies also capture some of what it means to be black. Although many of my informants remember the "black exploitation" movies of the 1960s and the 1970s, many noted the influence that black movie and television stars and series can have on black youth. Much of the expressive culture that is black is conveyed nationwide through the media, reinforcing a national black style yet usually neglecting its origins on the streets of Harlem. Although they spoke of the importance of the media in educating blacks about being black, my informants also criticized the media for misrepresentation.

HERBIE: Being black is the most important thing in my life. I am black. And I can't do anything abut it, so I might as well enjoy it.... Of course, you know you're different. You just gotta look at TV to see that. I mean even when they do us they get it wrong. Even when they use black actors, it's just like white people's ways. They really don' know what it's like to be black. That's our secret I guess. That's what makes us different. So, yes, we know we're different.... Sure, they did it OK with "Good Times." Now that was in Chicago. And you could tell that. But that was close to what you'd see around here. I mean they caught some of the emotions. They made you laugh and cry. And that's what we did. We laughed and cried. Just like everybody else, I guess. We laughed and cried about it all. That's how you got through.

Being black also includes the realization that you are different. Of course, it is regarded as more than just an issue of color.

SHAWN: McKay and Ellison taught me about that [racial difference]. I learned that from them. More than being black or Negro. It was being different. Different from other colors. But they mean different in other ways too. Not just color. But black things I really learnt from my family and my friends. And at school. I mean you gradually learn those things as you grow up. But certain events or books teach you certain things. They can be more earth-shattering than things you do. Like *The Autobiography of Malcolm X*. That book affected me more than anything else I've read. It moved me so much. I took a real close look at the Black Muslims after that. I almost became one. But I respect them enormously. They're tough.

Thus, from a variety of sources, much different information is received about being black—from family, friends, the street, television, school, and books. Actively seeking further information from libraries and knowledgeable people enhances this experience. One of the most important ways to learn about being black is in confronting different races. Out of this confrontation, knowledge comes early and often painfully.

## Skin Color

The search for a black identity in America includes the recognition of race, an important dividing line in this country.

LUTHER: I knew I was different when I first went to school. I had a white teacher. She was the first white person I had to deal with. And she talked funny. I used to laugh at her. Well, she had enough o' me. And my mother got called up 'n' all. I really didn't know what was goin' on, but I knew I was in trouble. My mother explained to me, after she beat the shit out of me. It really wasn't my fault. She told me we was different, and they didn't like us. So I has to be careful. I remember that well, 'cause in the end we all ended up laughin'. My mother laughed so much, she forgot to be angry wit' me. I was walkin' around like my teacher. And talkin' like her, and ev'ryone was laughin'. I guess that was the first time I was imitatin' a woman. It must have been good, 'cause they all laughed.

Knowledge of race and ideas about other races are learned at home or from peers. However, difference is learned through contact, sometimes confrontational, between members of different races.

HAMILTON: We've all been called names, child. But when a white child does it, it really gets you pissed. Now that don't happen too much, y'know, 'cause we not stupid enough to expose ourselves to that imagery. You know, you keep away from places where that's gonna happen. We was always told don't you go here or there. We was always told that. So you knew that if you went there then you could expect some shit. But in New York you can't keep away from everyone. So, you gets it.... The one time I remember it really bothering me was in school. I remember they used to bring some older white children uptown to help us with our homework. It was like a program to help the poor kids after school. You know, they'd come up and teach you. It was OK, but some of them were worse than the teachers. But I remember once a group of these children walking down St. Nicholas Ave. Looking for the subway, I s'pose. And they had to walk around me and my sister. We was carrying a bag of groceries or something. And one of these guys said something about having to come up here and help these "colored" kids but we didn't respect them. Then he bumped into my sister and walked away. I called after him, and called him names, but the others took him away. I was ready. I was ready to knock him upside his head. Especially when he hit my sister like that. But that's how you learn you're different. That's how you know what black is all about. It's about not bein' white.

This confrontation is resolved by seeking out an alternative, positive identity, that is, being black in a white-dominated world.[3] However, most informants did not raise the issue of race. When they did, it was as "color."

DARWIN: They make it a racial issue, simply by labeling us black. I believe that Negro is a true racial label. If they want to divide us up racially, we should be Negro and they should be Caucasians. But they call themselves white, so we have chosen to call ourselves black. To be different.

But being black is more than an issue of color. As defined by my informants, "black" describes not only skin color but a cultural milieu. As Cleveland put it, "Black is our color. It's race. But it's more too. It's cultural. Black stands for different cultural things. Not just skin color."

Pride in black culture reinforces a positive image of being black for most of my informants.

TERRY: My first encounter with the police told me all that I'd heard was true. I was walking along 125th Street with my brother and suddenly they swooped down on us. This car pulled up and they jumped out and had us up against a window. A shop window. They handcuffed us and took us to the precinct. We were there for hours before they even spoke to us. I think they were looking for a couple of guys that had stolen something. Something like that. But when they put me in this room with the two cops, one was a detective, I think, they started asking me questions. But before I could speak they'd keep asking more questions and talking about Negroes and how we were the scum of the earth and how we weren't fit for living, and how they had the right idea down South by lynching all the niggers. When they said that and I couldn't even answer, I knew everything I'd heard about whites was true. They were different to us and we were black and different. I felt a sense of pride too because I knew we were fit to live. We have our own culture. Right here in Harlem. And they didn't even know that. I often wonder whether those cops ever went to any jazz clubs, or to the Apollo. Or the Cotton Club. I wonder if they ever knew anything about us apart from the few bums they had to deal with on the street.

The gay community is not without racism either. Most gay black men have experienced rejection by other gays because they are black.

BLYDEN: White gays are strange. They treat you all nice and shit, but when they don't want you around, they'll let you know. Like when I went to Fire Island. Just once. I sat on the beach all day, drinking my cocktails and feeling just lovely. But I wasn't picked up, like the other children. I was just left alone, all day. I didn't get invited to any of their parties. And even in the clubs, I felt like I was from another planet.

This means that for a gay black man, often his color, not his sexual preference, defines his position in society.

BRANTLEY: I'm more aware of my color than my sexual orientation. My mother taught me what it was to be black in this country. And now I understand what she meant. It's the color which is thrown up in my face when I move around town. People see my color, not my sex. They see I'm a black man, so they step aside, they won't serve me. Or not with the courtesy or enthusiasm that they serve white folks. That's what defines me. My color. Even though I choose to be gay, and a gay black man, it's my color that decides where I go, who I can go with, or what I can do.... White men expect certain things from you, if you're black. They believe you're either rough street trade and that you're gonna rob them, or they're expecting you to be all macho and butch. Aggressive sexually. I can see that a lot of white men that I know, that move in the circles that I do, don't know how to deal with me as a physician. I'm clean shaven, well dressed, quiet spoken. That's not the image they have of a black man, one way or the other. So, that's what it's like to be black in a gay world.... I really only feel that when I'm downtown.

Because gay black men are constantly defined by their skin color when they socialize in mainstream gay life, they choose to live in black society, among black friends and lovers, to be free from the stigma of racist attitudes in their daily lives, and their choice of black men as lovers is often an expression of love of blackness.[4] In this context, black culture becomes not only a source of pride but also a source of comfort in a society where racial and other stereotypes are so pervasive.

Skin color differentiation reaches deep within black society. The significance of different shades of black within the black community was evoked by Spike Lee's movie *School Daze*. The competition between light-skinned and dark-skinned black college students aired a painful issue for many in the black community. For one man, this antagonism was evident even within his family.

PAUL: I was the dark one in the family, y'know. So I knew right from the start that I was different. I really knew what it was like to be black. My brothers took after my mother. They was light. Very light brown. And I took after my father. I was always dark. They used to call me names. When I was real small it used to upset me. 'Cause I was different. And they were my brothers. But we never was close. I think it made my parents closer to me. Especially my mother. But they could do it too. You know, if they was angry or something, they be callin' us names. And I was always the black one. Like if I did something wrong, I'd be "the good-for-nuttin' black one." ... I don't know but they must feel they was right doin' it too. I never was too good at school. And then I turned out gay. I bet they're laughin' about that now.

Thus the stereotypes about blacks prevalent in mainstream American culture have been absorbed into black culture itself. In black society, light-skinned or "mulatto" blacks are often regarded as closer to white and therefore more easily accepted by white Americans, while dark-skinned blacks are often regarded as more African, more streetwise, and less white in dress, speech, and aspirations.

DONNY: Now those dark boys. We were told they were good. Like Paul. Now Miss Thing's husband is fierce. You know him. He's a fierce child, honey. So you know Miss Thing is gettin' it real good.... My mother. And my sisters. And their friends. They told me. I remember. They said that the black ones would be good in bed, but the light-skinned ones was husband material. Now that's true. They're the ones with jobs and education.

That this distinction has become culturally accepted among black people is an interesting, if painful, expression of the intersection of race and class. The arbitrariness of such categorization is seen when its lines are crossed. Barry, for example, felt he had to defend a dark-skinned friend: "Child, he's family. You know that, don't you. He is. Don't be fooled by his big, dark self. He went to college.... Just because that child gives you street, he ain't no bum."

Although color differences obviously exist, attitudes toward different colors and shades, and expectations of the same, are instilled during socialization. As a result, a deep distrust of white people and white society and different attitudes toward differing shades of black run deep within the black population (Gwaltney 1980). However, while race itself is not that much of an issue for these gay black men in their daily lives, shade differences within the black population do exist and tend to reflect a socioeconomic differentiation.

## Class

Although class differences do appear within the population studied here, participation and social position in the gay scene do not necessarily reflect that.[5] In other words, not all hustlers came from the projects or single-parent homes, nor were they all high school dropouts. Michael, for example, comes from a well-established Harlem family. His flamboyant lifestyle, a combination of staying out all night, drug use, and failing grades, led his parents to cut off funding when he was only halfway through college. Hustling redressed this problem, until drugs caused him further financial difficulties and the "temporary" abandonment of his degree.

The non-hustling gay population also includes many men from lower socioeconomic classes. Barry was raised in the Grant Houses, a project on Broadway, by his unmarried mother. He still lives in city-operated housing, despite stints at rooming with other gay friends, and he is forever looking for better-paying work. However, he pays his rent and maintains financial independence, with a little help from friends. By contrast, Louis and Paul, who were raised in home-owning, two-parent families in Harlem, own their own apartment. They rely on nobody for financial aid but do dispense some to close friends like Barry.

This mixing of different socioeconomic classes of men in the gay scene in Harlem was explained as one reason gays referred to themselves as "family."

DEVEN: We're all family in the life. No matter where you come from, or what you do. You one of us, then you're family. That's how we survive. That's what's keepin' us going. We just like a family. Takin' care o' each other. Lovin' each other. Don't matter if you come off the street. Or live in a shelter. Even these hustlers. They're all over the place now. No matter. They be family.

This socioeconomic leveling brings people of all classes into each other's social networks. Although there is a class structure in Harlem, and gay men there do originate from different classes (which they still reflect in terms of their education, occupation, income, and residence), when it comes to gay social life, class lines fade.

Because most of the gay black men in Harlem I encountered during this study did not come into contact with people of other races very often, issues of class based on race did not often arise. Admittedly, some thought that white people are richer because they are white. Some Harlemites employed in occupations downtown worked alongside people of a variety of racial, ethnic, and class backgrounds. But the majority did not, and they certainly did not socialize outside their community in their leisure time.

## Women

If there is a definable group of people with whom these gay men socialize in Harlem, outside of the gay scene, it is women. Most of the gay men I interviewed numbered many female friends in their social networks. Friends from school days or the neighborhood, and occasionally from the workplace, participate in the social lives of these men,[6] sometimes accompanying them to bars, dance socials, parties, family gatherings, and on shopping expeditions. But it is female relatives, especially mothers, grandmothers, and sisters, who top the list.

It is from their female friends and family members that gay black men learn about black men and how to deal with them in relationships. Although some dismiss the opinions women have about men as irrelevant to themselves as gay men, most concede that many of the opinions they themselves hold about men have been learned from their mothers and sisters. In *Soulside* (1969), Hannerz notes that men are placed into two basic categories—"good men" and "no-good men"—although "no-good men" are often regarded as "real men" by gay blacks. In other words, men who hang out on the street or pursue lives as hustlers are perceived as more masculine and aggressive than those who are more inclined to maintain permanent relationships and steady employment.

The support these gay men receive from women when they have trouble with men is reciprocated with financial assistance, baby-sitting, or "father" role playing. In many instances, gay black men acted as "fathers" to their sisters' children. These men are probably the "uncles" in Stack's *All Our Kin* (1974). They contrast directly with the received image of black men, who are pictured as not playing an active role in children's socialization.[7] While only one respondent currently resides with his sister, several indicated that they had played a significant role in the socialization of their nieces and nephews.

BRIAN: When V—— was raisin' her boy, I stayed by her for about five years. After that she married T—— and they had their family [three more children]. But Mickey's my boy. He calls me "uncle" now, but before he called me "daddy." I was like a father to him. His own father never showed up. I was the man in his life.

Sometimes a gay man and his lover will both be involved in the care of a sibling's children.

EDWARD: I still take M——'s children on the weekends. Sometimes we go to the movies, or hang out in the park. I'm too old to play ball with the boys, or rather they be too big now, but I still go down the park with them.... Their [other] children [three girls] always come by on the holidays and stay with us a while. They love to hang out with A—— and me. They know what's goin' on. They old enough. But they still come and stay.

Mothers and grandmothers remain the most important family members in the social networks of the gay men I interviewed. Along with maternal and paternal aunts, they influenced where the men lived, what friends they brought home (into the family setting), and how often and when they went to church. All demanded and received attention from their sons, grandsons, and nephews, sometimes asking for financial assistance, in addition to other forms of care and company, which was always provided willingly.

This intensity of gay black male interaction with family members is unique among other gay men in New York City. Because most gay men in New York come from elsewhere,[8] kinship is not such an important aspect of their day-to-day existence. In Harlem, family is very much the center of daily life.

## The Black Family

According to these gay black men, the aspects of black culture that have the most influence on their social lives and identities are their experience of family and their expectation of extended familial relationships.

STANLEY: I grew up right here. In this building. We had an apartment upstairs. I think Dad's parents lived here at one time as well. I remember [Shirl, Stanley's mother] telling me that when she married Dad, she moved in here with him. His brother also lived in the building. So I grew up with my family around me. I had cousins right here in the building. Mom's sisters all live in the neighborhood with their families. They're still here. Mom lives with one of my aunts now. On 163rd [Street].... I have an uncle who's gay [father's first cousin] and one [first] cousin that I know of. He's a few years younger but I used to see him around the bars with his crowd. He comes over whenever we have a party. We're closer now than what we were before. In fact, [London's] gonna move back up here soon. He likes to be near the family. Especially now his roommate's gone. They were real close. I guess he misses having a close friend. And I'm the next best thing.... My mother comes to all my parties. She never misses one. And she's the life of the party. Always dancing with the boys, and drinking up a storm. They all love her. She's always been like that. She's always been good to me and [Mickey]. She gave us a beautiful decanter for our first anniversary. And she made the curtains in the living room.... My brothers. Well, they're OK. C——'s really great. He and his wife live on 145th Street. They got two boys. So I see them a lot. Over at Ma's. We all get together for dinner on Sunday over there. Some of my cousins will come. Bring their kids. Ma's really popular with all the family. I don't see D—— that much. He lives in the Bronx. He and his woman have been having some problems. She's very religious and he likes to hang out. But I don't know what crowd he's hanging with. But I know he's having problems.

Stanley comes from a family with three boys. All have worked with their father, who is in construction. In his retirement, the father has entered the real estate business and now lives off his investments. He owns the building where Stanley and his lover reside. Several of

Stanley's parents' siblings and his first cousins also live in the building or in other buildings owned by his father. Several generations of occupancy in the same building or on the same block give a sense of continuity, of "roots," that has been important in Stanley's sense of identity.

Stanley and his brothers receive an annual payment of $20,000 from their father, which Stanley says he is reinvesting, for the most part. He is interested in buying property in Florida, where his lover grew up, so that eventually they can live down South. Although he was born in Harlem, Stanley loves the South. His grandparents came from South Carolina and Louisiana, and he has relatives in both places, which he visits now and then.

Stanley's parents are divorced. His father remarried a younger woman, whom all of the family like. Family gatherings include both parents, Stanley's brothers and their spouses, and many of his twenty-four first cousins and their families. Stanley also has second and third cousins living in the building and the surrounding neighborhood. He considers several of these relatives to be part of his social network, not only because he likes to keep in touch with all his family but because he is in continual contact with them in the neighborhood. This is typical of many of my informants. It is important for their identity to have a sense of family constantly reinforced by frequent interaction. It promotes security and a sense of well-being.

Likewise, Nate is surrounded by kin in Harlem. He too makes efforts to keep in touch with his parents, who are still together, and his four siblings and their families. He visits frequently with his grandmothers and a couple of his six maternal aunts. Like Stanley, Nate realizes the importance of female relatives as anchors of strength in the black family. Their opinions and example of family leadership, nurturance, and household management are imitated by these gay men in their own homes. As mentioned above, gay black men tend to have close relationships with women, especially female relatives. Many informants frequently referred to the open expression of emotion that made these relationships special.

BASIL: I never forget the first time I cried in front of my mother. Not the thing to do for a growing man. But she let me howl. It was great. I thought she would get mad at me. But she didn't. I told her it was over some girl. But I think she knew even then that John and I had broken up.[9]

Nate's other family members are also important. Two uncles live in the Bronx, but he counts some of their children among his closer friends. He visits weekly with one cousin who lives in Harlem to play cards and party. While his family is aware of his sexual orientation, none of them has participated in the gay side of his social life, certainly not to the extent that Stanley's family has absorbed his lover and gay friends into its extended familial network. Nate prefers to keep his gay social life separate from his family obligations. The necessity of maintaining a semblance of independence is important to him as a man, and in order to protect the privacy of his gay sexual activity, but he admits to the strength and importance of his familial relationships. They are an integral part of his being black.

NATE: I been livin' by myself for twenty years. It's the only way. I had a child live with me for a while ten years ago. But it didn't work out. I wanted to go out but he wanted to tie me down. Worse than a woman. So it didn't work out. So, I just keep to myself. I go out and have friends to go out with but I just keep to myself.... My family's very close, y'know. We all stay close to home. My sisters are married. One lives here and the other one lives on Long Island. But we are very close. My brothers both live nearby. T—— was out in California for a while but he and his wife are back here now. He works for the government. B—— has been around the streets forever. He has children all over the place. I don't even know how many. But he brings them by my mother's all the time. She knows all her grandchildren. But I don't know them.... Both my grandmothers live in Harlem. Dad's mother stays with my mother. She's getting old, so they look after her. Sometimes my uncle [father's brother] takes her for a while.... I spend a lot of time with my aunt [mother's sister]. She's not married. She likes to party and always has us over there for a drink. She lives in the old people's [maternal grandparents'] house. She looked after my grandmother 'cause she's a nurse. But now she's in the hospital.... I see a lot of my cousins. There's hundreds of them. They're all around Harlem. I can't go nowhere without they be seein' me. Even in the middle of the night when I go up to [Mickey's Place], someone'll call out, or tell my mother they been seein' me.... I'm close to the family. You know, on birthdays and things I'll go and party with them. But I don't go out too much with them. I just keep to myself.

The fact that so many of these gay black men were raised by both parents may reflect to some degree the socioeconomic standing of the members of my respondent sample, who are largely middle class or at least have stable working-class backgrounds. The broader community of people whose lives I came to know reflect a wider range of socioeconomic classes. It is true that those living in the south part of Harlem, below 125th Street, or in the city-operated projects, are more likely to come from single-parent families with less stable sources of income.

Single-parent, often female-headed, unstable, or unstructured families are also evident in my data, most predominantly among my informants from the lower classes. These families best fit the description of "kin-structured local networks" that are the basis of Stack's (1974) thesis. Yet all of the gay men in this population (irrespective of socioeconomic standing) participate in extensive social networks of financial, emotional, and other support. Every informant listed a variety of kin, always including parents and siblings and usually including grandparents, aunts, uncles, and cousins, in their social networks. While it was not always apparent to what extent the "survival" of individuals and individual family units depended on these close familial ties, most informants indicated a certain emotional dependence on family and insisted that family values instilled in them as children constituted the single most significant influence on their black identities. These values included the importance of kinship, "good neighborliness," hospitality, generosity, education, work, and church.

## The Black Church

The value system of black society inculcated through the family, education, and the church constitutes the foundation of black identity. Outside of the family, the most significant black social institution appears to be the church.

CECIL: The most important black institution for me is the church. I don't care which church. But you better be in the church. That's such an important part of black life. It's your whole bein'. Without the church, you ain't shit! And so that's what you see in Harlem today. A whole lot o' shit. That's because they give up on the church.... In the South, that's all we had. All that was ours. I mean they robbed us of everything. Even our names. But we've got our church. That's our sanctuary in the storm. Praise the Lord.... If more of these children had stayed closer to the church, there'd be no problems. And it don't mind what you are. 'Cause the church will take you in and feed you and care for you and guide you on your way. That's its significance for the black people.

August Meier and Elliott Rudwick (1976) discuss the significance of the church in the lives of black people, not only in the South (see Powdermaker 1939) but also among transplanted migrants in the northern urban areas.

In the black church the migrants carried with them an institution that helped them adjust to the dismal realities of urban life. The church, as it had in the South, remained the center of black community life. Migrants sought to re-construct the institutions they had known in their southern homes. Indeed, throughout the North and West one could identify church congregations composed of people from specific locales in the South. (Meier and Rudwick 1976:249–250)

Similarly, when blacks migrated within New York City from the Ten-derloin to Harlem during the last decades of the last century, they followed or were closely followed by their churches.[10]

C. Eric Lincoln, following on the heels of E. Franklin Frazier, writes of the importance and centrality of religion in the lives of black people.

To understand the power of the Black Church it must first be understood that there is no disjunction between the Black Church and the Black community. The Church is the spiritual face of the Black community, and whether one is a "church member" or not is beside the point in any assessment of the impor-tance and meaning of the Black Church. Because of the peculiar nature of the Black experience and the centrality of institutionalized religion in the develop-ment of that experience, the time was when the personal dignity of the Black individual was communicated almost entirely through his church affiliation. To be able to say that "I belong to Mt. Nebo Baptist" or "We go to Mason's Chapel Methodist" was the accepted way of establishing identity and status when there were few other criteria by means of which a sense of self or a com-munication of place could be projected. While this has been modified to some degree in recent times as education, vocational diversification, and new oppor-tunities for non-religious associations have increased, the social identity of the Black American as well as his self-perception are still to an important degree refracted through the prism of his religious identity. His pastor, his church, his office in the church, or merely his denomination are important indices of who he is. (Lincoln 1974:115–116)

Church affiliation is still an important mark of identity today for gay black men in Harlem. Among those gay men who continue to attend church, the majority agree that the strong socialization into church participation when they were young explains their continued atten-dance, along with the kin pressure from mothers, grandmothers, or siblings. Friendships with other congregation members, especially other gay men, is also an important motivating force for participation. This sense of community evoked by the church is explored in Melvin D. Williams's ethnography of a black Pentecostal church.

The Zion members must depend upon a social network of relationships that extends across neighborhood and subcultural boundaries to reach potential recruits wherever they can be found, as well as to nourish them as members once they are committed to the church. These relationships and the way they are linked make Zion a community. (Williams 1974:157)

For gay men with children, the desire to raise sons and daughters "right"—that is, in the church—is strong. Willis leaves his son at a day care center operated at his local church and vows that "young Will" is bound for Sunday school when he is old enough.

Even non-Christian belief systems such as Buddhism and Islam are entered into with extraordinary passion and devotion. Both informants who converted to Buddhism say that this "spiritual" religion—they pray in private daily rather than attend church weekly—enables them to live "good" or "decent" lives as gay men in a black community. Since Christian preachers frequently rail against homosexuality, some gay men seek out alternative belief systems. (This was also cited as the main cause for the disaffection of seventeen informants from any form of religious participation.) However, for the majority, church or at least some religious affiliation is such an important identity marker and the church such an important social institution that they continue to participate even in the face of the anti-gay rhetoric of many preachers.

The two Black Muslims in my sample were born and raised in the Nation of Islam.[11] One of them remains true to his faith, in defiance of the unusually strong stance against homosexuality taken by this Islamic sect. Mohammad attends mosque infrequently but stays close to his faith through his family ties. He observes Ramadan (the Islamic month of fasting) and tries to pray at least three times a day. He has a prayer rug laid out on his bedroom floor as a constant reminder of his need to pray. He hopes that he will get to Mecca at least once in his lifetime. He has a paternal uncle, a former member of the Fruit of Islam, who made his pilgrimage in the 1960s. This uncle serves as his inspiration in his faith.

MOHAMMAD: I respect Christian and Jewish holidays too. You have to. This is a Christian country. A so-called Christian country. But I stay true to the teachings of Mohammad. That's how I was raised and that's how it is. I know I'm not the best. I don't always observe things. But I am good during Ramadan. And I want to go to Mecca. I give to the poor. But I don't always pray every day. I go to mosque. But I'm black first. And there are things that are important to me there as well. Like Kwanzaa. I celebrate Kwanzaa with my friends. I have a large group to my house one night during Kwanzaa. Every year. Really that is most important to me.[12]

What is peculiarly important about the black Christian church is the prominence of the black pastors, not only as preachers within the church but also as political leaders in the black community. Lincoln waxes eloquent on the history of black political leadership in the church, especially when referring to the civil rights movement of the 1950s and 1960s (Lincoln 1974:114–122). Such political leadership has a long history. Even Frazier (1974) notes that the "Negro church" provided an avenue for black leaders to emerge in their communities during Reconstruction, outside of the existing white power structure, to which blacks were not admitted.[13]

The church has played a central role in the organization of political life in black society since the days of slavery (Berry and Blassingame 1982:107). And it remains politically prominent in the lives of contemporary urban blacks.

CLEVELAND: For me the church was very influential. Right from the youngest time I remember having to go to church. As I grew older I realized that there was something there for me. The preacher was always talkin' 'bout our rights and how they were comin'. I didn't know what he meant at first. As I grew older I knew what he was talking about. Especially when I came to New York. That's when I heard about Martin Luther King, Jr. That's when I heard about the marches and the sit-ins. I wasn't aware that we were treated so badly until the preacher started informing me. I just wasn't exposed to any of that shit. You know, I was raised in a family and among my family and friends. That was my world. I never came into contact with any of these so-called racists. So, at first I didn't really understand. . . . By the time I was in college, I understood what it was all about. Why black folks had suffered so. Why King and Malcolm had to die. Why the preachers talked the way they did. They were a big influence on me. Especially in the South.

Because of the strong impressions made by preachers and the importance placed on religious services in their youth, many gay black men feel motivated to attend and participate in their respective churches. Even the anti-homosexual teachings of the Bible and the blatantly homophobic sermons of many preachers have not shaken their faith. More important is that the church has become a place for social encounters with other gay men.

WILBERT: All the friends I have in New York are gay. They all come to church. My best friends sing in the choir. [Leslie] and [Clayborn]. They're the first two good friends I made here. And I met them at church.... Child, you don't know. Hundreds. Hundreds and hundreds. All the choir boys are sissies. Ain't nothin' but sissies.... There's a strong network of us in the church. And other churches as well. I mean we know the children in the other Baptist churches too.

Gay friendship networks within most churches reach out to other networks in churches of the same denomination and even into churches of different denominations. In his "church girl" network, Moses counts both Methodists and Baptists. What is important to him about his friends is that they are associated with a church. This affiliation not only identifies these men as being religious but also as "decent" gay men. Moses judges gay men on this affiliation, and if he finds them acceptable, incorporates them into his wide circle of church friends and the social events they attend.

In addition to establishing networks of friends, many men make sexual contacts within the church population. In fact, many have their first sexual encounters through church contacts. Edward recalled the circumstances of an early experience: "My first sexual encounter was with a fine young man. Older than me, mind you. He used to sing in the choir. By the time I was in Bible class, we had a real strong thing going. He led our group.... This was when I was about twelve or fourteen."

Now that education and occupation, among other variables, have become identity markers, the significance of the church has declined somewhat. But the social institution of the church remains an important focus for gay socializing for many men in Harlem who continue to express their identity through church attendance. The sense of continuity through generations of family participation in a particular church provides the black man with a sense of familial and historical roots and enables him to participate in that ongoing history.

## Black History

Knowledge of the past experience of black Americans is deemed an important aspect of being black by my informants. Significant events in the history of Harlem—the days of the Harlem Renaissance and thereafter,[14] the jazz clubs of the 1930s and 1940s,[15] and the civil rights demonstrations and riots in the 1960s[16] are well known to gay black men. Each event or era represents a positive example of the potential of blacks to achieve historically significant steps in the acquisition of political power and artistic achievement. The lore surrounding these events has usually been passed down by word of mouth, especially by older family members to their children and grandchildren. Yet several of my informants can recall the riots of the 1960s and the looting.

WILLIS: I remember seeing the crowd running down Fifth Avenue. They were carrying sticks and things, and breaking the store windows. When they got down near by our house, my mother made us come in from the window.

One informant who witnessed the assassination of Malcolm X has the experience indelibly printed in his memory.

HERBIE: I was really quite young, about thirteen or fourteen, but I remember that well. It was very confusing. I remember the shots. I don't think I really knew what had happened. Not at that moment. All the shouting and yelling. That's what I remember the most. And outside afterwards, the crowd went crazy, smashing up cars and things. My older brother [first cousin] took me outta there.

The furor surrounding Malcolm X's assassination left many people in Harlem confused and obviously angry. Many are still upset that his memory has not attracted the attention of government or the general American populace as has the memory of other leaders. For those who witnessed Malcolm's demise, his example lives on, informing their oppositional stance to the system, the "man," and most things representative of mainstream American culture.

Although many were too young to actually participate in the civil rights struggles, every informant had been made fully aware of the significance of that period for black people in America. The culmination of the civil rights era in the political enfranchisement of blacks engendered hope that equality in other areas of life could be achieved. The lesson inherent in the recounting of the sixties is the need for constant struggle, which the young are urged to continue.

The most important historical period in American history for black people is the era of slavery.

DEMOND: I see slavery times as being a time of great strength. Especially for us. It taught us the strength that we need to get by today. It taught us the strength of family. And of prayer. I think of slavery times as the times of big strong men. Of healthy babies, and strong, capable women. It was a period of great strength. And today I draw on that strength. I think of the hard times we're in now. And I think, well, they got through it then, just with the simple strength of their bodies. That gives me the strength to get by here.

Slave culture has been the object of study by many academics—folklorists, historians, political scientists, sociologists, anthropologists, and psychologists—as well as novelists. A significant contribution to this vast collection of material, data, analysis, and assumptions was made by Lawrence Levine (1978) in his well-analyzed documentation of expressive elements of black culture from the Civil War to 1950. His work has incorporated previously unpublished or inaccessible writings, hymns, songs, poems, and "toasts,"[17] which in various forms represent the thoughts, aspirations, and interpretations of the current social lives of the narrators. These elements of expressive culture provide us with a historic record of black life in the United States. Although not written down, they are nonetheless reliable and credible to present-day black people. This belief enhances their sense of tradition and informs their identity with a sense of roots—albeit in slavery.

Slavery remained alive, too, in the specific details and descriptions embodied within the stories of the slave past. The narratives of ex-slaves and the stories, anecdotes, and legends of their descendants are filled with information about the everyday conduct and culture of slaves and the mechanics of the slave system. (Levine 1978:388)

The oral traditions kept alive knowledge of the slavery experience and also encouraged a tradition of resistance to the slavery system. They combined fact and fiction to produce powerful images of resistance and escape from the harsh realities of slavery.

Historians have much to learn from these prolific reminiscences not merely because they are so often accurate but also because they are so often legendary; because they blend and interweave myth with fact. The folk are not historians; they are simultaneously the products and creators of a culture, and that culture includes a collective memory.... Historians have debated and will continue to debate the exact amount of resistance that occurred during slavery, and for an understanding of the slaves this debate is crucial. For an understanding of the post-slave generations, the history of slave resistance is less important than the legends concerning it, though the two by no means invariably contradict each other. Looking back upon the past, ex-slaves and their descendants painted a picture not of a cowed and timorous black mass but of a people who, however circumscribed by misfortune and oppression, were never without their means of resistance and never lacked the inner resources to oppose the master class, however extreme the price they had to pay. (Levine 1978:389)

This model of resistance is critical to my gay informants and is expressed in their attitudes toward mainstream American culture. In turn, their resistance against "whitewashed" norms instills a pride in black culture and motivates individuals to seek out the attributes of being black. It provides them with an imagery of strength and the capacity to overcome hardship. Coming from Harlem as they do, they have seen enough hardship to identify with slave traditions of survival against the odds.

## Africa

The active search for knowledge about being black has led many of my informants on a search for Africa: African history, the collection of African artifacts, masks, statues, *kente* cloth, and a desire to visit. The Public Broadcasting Service's television series based on Ali Mazrui's book *The Africans* (1986) was seen by many of my informants and was often the crucial experience in this search. These gay men claim that Africa is important to them not only as an affirmation of their distinctive race but also as evidence of a golden age when blacks ruled kingdoms and cities through trade networks every bit as significant as those of the Europeans'. During the 1960s especially, knowledge of Africa became tied to black nationalism and pride in being black.

The sense of African roots is part of the development of an ethnic identity, which Geneva Gay has outlined in her interesting essay on the sociopsychological process of ethnic identification (Gay 1987b:35–74). It can best be likened to the establishment of an African nationalist identity, which black Americans sought during the civil rights era (Essien-Udom 1962), one expression of which was the establishment of the Black Muslims (Lincoln 1961).[18]

The intensity of the search for African roots is deepening as witnessed by the interest in things African in the black community at large and among my gay informants in particular.

BINGA: I've always worn this stuff. My mother had me wearing this cloth when I was a kid. I remember the children at school teasing me because they thought I was an African. And when I told them I really was, they thought I was crazy. At least they left me alone.... Now, I choose my cloth carefully. I am sure we came from Ghana. Or the Gold Coast, I think it was called. I'm sure, because the more I read about Ghana, the more it sounds like my family. You know, the way that the families are extended. I was raised with all my cousins. And with my father and my uncles. They took a real interest in us children. They taught us so much. I don't know where they get the idea of all these women running things in Harlem. The men are here, baby, believe me. And they ruled us. I mean my father was the head of our household. He was the one that punished us. And always chasing us for our homework. He was crazy. But he was the force that made us get there.... He was a true African king.

This fierce, ethnicity-based "nationalism" (Berry and Blassingame 1982:388–396) that accompanies the search for an African heritage had already found expression in other areas of black culture: in the civil rights movement and in the traditional African cultures of the Sea Islands, for example (Jones-Jackson 1987). Clinging to African elements of culture is not only an important feature of the Southerners' lives but also provides a reawakening of an African consciousness for many Harlemites. On the individual level, this search for African roots and participation in activities related to African themes gives these gay men a sense of pride in being black.

GARVEY: Having a real sense of yourself. I think that's important. That's truly bein' black. Knowing who you are, where you're at. Where you come from. That's really important. And I don't mean which state you come from. Or what state your grandmother came from. Or whether she was a slave or not. That's important. But I mean a real sense of your African roots. Knowing that you have a whole history behind you. You know you can tell if someone's got that in them. They have a pride in themselves. You can tell that.... I know that's true. But in the Carolinas, the children are on this Yoruba trip. Child, we really don't know exactly where we came from. I mean even Alex Haley has doubts about his origins. But what he did was fierce. I mean it got a whole generation of us lookin' back to Africa. And if it's Yoruba that turns you on, hey, then go for it, y'know.

## The South

Knowledge of the South and especially experiences in the South are regarded as important aspects of black culture. In fact, many of my informants spoke of the southern origins of much of what is regarded as black culture: extended families, soul food, church, and much of black folklore.

Roots in the South, either through ancestry or birth, are important to all of my informants. Even those informants raised in Harlem usually spent summer holidays with grandparents or cousins in the South.

ZACHARY: I go back to see the old girl [his grandmother] often. Especially now she's going blind. We have a lot of fun together. She fills me in on all the news about all the children I grew up with. They're all over the place now. Only one or two of them left in North Carolina. None of them at home. I don't know what's going to happen to the community when all these old folks die off. My mother says she ain't goin' back. She's crazy anyway. But I think I might come back. It's so peaceful. And the house is huge. I could find some work down here. At one of the schools in the area.... All those herbal things I use on my massages are from her. I've been adapting some of them for some of the young guys I'm working with now. Many of them are in awful pain because of this disease. And to have the touch and care of someone else is all they need to give them peace of mind. That's what we're about with this stuff.... I got all of my healing training from my grandmother. She taught me the massages. And the voodoo. Some old African stuff. Yeah, she was Geechee. She was born on one of the [Sea] islands. But she never gave it up. She always kept close to their beliefs. Some of that stuff even scares me. But she says of all the children in the family I'm the one with it in me. So I guess I have some powers or something.

Some informants still visit relatives and friends in the South, even as adults. Some are even considering the possibility of living or retiring there.[19] The South is regarded as "home" by many of my informants, even if they were born in the North. Because the South is perceived as the root of black culture and because of the large black population in the South today, it is regarded almost as a homeland. In the North, a certain body of lore has arisen about the South and its potential as a separate black state, where, if Atlanta is any standard to judge by, black men can be successful and prosperous in a black-run land. With these visionary tales and the strength of historic familial connections, the South has become important to being black, as least for these gay black men.

## Folklore

One of the South's enduring traditions that is being re-discovered in northern black areas is storytelling.[20] One gay black man in Harlem, Manu, has become a storyteller and has visited other story-tellers in Baltimore and Philadelphia in order to learn tales. Most of those he tells are of African origin or concern African roots. Several museums, such as the Smithsonian Institution in Washington, D.C., and the American Museum of Natural History in New York City, sponsor performances by these storytellers. Storytelling, an age-old African tradition, has always been an important part of black culture in the United States. Together these tales form a body of folklore essential to black culture.

Apart from the social commentary and didactic intent of much of the storytelling, today as in the Old South, the stories entertain. They allow the narrator and his or her audience to rise above their lot, albeit momentarily, and take pride in the heroes of their race. In black culture, legends of resistance against slavery and oppression are full of culture heroes such as the slave trickster—in part, an extension of the African "Anansi the Spider"—and the "Signifying Monkey" and "Brer Rabbit" of the South. In the real slave world, too, as Levine (1978) points out, there was no dearth of stories or anecdotes of slave ancestors who had stood up to their masters. Freedmen also featured in these tales. Thus the transformation of the slave culture hero into a man (or sometimes a woman) standing for civil rights in the postbellum South was relatively straightforward.[21] "Henry Peterson" and "Trickster John" were such heroes I heard about from my southern-born informants. "Shine" appears to be an urban creation. Most of these heroes were, in fact, "bad men"—"hard, merciless toughs and killers confronting and generally vanquishing their adversaries without hesitation and without remorse (Levine 1978:408). Their stories are still relayed today. Dennis Wepman, Ronald Newman, and Murray Binderman have collected them in *The Life* (1976). The narrative poems in their book are a representative sample of "toasts," as important to black hustler culture in performance as in content. Here the "Signifying Monkey," "Dumbo the Junkie," and "Stagger Lee" feature again. As Wepman explains, the toasts, as a cultural record of "the Life," promote the masculinity of both the performer and the culture hero: "The Life is a glorification of virility, masculinity, male assertiveness" (ibid., 4).

Masculinity is a recurrent feature of all the folklore stories since the majority of heroes are men. This may be because men are more often the storytellers, because the events confronting the characters are more often encountered by men, or because the stories express the "shadow values" of black male culture (Liebow 1967). Gay black men are also enthralled by the overt masculinity of these characters. When Edward told me his version of the John Henry story, he provided details describing Henry's physical attributes and the aspects of the story that emphasized the latter's masculinity. In fact, the most important culture hero about whom I heard most frequently was John Henry. Fifteen informants were able to reiterate the famous story of this black man's strength, in part if not in full, in the prose in which they had learned it. Not only is John Henry's sexual prowess the subject of many stanzas, but John Henry stood alone, stoically, against the white man and his machine.[22]

John Henry's epic contest is never purely individual. He is a representative figure whose life and struggle are symbolic of the struggle of the worker against machine, individual against society, the lowly against the powerful, black against white. His victory is shared and his demise is mourned.... It is this representative quality that gives his struggle epic proportions and makes John Henry the most important folk hero in Afro-American lore. (Levine 1978:427)

Many folk stories also revolve around male-female conflict, so often the basis of analysis of black social life, especially in the urban setting.[23] Yet it is the male culture heroes who have had the biggest impact on gay black men and their aspirations.

By tracing John Henry's legacy to modern secular, real-life heroes, such as Joe Louis, Levine explains how easily masculine sports heroes become today's culture heroes. Thus, when asked about significant black men in black culture today, all of my informants went beyond the arena of politicians, civil rights leaders, and artists to include the likes of Mohammad Ali and Mike Tyson, Dave Winfield and Dwight Goodin, Carl Lewis and Bo Jackson, but most repeatedly the basketball players Magic Johnson and Michael Jordan. In Edward's words, "Honey, they are the fiercest [best]. Indeed. Child, you can't find a finer lookin' man than a basketball player. And it ain't because they can't be had. They just fine."

Folklore, then, provides these gay black men with not only a sense of history, which is important for their black identity, but also an image of the ideal man in the culture hero: a physically strong, sexual, masculine man.

## Role Models

Besides preachers, sports figures were included in lists of prominent black male role models for these gay black men. Not only are they constantly present in the media but they are also invariably good-looking men.

LEONARD: When you look at black role models you invariably come up with the sportsmen. I mean that's the kind of man that American society likes. He's the kind of man's man that it's all about.... I guess the football players are the most important. And the baseball players. Because those are the main sports. They are where even white men will be fans of black players. But if you ask me, in fact, in the black world especially, ask any woman, or any gay man, and they'll tell you it'll be the basketball players. They're the finest-looking men. And they are the real athletes.... For the most part. You get young guys like Michael Jordan and Magic Johnson. They serve as pretty good role models. In my day it was Kareem [Abdul Jabbar] and Julius Irving. Because they went beyond the court and took some interest in black youth. Working with youth clubs and stuff. But you gotta remember that they are one in a million. So all this talk about role models. It only does so far. And we know that. Only one in a million black child is going to make it. That's why we pay that no mind!

Several informants rebuked the media for "all the fuss" about the lack of suitable male role models for young black men. Donny retorted once, "Role models for what?" He and others were adamant that excellent male role models exist in black society, especially their fathers and their teachers and preachers.

LEONARD: There have always been role models for us in Harlem. I mean even if we didn't fit into their shoes, directly, there were always men to look up to. I just wish the kids today would aspire to these heights. Instead of wasting all their money on drugs and that bullshit gold. There's so much they could do. Especially now. I sense a second renaissance in black art. Even the white art establishment is after it. They know we've got lots to offer. And especially with the Japanese chasing after us up here. The white folks'll be smellin' money. With the Japanese tourists. The next thing you know they'll be cutting business deals with the restaurants and artists up here in Harlem. I know it's gonna happen. But whatever. If it funds a renaissance, then that's fine by me.

While prominent black women in history featured as role models for some of my informants—especially the liberationists Harriet Tubman, Sojourner Truth, and Ida B. Wells and the writers Nikki Giovanni, Audré Lorde, Alice Walker, and Maya Angelou—it was the male political leaders—Booker T. Washington, W. E. B. Du Bois, Adam Clayton Powell, Marcus Garvey, Andrew Young, Jesse Jackson, Ralph Abernathy, Martin Luther King, Jr., and Malcolm X—who were most frequently perceived as role models. Some of the black power leaders, such as Stokely Carmichael, Bobby Seale, and Huey Newton, were also named. Most important were the writers and dancers of the Harlem Renaissance: Langston Hughes, Countee Cullen, Alain Locke, Wallace Thurman, Walter White, Claude McKay, Douglas Aaron, and Richard Bruce Nugent, and their successors James Baldwin, Alvin Ailey, and Arthur Mitchell. The impact of these prominent black Americans and the historical events that surrounded their experiences was most pronounced among those of my informants who were themselves employed in the arts. Garvey, who works as a choreographer, described his feelings.

GARVEY: I perceive Ailey as the most inspirational for me. He took jazz and modern dance to black society, and then back to white society, but filled with that special exuberance he had. It was African. African deep [thoroughly]. The Dance Theater [of Harlem] give you that too. But in a more classical manner. They are the most widely accepted because of that. But Ailey has paved the way for so many of us now. He's really the one.

Political leaders also appear to have had an impact on gay black men in Harlem. Without a doubt, the importance of Malcolm X to this population is unrivaled. His aggressive, confrontational style of politics is often praised by black New Yorkers.

FRANKLIN: Malcolm X, definitely. The most important. I mean just the fact that he died right here in Harlem is significant. I know a lot of us knew him or saw him. I heard him speak once. He was so strong. And so powerful. He was someone who you could identify with. Very easily. He was speaking from us. Now, Martin Luther King was important. But he was southern. He was church. He didn't have the appeal that Malcolm had with the people here in Harlem. King was respected and just as loved, believe me. But Malcolm was one of us. He knew the streets and knew the boys he was recruiting into the Nation of Islam. And he knew how to hook the rest of us into his philosophy. They were violent times. We all knew violence. Especially in the ghetto! So his message meant something very real to us. It certainly had more appeal to us in the cities than Martin's did.... I would say that Malcolm X was the most significant of all of them. For me anyway.

The impact of political leaders as role models is especially evident in the following remarks.

LOUIS: Malcolm X was the most influential political leader we've ever had in Harlem. But, you know, there've been other leaders up here. Adam Clayton Powell. Senior and Junior. And Marcus Garvey. I don't think enough people really understood what that man achieved. Especially the people from the civil rights movement. They could have honored Garvey a whole lot more....

Sometimes I thought about running for office. You know, like the city or the state. I think Harlem could deal with a gay politician. I think that people in Harlem would back you no matter what. And they'd still be proud of you, and support you. That'd teach America something.... Yes, mind you, the churches would stop that [a gay candidate]. They really are the powerhouse in Harlem.

It is interesting to note that Louis entertains ideas of a political career. It shows the impact that Malcolm X, Louis's culture hero, and other leaders have had on this man. In fact, Louis is quite sure that gay people in America will achieve recognition only if they unite behind some dynamic leader. He noted that the gay movement does not have the charismatic leadership that it once had, nor that which the black movements had in the 1960s. But he adds that the politically powerful churches are likely to sabotage any attempt by a gay man to achieve elected office.

This fear of the power of the church not only reinforces respect for the institution in the black community but also shows respect for the charismatic preachers who lead the churches in Harlem.[24] Their leadership has been, and still is, an inspiration to many of the gay black men who are currently church participants.

CLEVELAND: I guess you could say that they were role models for most of us. We felt very close to our preachers. They were community leaders, especially down South. And with the family pushing us, we became very involved with the church. I guess I was in the choir before I knew it.

Both in the South and in Harlem, preachers are seen by gay men as role models—men who are educated, successful, and powerful.

Prominent men in Harlem are often political or religious leaders who manipulate the media to promote their prominence. Many informants were critical of such leaders, who they feel often detract from the positive aspects of being black.

TERRY: Some of them are crazy. Now, that's the problem. Because they're crazy, and they represent us, that's why the media makes a fool outta us. Showin' C. Vernon Mason and that Maddox guy. I mean they're lawyers. OK. But all the young kids gonna hear about them and start carryin' on like that. Miss Sharpton's a trip. With that [hair]do. Child, she's missed her callin'. She should be on stage at the Apollo. Really though, the impression they make 'cause of the media. That ain't right. They need to see what these young men are doing' for our kids at the YMCA. Running all those dance and theater workshops. Now that's important. And those brothers feedin' the kids with AIDS. They're the role models today. But you don't see them on TV.

In addition to the role models of prominent black men, those in the immediate neighborhood, through community participation, offer examples of what it is to be a good black man. At this same community level of interaction, black people learn many of the expressive traits of being black.[25]

## Expressive Culture

Peer pressure in the black community to conform to "being black" is given prominence in the discussion of socialization in the works of other ethnographers.[26] Many demonstrate in their descriptions of life on the street the powerful socialization of their subjects in day-to-day interaction with other members of their communities.

In Harlem, much of the expressive culture of blacks is transmitted verbally and by example in the performance of daily life on the streets and in the courtyards of project and tenement buildings. Language, speech performance, nonverbal behavior, and clothing and hair styles define what it means to be black. They are learned from peers with whom individuals hang out after school, in playgrounds and parks, in the bars and dance halls, while shopping or sitting on the stoop.

My research in Harlem has provided a vast pool of evidence of black expressive styles. These range from spoken expressions and reinterpreted standard English vocabulary to nonverbal gestures, dance and walking styles, hairdos and fashions. Gay black men appear to be at the source of much of this stylistic creativity, as with so many of the styles of behavior and clothing that originate within this population. To this extent, gay blacks have their own "diction," which feeds on and into black society. While non-gay Harlem would probably be reluctant to admit this, evidence exists that indeed it does (see chap. 9).

Gay black men in Harlem learn the expressive culture of being black from family and friends in their hometown community. Specifically, gay black aspects of that expressive culture are learned in the gay scene, in the bars and discos, at parties and card games. The creativity gay blacks express in their daily speech and nonverbal communication with each other, their fashion and dance statements in the gay community, and their contributions to the arts of black American culture place them at the cutting edge of black expressive culture and demonstrate the significance of their position at the intersection of gay and black cultures.

## "Being Black": Summary

Because their socialization into black culture has been so thorough, gay black men in Harlem are able to identify as black men. Although they are known to be gay or "sissies," they know how to act as black men. Also, because they avoid contact both with the white world beyond Harlem's borders and with mainstream gay society, they have accepted "being black" as their primary identity. From all of the varied sources referred to above—family and friends, books, television, and the example of community leaders—gay men in Harlem have learned what it takes to be black. "Being black" is more than an issue of color, although that in itself is a significant attribute. For Byron, for example, "being black" is more than just having "black" skin: "Black means a whole lotta things. It means my color. It means my race. It means my family. It means my church. It means Harlem. It means me. I'm black. That's what it means. Everything."

Roots in and connections to the South, knowledge of slavery in particular, are important components of being black. Knowledge of black folklore and pertinent historical events and participation in a black church, at some level, are also important. Most significant are some of the contemporary cultural traits that are learned in the home, at school, or on the streets where one lives. And peer pressure on the streets is especially important in the creation and perpetuation of expressive black cultural elements.

Participation in expressively black styles of walking and talking is one important part of "being black." Living in a black extended family and in a social network of black acquaintances also contributes to black identity.

WALLACE: Black lives? That means the way you live. The way I was taught to live my life. The way I was raised. My mother taught me that. You know, the importance of family. The importance of church. The importance of schoolin' and work. How you need good friends around you. How to choose those friends, carefully. All those things are our lives. That's what makes our lives. It's a bit different in the city. You know, the most important thing here is money. You gotta have money. To survive. So, it's a bit different here. Your friends can be more important than your family. You know, because your mother live somewhere else. Or your brothers are running in Brooklyn or Yonkers, or someplace. So your friends become your family. That's why I take good care of my friends. They be my family.

Gay black men's preference for residence and a social life entirely within a black environment further serves to explain the perception they hold of themselves as being primarily black men.

However, if these men socialize outside of the black community, they are most likely to do so in an alternate gay scene rather than in a non-gay or gender-mixed scene. In other words, gay culture, while of secondary importance to being black, is an important source of cultural identity for these men.

# 6

# "Gay Is Lovin' Men":
# Gay Identity in Harlem

Many black Americans manage multiple identities. In white-dominated corporate America, for example, black executives may find it expeditious to play down their black identity. In the cultural context of American society, gay black men often are adept at identifying as American, black, or gay, as the occasion demands, and negotiate between one identity and another depending on context.

In Harlem, where a wide range of types of people are accepted, being gay is not necessarily regarded as being deviant. (Compare this with being gay in mainstream white America, where white gay men are trying to overcome the deviant label by pursuing the status of gay as "ethnic" in order to rationalize and justify the equality of their existence alongside other Americans.)[1] Being gay in Harlem means being different, but in a community characterized by diversity.[2]

Whatever the psychological dimensions of a gay identity, it too, like black identity, comprises social and cultural dimensions. These social and cultural elements of gay life and their importance to the construction and maintenance of gay identity are the subject of this chapter.

## Being Gay

FRANCIS: Gay is lovin' men, honey. All kinds o' men. Lovin' men. Now, that's bein' gay.

In Harlem, gay men primarily regard being gay as synonymous with being homosexual. Same-sex sexual behavior was invariably raised as

125

the single practice that distinguished gay men from other types of men ("bisexual" and "straight") in Harlem.

ROLAND: [A gay man] has sex with the same sex. With other men. He prefers to have sex with other men.

GILBERT: [A gay man is] a man who is interested in another man, sexually. He can be feminine or masculine. It doesn't matter. Some men like different things in sex. But they're all gay.

LESLIE: [A gay man is] a man who has sex with another man. It usually involves emotional commitment. A lover relationship.

The most important aspect of gay identity for these gay black men is sexual behavior. It is the one common attribute they share as gay men. All of my respondents indicated that in order to be gay, that is, to be distinguishable from non-gay people, one had to engage in homosexual intercourse with another man.

For some men, however, having a gay identity meant more than just having sex with other men. Being gay also included participation in a gay social life.[3]

BYRON: [A gay man] is homosexual. He has gay friends. He goes to gay places. Does gay things.

LUTHER: Gay means homosexual, you know. A man who likes to have sex with other men, and who lives a gay lifestyle. He has gay friends and does gay things. Like goes to discos and parties.

GILBERT: A gay man has sex with other men. Hangs out in the scene. Has gay friends. He's out to his family.

ORVILLE: [A gay man is] a homosexual. But it really refers to younger men.

NATE: Most of them are sissies. Real women. I mean, most gay men act and carry on like women. Now you have the hos [whores] and the church women, the wife type and the nymphomaniac. That's what gay men are like.

SHERMAN: Sometimes [a gay man is] a flamboyant male. A man who dresses well. Has great compassion. He lives a gay lifestyle. In gay bars, and parties. He can also be conservative, though. You know, a quiet man. It depends on his personality. And his role in the community. They're all different types of men actually.

LOUIS: To me, personally, it means that you live a separate lifestyle. It's more than just the sex. Gay sex is important. An important part of it. But it's not all. Because being gay means that you do other gay things too. Like having other gay friends. Going to gay places. I mean you really could see that in the seventies. You know, 'cause all the discos were really gay. That was a gay thing. And gay liberation. That told us so much about being gay. So you could see things that were gay. Just gay. Different to the rest of New York. So being gay is all that too. It's history now, too. We have a history.

Many gay black men in Harlem agree that engaging in homosexual behavior was the starting point of their homosexual identity formation.[4] Such homosexual experiences are followed by a variety of social experiences that lead the individual into the gay world. It is in this "cultural scene," composed of both private and public contexts, that the individual learns how to be gay.

The life history of Louis that I give below is an attempt to show how a gay social and political identity emerged in a man raised in a prosperous and stable black family, the kind rarely mentioned in the literature on black society.

Louis was born in 1950, the third of five children and the elder son of May and Charlie Williams. Charlie was a prosperous realtor, born and raised in Harlem. He had completed high school and worked all his life in his uncle's business, which he was eventually to inherit. He hoped one of his sons would take it over, but one was interested in the arts and the other in basketball. May had come north from Georgia, following in the footsteps of two older sisters. One of them had been a successful jazz singer in the after-hours world of wartime Harlem but had succumbed to alcohol "and stuff" in 1946. That was about the time that her other sister had started taking her to Convent Baptist Church, "with all those monied folks." That's where she met the handsome Charlie. "You seen Louis. You ain't seen nothing," she once remarked. "You think Louis is pretty. Child, you shoulda seen his Daddy!"

Charlie's parents weren't too sure about a southern girl as a wife for their city son, but she regularly went to church, so that helped. They contributed to the couple's first home, in a tenement just north of 110th Street. Four children in four years meant that the family quickly outgrew their first apartment, but by then Charlie was doing quite well with "Uncle's help," so the family moved to 140th Street. This is the home that figures earliest in Louis's childhood memories.

The apartment was huge. It had a long entranceway, off which one could enter the three bedrooms or the two bathrooms. In the "rear" were a large living room with an alcove where the television was located, a dining room, and a large kitchen, which housed a breakfast table. Louis shared a bedroom with his younger brother. His two sisters at that time shared a bedroom also. (Louis's third sister was born some fourteen years after him.) He recalls that he got along well with his brother. Both of the boys were out and about a lot. His brother played ball in the park most evenings and weekends, and Louis was able to have his friends over to play in the bedroom. Mostly they played cards or read, and sometimes his best friends would stay the night.

Louis's parents entertained a lot. He suspects that was because of his father's contacts in the business world. His mother was a wonderful cook. He remembers her peach cobbler with special affection. And he insists, "An' nobody, just nobody, cooks ribs like Ma!" On Sundays, Louis's aunt and her church friends would come to eat. That was always a great time to be home, because his aunt would bring over gifts for the children. Mostly they would be small toys or candy, but once she gave the children a bicycle, and Louis was put in charge.

Louis remembers his older sisters were always in school. Naomi and Rona had many friends who were always coming around. He didn't like them too much because they were always making noise and teasing him. His sisters were always allowed to stay up later and watch television. When Naomi was in eighth grade she had a boyfriend, Willie. He was a basketball player whom Louis admired very much. He was tall and dark and very handsome. He favored Isaac, Louis's younger brother, because Isaac was so good at playing ball. Louis also liked to play, but he was heavier and couldn't match Willie or Isaac on the court. But he persisted because he liked Willie so much. Willie and Naomi eventually married after they finished high school, and Willie became a successful professional ball player.

Ruth also married and has four children as well. She and her family live in New Rochelle, near Louis's mother. His brother lives in D.C. and works on and off as an electrician's assistant. "God knows how many nieces and nephews I got in D.C. Isaac has a different woman he's livin' with every time I see him. His trouble is that he's so fine and all these girls chase after him!"

Louis remembers the summers as a child especially. He would be allowed to play in the playground on the corner. It had swings and "things to climb all over." Trees shaded the mothers, grandmothers, and older sisters who took care of the children "in the park." His favorite part of the playground was where the fountain sprayed over the children. Sometimes if he and his sisters were really lucky his mother would take them to Riverside Park or Central Park. One summer he remembers going to the Bronx Zoo. But it was hot and smelly. He remembers riding the elephant and watching the monkeys, but overall it "wasn't all that."

Louis had two very close friends during his early years at 140th Street. His best friend, Billy, lived in the same building, downstairs. Billy was a quiet child. He always liked to read, and sometimes he'd watch television with Louis. In fact, anything that Louis did Billy liked to do as well. Louis liked his friend. He was very good-looking and always supportive of Louis and his wild dreams. Early in life Louis had decided that he would become a famous singer or film star. He used to dress up and pretend to act parts, sometimes in front of the mirror, but most often in front of Billy. Billy would always cheer and clap, and sometimes tell Louis how he could do something better. Louis and Billy attended the same elementary school, a few blocks away from where they lived. They used to walk to and from school every day. One of Louis's older sisters would escort them. Another friend, Johnny, whom Louis had met at school, would join them on the way. Johnny was a year older than Louis and Billy, physically much bigger and more rugged in appearance. Even at elementary school, the girls followed Johnny around. He played basketball and football at school and always drew a large crowd to watch him perform. This was how Louis had heard of him and eventually got to know him. Louis also liked to play basketball, and he and Johnny became a very popular pair both on and off the court.

Louis notes that around about sixth grade he realized that his feelings for his two closest friends were different from the feelings he had toward a lot of his other friends and acquaintances at school and in the immediate neighborhood. He didn't understand them at the time, but at some point, in a bathroom at school, Johnny approached him and touched him. Louis recalls, "I always remember how good that felt. I mean I felt sick inside, you know. I suddenly felt I was in love or something. I just know I felt wonderful."

At some point over the next few months, as their sexual involvement increased, Louis told Johnny that he was in love with him and that he wanted to marry him. Louis had just simply decided that this was the person with whom he wanted to spend the rest of his life. He compared the simplicity of his love at that time to the love of Fabian and Annette, or Bobby and Debbie, in the movies. But he says that it did consume him and made him intensely jealous of all the girls who hung around Johnny at school. He used to get mad at Johnny for even talking with the girls. And Johnny used to get mad at him, eventually saying that Louis was worse than a girl. It was this statement of Johnny's that caused Louis to think that he really was different. Up to this point, Louis's upbringing typifies that of many of my informants who grew up in the 1950s and 1960s. His introduction to same-sex behavior at the hands of a schoolmate is also typical. That experience was the turning point for him and others, an "awakening" as Willis called it, because the realization hit home that they were "different."

In the early 1960s, the word *gay* wasn't used to describe homosexual men in Harlem. But Louis remembers, when he was in high school, the first time that someone called him "homo."

LOUIS: I had been hanging around with Johnny so much and really sticking close by, so close I guess it was obvious that the two of us were too close. What pissed me off most was that Johnny heard it too and didn't do nothing. I mean he was my hero and I was hurtin' and I guess I expected him to fight this guy.

Louis stayed home from school the next day, feigning illness. That evening when Johnny came over Louis told him that he didn't want to see him anymore. Johnny told him to "get over it," that he had to understand that he, Louis, really was a "homo." Louis was very distressed. He didn't know what it meant. He knew that he was different, but he was happy the way he was. He knew that something was bad about being a "homo," but he felt he had no one but his good friend Johnny to talk to about it. They never did have sex again, but they remained close friends until Johnny went to high school in the Bronx.

Thereafter, Louis concentrated his efforts on his friendship with Billy. Billy was attractive but not as "manly" as Johnny. But there was something that Louis felt about him too. One day on the way home from school, the boys went to Riverside Park to watch the older guys play basketball. They were there quite late, when Billy told Louis to wait a while. Billy went off down by the river and didn't come back for a long time. Just as Louis was about to go looking for him, Billy emerged from the bushes with a man. Looking back, Louis thinks the guy wasn't all that old, but at that time he thought the guy was too old to be hanging out with Billy. Immediately Louis thought that Billy was up to something. On the way home he asked Billy what was going on. But Billy was evasive. He told Louis that the guy was a friend from the neighborhood. But Louis hadn't seen him before. He persisted until Billy finally told him what they were doing. Louis was shocked and pleased. He couldn't wait to blurt out that he and Johnny were doing the same stuff. Billy said he knew but that he hadn't talked to Louis about it because he wasn't sure whether they could still be friends.

Sometime after that evening, Billy took Louis down to the park and eventually, after seeing the same man again, took Louis into the bushes. Louis enjoyed having sex with Billy but said it wasn't the same as with Johnny. He played a different role. And Billy was too close a friend (and confidant) for them to get into too much. They decided not to do it again but to be special friends. "Girlfriends!" Louis laughed.

This initial sexual encounter typically cements a lifelong commitment between two gay friends. Several informants related similar incidents in their development as gay men. Also, we see here the beginning of a gay social network that was to expand through high school and college years. Typically many of these friendships are maintained in adult life.

Louis and Billy both attended George Washington High School in Harlem. They were in the same class right through school, and both were better than average students. Louis won a scholarship to go to college, but Billy did not even graduate.

LOUIS: Most of our crowd just studied. We all liked our books. None of us was really sports-oriented. We left that to the boys! We supported them and all, 'cause we liked the sports, and the boys, but we only did that because we wanted them. You know. If we got up to anything those days it would be on the way home from school. 'Cause once I was home I wasn't comin' back out. Not in those days. It was "Do your homework, boy!" But it got me into books, and dreaming. Hours and hours of dreaming. That's why I'm here today. Doin' what I'm doin'. Because of those years.

Occasionally at school Louis would engage in sex, usually with some younger guy. He had two good places to take boys when he wanted to have sex—one in the gymnasium, the other down a tree-filled bank.

LOUIS: I didn't do much at school, really. Not really. I mean I got caught once and that made me cautious. I was having a good time too. The best I'd ever had. And this kid was screaming. He was screaming so loud that's what at-

tracted them. One of the teachers and some students, I think from the basketball team, came and caught us.

But Louis and Billy discovered (or heard about from friends at the
same school) several places they could go and see or participate in
sex on the way home from school.

LOUIS: Our favorite were the parks. You could spend hours there, just watching. And some fine motherfuckers would come on up in there. I even had sex
once with the captain of the school basketball team. I fucked him real good.
He never spoke to me at school, but I had him. If only all those sissies, and
those girls, knew that!...I had a teacher. I had some prominent people from
around Harlem. I had a TV star.

One particular park seems to have been their favorite. It also features in the life histories of many of the other gay black men I met in
Harlem. For some of them it is still an important meeting place for
sexual encounters, although the current drug epidemic in Harlem has
made the gay area of the park somewhat unsafe. Louis and Billy would
go there two or three times a week on the way home from school.
They spent hours wandering around the paths and watching older
men engage in sex. Louis recalls that it was quite an education.
Although he had worked out what to do, actually to see the particular
act take place was quite thrilling. Occasionally, the guys would go to
the park on the weekends. But Louis thought that it was too crowded,
and they might have been recognized: "They was all up in there.
Everyone. You never know who you gonna run into. And it was too
crowded. I didn't like that. They was comin' at you from every direction." But the park was where Louis first engaged in oral sex—"a
scary thing, the first time"—and where he and Billy made many of
the friendships with gay people their own age that persist today. Public settings for sex such as this feature prominently in the life histories
of many gay men. Apart from the fact that access was free, and no age
limit was enforced (as for bars), sexual experience was gained, anony-
mously, and entry into gay life established.
    About this time, 1969–1970, the word *gay* became familiar to
Louis and his friends. During the summer before their last year
in high school, some gay people had rioted downtown, night after
night, and fought for their rights to hang out together, to be gay
together, and to have sex and relationships with whom they liked.
These, of course, were the Stonewall riots, a memorable event in history for gay people the world over. What this event did for Louis and

other young gay men in Harlem was to enlighten them about the fact that a whole section of town was gay. Just as Harlem was for blacks, so Greenwich Village was for gays. Louis used to think that he had been born into the wrong part of town. He should have been born and raised in Greenwich Village.

LOUIS: I used to dream that I had been born in Greenwich Village to these two fierce gay men. They had a beautiful house and I had a very happy life. I dreamt I went to a gay school and met all these beautiful boys, and I fell in love and got married.

But Louis had never been to Greenwich Village.

In July or August 1969, before entering their senior year at high school, Louis Williams and Billy Pritchard emerged from the Interborough Rapid Transit subway line at Christopher Street for the first time. Louis recalls it as a colorful sight.

LOUIS: The place was full of hippies. I mean I'd seen them on TV, but here they were live. Hundreds of them holding hands and kissing each other. And a lot of them were men kissing men. I remember us like country boys, standing and staring. All these men. Even black ones. And black and white ones together. I remember that really affecting me. To see black and white men together. That was a trip.

The guys didn't venture too far from the subway. They found the Stonewall Inn, in Sheridan Square, and paid homage along with the many others who were milling around outside the boarded-up bar. They soon returned to the subway, having explored enough for a first visit and because they were a little scared in case they got into trouble. Being raised with a heightened awareness of racial differences, they were not sure how they would be accepted downtown. The fact that black and white men were together questioned basic assumptions that Louis held about life. Although being gay obviously cuts across racial barriers and has instilled in Louis a sense of pride in being gay, he has never had a white friend, let alone a white lover.

An important event in the development of being gay for all the informants was a "first visit" to a gay section of town or to a gay bar. All expressed some sense of relief, not just at the security of being away from prying family or suspected homophobic neighbors but at the discovery of others like themselves, doing normal things like dancing, drinking, kissing, holding hands, relaxing, and having a good time.

When school started again, Louis and Billy shared their experiences with their gay friends at school. There was much talk about setting up a gay liberation club at school, but they were not sure how "scandalous" that might be. Harlem wasn't ready for them, yet. Some years later such a club was formed at that high school, and on the club's unofficial "honors list" are the names of Louis and Billy, as Stonewallers.

The last year at high school was difficult. Louis wanted to go to college and was aiming at a private school in upstate New York, a liberal arts college that would provide him with the education he would need to become a star. But gay life was developing all over the city. More parks and bars, and even the bathhouse, in Harlem, beckoned to him. Louis remembers it all "bursting forth."

Louis: It was really me bursting forth on all of it. I mean suddenly I found all these things to do. I started drinking a lot, and going to the bars down on 125th Street. There were a whole lot of them. And all the noise and bright lights of the gay scene at that time. And all the men. I could have sex anywhere, anytime, with anyone I wanted. People begged me to go home with them. But I never did. I mean I had sex with them all right, but I wouldn't go to their homes. I was frightened they wouldn't let me go. And I didn't know who'd be at home with them. But I had a ball.

Louis didn't fall in love at this time—fortunately, he says—so he was able to strike a balance between going out, mainly at night and on the weekends, when it was all happening, and staying in when schoolwork demanded it. However, his friend Billy did fall in love.

Louis: Billy met a guy who was working at Macy's. He was handsome, and he had lots of money. At least we thought so. Anyway, I've forgotten his name, but he used to take us out. We'd go to parties all over town, even to his friends' in Brooklyn. Sometimes we'd stay out all night. But that was mainly when we went to the discos. We were trying all sorts of drugs and drinking. But I said only on the weekends. That was where Billy went wrong. He was going out with these guys all through the week. He didn't come to school. Until he got into real trouble. And his parents found out. And he got a beating. So, he moved out and lived with that guy in Brooklyn. I used to see him sometimes, but I haven't seen him in years now. I don't even know if he's alive.

It was at this time that the education, career plans, and other dreams of many of the gay men I interviewed were derailed. The 1970s, and all that those years meant for gay men in New York City, undoubtedly played a part. Gay liberation, emerging gay social and political organizations, and the establishment of a large gay scene of bars, clubs, and discos provided these men with places to be gay. Suddenly many men found that they could live "gay" lives, even openly, in the company of many like souls. Most of this new lifestyle, however, was conducted late at night because of the marginalization of gay culture by mainstream New York society (and because many gay men wished to remain discreet). This after-hours lifestyle often interfered with other aspects of gay men's lives. Many did not realize that it would cost them money, time, and sometimes their jobs or schooling.

According to Louis's mother, Billy's expulsion from school and his running away from home was the moment when she realized that Louis too was possibly gay. However, after that incident, Louis settled down, stayed home more often, and studied hard. This reduced her concerns about his gayness. She noted that he was young, and it might be a stage that he was going through or a matter of his hanging out with a wild crowd. She never discussed the issue with him and soon forgot about it.

Louis says that Billy's moving away meant that he did not go out as much and that staying at home probably did help his schoolwork. He was delighted in the spring of 1970 to hear that he was going to college. He was so excited about his good fortune that he had trouble settling down to the last weeks of school.

The next four years were a mixture of pleasure and pain. College days provided Louis with an opportunity to shine academically, especially with his acting, directing, and writing. He also enjoyed an active sports life, but his interest was mainly in the other players. Louis described many of the sexual encounters he enjoyed at college. The dormitory situation provided the growing network of gay friends with many opportunities to engage in sexual encounters. Some of these men went on to marry and have families, but many of them, with whom Louis keeps in touch, remained gay. In his junior year, Louis met Terrence, a "tall, handsome, light-skinned boy" who was a superb basketball player and a gentle, understanding friend. They became buddies on and off the court. Eventually they became lovers. Through the following summer, which Louis spent in Washington, D.C., where Terrence came from, the two developed the basis of what was to become a ten-year affair.

After college, Louis moved to D.C. for six years and lived with Terrence. They were a popular couple in the gay community and well known in the discos and bars. They both worked office jobs for different government departments. Louis recalls this as the happiest time of his life. He had the security of a relationship and of a well-paying, full-time job. Unlike many of their friends in D.C. who were struggling to break free from family constraints and improve their socioeconomic status, Louis and Terrence had it made. However, after six years, during which Louis freely admits to a very promiscuous sex life outside of the relationship, the yearning to return to the arts became too great. Not foreseeing the opportunities he desired in D.C., Louis set his sights on New York. Fortunately, Terrence was a willing partner, and the couple moved to New York City in 1981. Louis's constant unemployment, the cost of living in the city, and continued promiscuity, especially on Louis's part, tore the couple apart. Terrence returned to D.C. Although they remain the best of friends and visit each other frequently, Louis is sometimes remorseful. Both men have moved on to other relationships, but Louis remembers that one with Terrence as being exemplary.

## Socialization and Coming Out

Socialization through social interaction has been the theoretical perspective adopted by many of the social scientists who have written about homosexual and gay men.[5] According to these social scientists, gay life, gay desire and sexual behavior, and the social etiquette of being gay are learned socially in the gay scene.[6] Some of my informants' experience supports this view.

GILBERT: Everything I learned from her. Mother [an older gay black man] taught me how to dress and how to pick up men.

LEONARD: Most of what I know about actually being gay came from hanging out in the scene. You know, gay talk.

For some researchers the process of entering and interacting in the gay scene and assimilating "gay" behavior is called "coming out," the final stage of gay identity acquisition.[7]

For most of the informants in this study "coming out" means much more than just entering the "gay scene." Coming out is a major event in their lives: they have to make a conscious effort to inform family, friends, neighbors, and co-workers of their homosexuality, as well as participate in "the Life." When they ventured to inform their families and friends about their gay identities, most were received with compassion and continued friendship. There were, of course, a variety of responses to the discovery of a gay son. In a few instances, some family members or friends chose not to deal with the issue further but still maintained social relations with the gay man in question. Thus, in Harlem, signs of disapproval are mild, if present at all.

ARNEL: It wasn't till some time after [high school] that one of the [three] guys [I had sex with] said we were all homosexuals. Then we knew we were different.... I had my daughter much later. When I had finished college. I was just sick of all this running around. And all these goddam men that you can't trust. So, I just started this friendship with this girl. She knew what the story was. We got sexual, only a few times, and now we has a kid. She's gone off to California, and me and Mom are raising her. But I didn't come out till after all that. I just didn't want to upset my mother. I love her dearly. Will do anything for her. To protect her. And I didn't want to upset her. But when S—— left me, and with the child, and I didn't really care, I thought I'd better explain the whole relationship to my mother. Well, she was a bit upset, but she said I was still her son and she still loved me.... Yes, I told them [his father, three brothers, and two sisters] after I told my mother. My father won't hear of it. It's not discussed in his presence. And the others just don't care. I mean it don't bother them. Even when I went back to Barbados and told Grandma, and my cousins, they don't care. You see, it doesn't affect their lives, so it doesn't mean anything to them. Well, now of course, they always askin' after my health. But I mean it really didn't affect our relationships.

Often the coming out process is provoked by the actions of others. Usually family members or close friends who may suspect an individual is gay will actually ask about it.

LOUIS: My brother asked me actually. I guess he'd heard something from someone. You know how us black folks is. You can't keep no secrets from no one! So I thought, well, I ain't gonna lie to my brother. We was pretty close, and he really looked up to me. But I thought, if it destroyed our relationship, bad luck! So I told him. Then I thought what a relief. It felt good. Especially 'cause you know, he didn't go off on me or anything. He took it quite calmly. And he knew a lot of my friends and be liked all o' us. So I guess he just accepted it. Then I thought well I'd better tell the rest of them, otherwise they gonna hear it from all over. So that same night I called my mother and sisters together and sat them down. I poured Mama a cocktail and just told them. The girls giggled a bit. And Mama gave me a hug and said she sorta knew. They thought it was alright. So that was that.... I don't lie to nobody. My co-workers, you know the ones that I work with every day, they know. And the neighbors know that [Paul] and I are together. You know, like when I got mugged that time and they helped me. I'm sure they wouldn't have bothered if I hadn't been more open and friendly to them.

However, for many gay men in Harlem, coming out was not a major concern, because their homosexuality, and later their gay identity, had always been assumed by family and friends. There was no need to "come out." Folks in their social networks had gradually taken for granted their sexual orientation.

DONNY: I was always a sissy, honey. I mean I always had girlfriends. You know, hanging out with the girls. I can remember Daddy sayin' that it wasn't healthy for a boychild to be hangin' round with all them girls.I used to do their hair and their nails. And go clothes shopping with them. You know, on Saturdays, we'd go out and buy clothes for them to wear. And at school all my friends were girls. Now some of the boys were jealous of that. Because I'd have all these girlfriends. But that was OK, 'cause I'd have all the boys hanging around and askin' me 'bout the girls, you know. But I'd have my hair done. And all my clothes were latest fashion. And I guess a bit too much for most of the kids. You know, they could tell I was gay. Even before I knew it. But I didn't think it was bad. You know like anything was wrong or anything. I just was like that.... I think because I thought it was natural then they all thought it was natural. No one ever caused any trouble. Sometimes the kids will call out "sissy" or "faggot," but I'd just say, "So what?"...I'm just myself. I carry on like this all the lime. My brothers and sisters know. I think they probably heard the kids at school or on the block, you know, talkin' about me. So, they just knew. I didn't have to tell nobody. Everyone just kinda knew.

Sometimes, this gradual assumption on the part of family and friends concerning a man's sexual orientation resulted from a man's participation in a prolonged relationship with a lover, especially if the relationship was live-in.[8]

STANLEY: I've always had a lover. Always. Ever since I left school I've been livin' with one lover or the other. I think that's how they found out. I mean, look at [London]. He's a real sissy. I mean, the way that child carries on. Well, I guess we were all like that too when we were younger. So, it has to be obvious. They have to know.... I did actually tell my mother. When this AIDS thing happened. But she knew already. She told me she knew because all my friends were like that. All the children I'd be bringin' home. They were all sissies. So she could tell. And she would party with us sometimes. And the children'd be carryin' on. So I didn't have to come out. All the family knew. So it was no big deal.

Some gay black men lead fulfilling lives as gay men without coming out to family or friends. Protecting family from any distress they may endure after finding out a son or brother is gay is the most frequently cited reason for not coming out to parents and siblings.

CECIL: My parents were so old by the time I decided to tell them that I thought in the end why do they need to be upset at this age. If they don't know by now it's not going to affect them by not knowing at all. I've been thinkin' about telling my sister, but she can be shady at times. So, I will, but not till after Mama and Daddy is gone.

Not wishing to offend people or their religious sentiments is another reason for not coming out to friends and co-workers. A gay man will be especially unwilling to come out if he suspects that people will not understand or if he fears they will not be tolerant.

QUINT: My brother knows. He was the one that took me into the Life. So we know about each other. But no one else in the family knows. No one. That's like it's our secret.... There's no need to go rockin' the boat. They don't understand things like that. Not down South. Especially with all that church stuff. They don't understand.... No one at the bank knows. I haven't told them. It's not their need to know. When I go out with them, I drink with them and dance with the girls. You know, but it is hard sometimes 'cause the girls in the office might wanna go out wit' you. And you keep turnin' them down. So they may be gettin' a bit suspicious. But I ain't tellin' them. It's my business.

As Quint says, the question of his sexuality and what he does in private is his business. No one needs to know.

Those who live away from their families, or maintain separate gay social networks, often feel no necessity to "rock the boat."[9]

CLEVELAND: All my friends are up here. All of them are in Harlem. I don't go out with anyone downtown. They don't come up here. I mean, if we go out after work, then we go to a bar for a drink. Somewhere near work. They don't come up here. And we don't go down there.... Yeah, they're two separate worlds.

Gay black men often raise this duality when they discuss their gay identity as opposed to their black identity, which has a visible dimension and cannot be hidden.[10]

As the quotations above indicate, "coming out" was not a major challenge for many of the gay men in Harlem. When it was, their experiences were often similar to the experiences reported for gay men elsewhere in the United States.[11]

The relatively calm response to news that a son is gay stems from the fact that being gay is not on the whole regarded as deviant in Harlem. And while some people do regard homosexuality as aberrant, the overtones are not as dramatic as in mainstream American society. Difference, not deviance, is the primary basis for social categorization. This is not to say that deviance is not recognized in Harlem. Truly deviant categories of people include those who live on the margins of black society and disrupt the lives of folks as they go about their daily business, for example, drug dealers and crackheads. Attitudes toward gays are best encapsulated in the following comment by a non-gay female Baptist churchgoer, who finds the sexual behavior between two people less important than companionship and other forms of social interaction.

MONA: It don' matter to me. You be what you want, son. It's you that has to make peace with the Lord.... For me, I's just pleased you got someone. That's what's important. Don' matter who. As long as you got someone.

Issues of sexual preference apparently are not a paramount concern to black people whose society has already been marginalized by mainstream white America.

## Cruising

The desire to enter into homosexual relations informs much of the expressive behavior of gay men, especially in gay public places. Many of the verbal and nonverbal expressions gay men utilize in the process of meeting potential sex partners bear some sexual innuendo.[12] Their "performance" in public settings indicates to gays and non-gays alike that they are homosexual, that they are expressly interested in a particular person, and that they are interested in a particular sex act with that person. The use of symbols (such as earrings and colored handkerchiefs) for a particular desired behavior is an important statement about identity; it indicates not only gay identity but specific sexual and social roles within gay culture.

ZACHARY: They [colored handkerchiefs hanging from a back pocket] indicated that you were active or passive in relation to a specific sex act. You know, different colors meant different acts. And if you wore it on the right it meant that you were passive, and vice versa. But more general things like the earrings were just general signs of being gay.

Gay men use many other verbal and nonverbal gestures to express interest in a potential sex partner. Often one man will approach another and ask directly if he is interested in having sex. Usually, however, the process of "cruising"—of showing interest and eventually picking up someone—involves a series of nonverbal introductory gestures.

ROMAN: [It's the] way he walks. And talks. Way he looks at other men. They get the message that you're interested. It's the way you carry yourself. And the things you say and do. Like, using your tongue to show him you want him. Touching him in a special way. Very affectionate.

WILBERT: [It's] not so much what he wears. Rather in the way he does things. Like walk. Or the things we do to pick up men. The small talk when we meet men. The way we look at one another. The way we touch. Or use our bodies. Like the one we saw that night on the bar. Sticking his butt out. He heard us talkin' about it. . . . And he knew we was lookin' at it. . . . Those sort of things indicate that you're gay.

Eye contact is the most frequently cited cruising gesture. Walking in the street, in a crowded store or disco, and most especially at a gay social gathering, or in a bar, gay men regard such stares as the first step in cruising. Asking someone for a cigarette or a light and buying someone a drink are also very common introductory gestures.[13]

All of these gestures add up to a wide variety of expressly sexual signs (see also Fast 1978; Read 1980). Yet most of these gestures, which appear to be more openly expressed in the gay scene in Harlem than elsewhere, indicate much more than just sexual interest. They indicate gender roles as expressed in gay society.

## Gender

Verbal and nonverbal messages not only indicate that an actor is gay but also usually reflect feminine or masculine role playing as dictated by the dominant heterosexual culture in which gay black lives are practiced. Many of the expressive elements of gay black culture elicited from my informants were explained as defining gender roles within gay society and within sexual relationships.

GREGORY: They'll do things like talk with female pronouns, or do womanly things, like stand with their hands on their hips, especially when they read someone. That'll give the general impression that they're gay. And to some men that they're interested in being the feminine part of a sexual relationship.

NATE: Some will give you sort of effeminate moves that show they sissies. Like stares, or sticking their tongue out. Or switching their butt. . . . It means

they're different to other men. They do things unmanly. By society's judgment. That's why a whole lotta people don't like gays. Because they break the
rules of behavior.... That's what I like about the Life. Now, I'm quiet. I hang
out and gets me my stuff. But I stand on the sidelines and watch these people.
They're so entertaining. Straight life must be so boring. Because everyone
conforms. These gay kids carry on. They give you the wrong colors at the
wrong time. They give you dance and great tea [gossip]. And their whole delivery is not how men are supposed to do it.

Kenneth Read's (1980) study is significant in the literature on gay
society. His description of the bar as a stage sets the scene for his analysis of social interactions between bar patrons as ritual—for example,
the obligatory repartee between "male" hustlers and "female" drag
queens. Read's dramaturgical analysis of the social roles of these bar
patrons as "players" (for example, King, who is "ordinarily masculine," and Pocahontas, who "has assumed all the visible attributes of
a woman's role") illuminates his thesis that these men's performance
of gender roles is but an act—a "symbolic enactment" of the heterosexual male-female role dichotomy. What is most important is that
these men are fully aware that they are engaged in role playing. In
fact, their acting leads Read to conclude that gender roles in mainstream American society are a "cultural myth," because they are
social constructions masquerading as biological truths that preclude
homosexual behavior.

The list of statuses for which the homosexual is ineligible, or for which his
eligibility is very questionable, is almost endless, and his ineligibility is "justi-
fied" by other myths, one after another, that embroider upon the fundamental
myth of gender and its notions of natural complements and oppositions (Read
1980:164)

The social construction of male and female roles will continue to be
debated as long as distinct biological differences inform people's con-
ceptions of the sexes. Most of my informants, however, have a very
clear perception of very real roles—in fact, of very real male and female identities, which they have learned from observations made during their socialization in black society. What is important about Read's
study for an analysis of gay life in Harlem is that it highlights the differences between the social roles expected of masculine-acting gay
men and feminine-acting gay men. In Harlem, these roles are recognized by my informants and are consciously reenacted in their role
playing in the gay scene.[14]

The conscious choice to play an exaggerated feminine or masculine (butch) role in gay black society, however, is chiefly a creative expression of sexual intention; that is, the feminine "sissy" character in a gay setting may consciously act this way to attract a "butch" homosexual male simply because he believes "opposites attract."[15] This gender role playing in cruising, though, does not necessarily indicate that such roles will be continued in other areas of social life.

ROMAN: I tease them. Play with them. You know, if I want them. To show them I'm interested in them. But being girl doesn't mean I'm a woman. I'm a man. A real man. ... I run my household. I work. I dress and act like a man. I'm a man. Only when I'm interested in another man will you see me being girl.

## Performance Culture

Being recognized for one's creativity is socially important. In fact, having a sense of style and innovation are key elements of gay identity in Harlem. The expressive aspects of black culture discussed in the previous chapter and the expressive elements of gay culture being discussed here do indeed reflect extraordinary levels of creativity at the hands of the individuals involved. Indeed, gay black men are often doubly skilled in verbal and nonverbal expression. The creativity involves clothing and hair fashions, dance, vocabulary skills, and verbal agility. Some of the elements of fashion that my informants claim as gay include the following.

LUTHER: Earrings. Pinkie rings. Those colored handkerchiefs. Buttons. Colors. Clothes. Drag. Hairdos. Long nails. Shoes. Color coordination. Slang. Wrist movements. Swishing. Dancing well. Dishing. Trashing. Reading. Vogueing. Cock rings. Nipple rings. Leather adornments.

SHERMAN: I mean there are buttons. Pink triangles. AIDS buttons. But mainly it would be fashionable clothing. A bit avant-garde. The way that he may put an outfit together. The way he wears it. The way that he walks and talks. That may indicate that he's gay.

KENT: Some of them will give you fashions down. I mean they'll rock you with some of the shit they come in here with.

BARRY: Jewelry, clothes, colors, gestures, snapping, limp wrists, calling each other "girlfriend."

COLIN: He always dresses well. Sometimes in drag, you know. Wearing jewelry. Rings. Earrings. Then there's swishin' and sashayin'. And language. You know, the way the girls call each other "girlfriend" or "sister." Manicured nails. Makeup. Hairdos.

Many elements of fashion and behavior serve dual functions for gay men. Through clothing and gestures, gay men are able to conspicuously challenge prescribed standards of maleness. On another level, many of the gestures and articles of clothing mentioned by my informants contribute to a kind of visual vocabulary used by gay men to distinguish themselves from others. By recognizing and imitating these visual cues, gay black men consciously identify themselves as members of a special in-group. Having an innovative sense of style, therefore, demonstrates not only a unique creative ability but also a mastery of that visual language which separates insiders from outsiders.

## Verbal Expression

In gay speech, common words or expressions take on uncommon meanings, sometimes inverting the original English meaning, sometimes highlighting an aspect of that original meaning. Such virtuosity has long been a feature of gay culture.[16]

*Shade, read, tired, over,* and *fierce* were some of the words I heard often in Harlem which retained special meaning for my gay black informants. To "throw shade" or to be "shady" means to display a skeptical attitude toward something or someone, usually by the nonverbal gesture of glancing away while rolling the eyes. It can also refer to an underhanded critique of one person by another, as Richmond meant when he said, "That whole conversation was shady. It ain't no way to talk about yo' friend." To "read" someone means that one is going to reproach the listener for some earlier activity or comment.

RICHMOND: I read the child, honey. I read her deep. She didn't have no right comin' in here and spooking me like that. She knows the door is shut for a reason. Yes, honey. Can't be she's never locked no door. You know if the door's locked then the children [gay men] are carryin' on. At least knock so they can know to pull their pants up.

If something is "tired," it is either unworthy of attention, trashy, or at best unoriginal, as in Terry's comment, "He was tired, honey. He had dirty old jeans on, and dirty sneakers." The adjective *over* (pronounced "o'fa") means that its subject is extraordinarily attractive and therefore the opposite of "tired." It is used most frequently in reference to someone's boyfriend or to an outfit worn at a disco and is often accompanied by a "high snap." Thus Winston noted, "That boy dancin' with Miss W——. Honey, that child was over! Did you see the thighs on him?" Finally, "fierce" has a meaning similar to "over," although it seems to be more commonly used.[17] Cletuh, for example, once commented to me, "Child, that's a fierce coat you wearin'. I'd like me a piece o' that. Who cut [made] that for you?"

## "Tea"

Verbal expressiveness is often colorfully used in the hyperbolic embellishments of "tea" (gossip), as in the following example.[18]

DARRELL: I been with all o' them. All of them. Some of them is OK. You know, they take care of you. You know, like give you carfare. Buy you something to eat. Maybe buy you a new pair o' sneakers. Maybe you can stay with them for a while. You know, move in. I had a guy once who'd let me live with him. But his place was small, you know, so I felt bad doin' that to him. Then there was another guy who bought me a gold watch. Yeah, he was real nice. Wanted to take me to Puerto Rico with him on his holidays. But that was too much. I had to stop him.

Sexual exploits are a favorite topic of gossip, but so are clothing styles, shopping bargains, information concerning new clubs, news events, and politics, church attendance, food served at a party, television shows, the welfare of acquaintances and friends, and their love lives, and severe but witty criticism of any of the above. Quint provided us with a harsh review of a bar he had never actually visited.

QUINT: We heard from [Nicholas] that the place was alright on Tuesdays, but otherwise only the old girls go there. I mean real old. Ancient. They can't even get up and walk let alone dance. Can you imagine a disco full of ol' queens like Miss [Moses]. All they can do is sit an' stare. They be fallin' over each other to get there, then they can't do shit once they're there. That place is too tired, child. Let's try the P.

Sarcastically criticizing a third party's behavior or dress is known as "dishing." This contrasts with "reading," which is more like a sarcastic reprimand. Both of these forms of verbal interaction are frequently found in "tea."

DONNY: Child, did you see the way that bitch read that boy. She was through [angry] with him. I don't know what the poor child had done by her, but she let loose. She read his ass.

RICHMOND: I was at Miss T——'s. We were taking tea. Oh, you shoulda heard us. We was dishing y'all. We spared none o' yo' asses. We did all o' yo' husbands. Miss D——'s. Miss M——'s. Miss K——'s. We did 'em all. Like that time when Miss D——'s boyfriend came up to the house all high and shit. She was livid. She was all dressed up and ready to go to Tracks and her husband was all fucked up [high]. Honey, Miss D—— read the boy for that. Embarrassing her like that. And in front of all o' us too. She was too much.

Most frequently, though, "tea" details the sex lives and relationships of friends and acquaintances. Below, Gilbert bemoans the fact that his best friend, Barry, asked an ex-lover of Gilbert's to a birthday party. The party was small and intimate, with large quantities of food and alcohol, good music, and conversation. But the only reference to the party was framed by Gilbert in his own interests.

GILBERT: That ain't right. You know it ain't. It ain't right that Miss Thing be doin' that shit. It was real shady o' her. She was my best friend. Now she be goin' and askin' them to her party like that. Child, she wears me out. Do you hear me. That was so shady of her.

Gilbert went on to discuss Barry's financial affairs in a bar one evening when a friend approached and indicated to Gilbert that Barry was having some problems with his landlord. The speaker had made no reference to money, but Gilbert, in the company of three or four others, saw fit to raise the issue. He was advising his other friends that, should Barry request a loan, they should not offer to bail him out, since he had not repaid loans Gilbert had made earlier.

GILBERT: She always be doin' that. You know, she needs help with that problem. She can't be goin' doin' her drugs, runnin' around wit' them boys, buyin' them drinks, and throwing grand diva parties, when she should be payin' her rent. That's the same old story wit' her. She always be doin' that.

As a senior member of the gay social scene in Harlem, Cleveland's opinions and advice were highly valued. He passed judgment on everybody's behavior in the bars and clubs, in church and at dances, and most especially in their relationships.

CLEVELAND: They always be up in church together. It don't take too much to work that out. Everyone sees them every Sunday. So they all know what's goin' on.... I admire her [Cecil] for tryin' to do somethin' for that boy [Cameron]. She dresses him nice. Gives him some spending money. But mark my words, he'll do something. He'll mess up. They always do. They're just plain no good. Ain't no good. And nothing you can do will change that. They just no good through and through.

Here Cleveland discusses the relationship developing between Cecil and Cameron. Cecil is a "church girl" and member of a clique of Baptist church supporters whose regular attendance and participation in church affairs in the neighborhood had earned them a special title. Cameron, a twenty-seven-year-old unemployed hustler who is kept by Cecil while struggling to overcome crack addiction, is a very popular member of the community. He is a tall, attractive man who has participated in the gay community since his high school years. A former lover had died and left him a considerable fortune (rumored to be a few hundred thousand dollars), which he squandered on drugs. Cecil met him in a bar one evening and has taken care of him since. This relationship was still going strong when I terminated the research and was well respected by other members of the community. For once, it appeared, Cleveland's predictions had not come true.

Recounting sexual conquests is one of the more common topics of "tea," especially in the social scene. Sometimes such gossip is based on the assumption that a sexual encounter has taken place. Often it involves "spooking" (catching someone in the act) or "outing" (disclosing that someone is gay). Richmond, for example, recalls, "And then the time when S—— and B—— were in bed, and Miss D—— walked in one them.... We laughed about that for hours. We just kept on with the stories. Right up till midnight."

Having homosexual experiences is not enough to establish one's gayness. For these gay men, being able to talk about these experiences with style and wit is also required to maintain gay social standing. As a vehicle for demonstrating knowledge and expertise and for giving advice and strong opinions on social relations among gay black men, the mastery of such "tea" is essential for the performance of a gay black identity. Being especially clever with the language of "tea" can also bring a man prestige within the gay scene.

## The Scene

Most gay black men regard active participation in the gay scene as an important means of expressing their gay identity. Socializing in bars and other public institutions, reading the gay press, and supporting gay businesses are activities that contribute to a gay "sensibility."[19]

In Harlem there are very few businesses identified as exclusively gay. Many customers may be unaware that the managers of some stores are gay, yet the businesses known to be operated by members of the gay scene, such as flower shops, hair salons, and mortuaries, are strongly supported by a gay clientele.

ZACHARY: I buy my meat from a gay butcher. I get my haircut by my dear sister B——. I go to gay films. I go to hear [Louis] and [Francis] sing. I go to the Cotton Club dances. I've seen [Hamilton] dance. I do anything if the girls are involved. That's being gay to me.

Supporting gay friends in their "endeavors" is also important to "being gay."

ORVILLE: I have always tried to support my friends in their endeavors. I always try to patronize gay stores, or places where gay people work because I feel that if someone hires an openly gay employee, then we should show our appreciation and support their business.... Like [Gregory]. I always go to him for my flowers. It's a bit out of my way, but he lets me phone in orders. Then I pay him when I see him.

Although no specifically black gay publication is available in Harlem, some of my informants ocasionally read mainstream gay papers, including the *New York Native* and *Outweek*.

Most important, maintaining a presence in the gay social scene is regarded as essential not only to the maintenance of that scene but also to the experience of being gay.

LESTER: Personally, I think it's important for us to keep going to the bars and places. I mean they're the main part of gay life. So many queens won't go out no more. I understand and all, but if we don't go, they're gonna close them all down. And then where will we all go? The scene is the most important part of gay life. It's where it's all happening.

The gay bars in Harlem, although not owned by gay men, are well patronized by a gay clientele. The bathhouse is also always well attended, and various other social clubs are frequented by gay men, especially if gay employees are regularly present or if gay entertainers are performing. These institutions constitute the core of the gay "scene," and some men deem participation in it to be an essential part of one's gay social identity.

MOSES: You ain't gay 'less you go to the bars. All gay people everywhere, all over the country, men and women, they be goin' to the bars. It's like the most important part of gay life. It always has been. That's how you know someone is really gay. When they start turnin' up at a gay bar. It's always been like that, too. Even for us. I mean we all knows one another from the church. But it was at the bar that we came to know each other best.... It's here where we relax. That we can carry on.... It's a way of life. The bars are a part of that. It's part of us. It's says what we are.

Yet it is important to note that in Harlem some men find it unnecessary to frequent gay bars to maintain a gay identity.[20]

LEONARD: I have many friends like that. Sure, they're gay. They have sex with other men. It's just that they don't hang out in the bars. You know, maybe they don't drink, or they don't like the stigma of being associated with the sleaze. 'Cause it can be sleazy. Look at [Pete's Paradise]. It's really a filthy place. They haven't cleaned that place in years. Not since I've been comin' out. And you can be damn sure they haven't painted the place since it opened centuries ago. So, yeah, I don't blame them. You know, for not wanting to come out. Not when it's like that. Plus all the kids doin' their drugs and stuff. And the hustlers. They can wear you out sometimes. There's really no small, quiet, intimate type place to meet friends. It's all loud noise and music and people and drugs.

In fact, most gay men in Harlem do not frequent the gay bars and clubs there, yet they maintain social networks of gay friends in the gay community. They socialize elsewhere in Harlem, in other ways.

MILTON: Most of my friends don't know about the bars and clubs. They'll probably be most interested to hear from you! You probably know more about the scene [in Harlem] than they do.... Most of them are from out of town. Yes. And most of them are middle class. You know, college educated, professionals. They don't drink in bars period. Let alone these after-hours clubs around here.... We spend most of the time having dinner together. Going to the movies or a play. Maybe shopping on Saturdays. Going to each other's homes for dinner. But most of the time we don't socialize in the scene.... What's really interesting is that many of these men, my friends, wouldn't be able to function in the bars. In the scene here. They've never been exposed to that culture. I mean they wouldn't know how to pick up a man in a bar. They don't do drugs or drink that much. I know they wouldn't enjoy themselves.[21]

## Other Gay Activities

Maintaining a household, being able to cook and entertain, maintaining a busy social calendar and a large social network of close friends, keeping in contact with family, obtaining a good education, and maintaining a stable career are also important features of being gay for the gay black men in this study. These sociocultural aspects of the daily lives of gay men are seen as integral parts of their ability to function as gay men. Such activities, which contradict the popular image of being a man in Harlem, appear to be similar to those of most Americans.

WILBERT: No matter what time I get home, child, I'll always get up for work. I'm good like that. I never miss work. That's my life. If I lost my job, child, I'd be on the street.... Of course, you know I wouldn't. I know my mother and father won't allow that to happen. But you know what I mean. I'd be so embarrassed. What would the girls think of me. That's one thing. Gay men are always hard workers. Always.

Keeping house and an extraordinary ability to entertain with food are regarded as especially important attributes of being a gay man.

WALTER: Now, those children can cook. I mean it's more than the fact that they run that restaurant. They got that from their Mama. She was a great cook. A great entertainer. That's where they got that from. Both of them.... Anytime they be havin' a party, the children will be fightin' to go. 'Cause you know the children will have food down [well prepared and plentiful].

Most important, loyalty to and support of consanguineous kin are significant features of gay black life. According to my informants, this deep concern for kin is born out of being gay and a need for security.

PAUL: You look at [Louis]. He's paying for his sister to go to school [college]. A whole lotta his friends are doin' just that. Payin' for their sisters and brothers to go to school. Or helping out their best friends who're in school. Or their kids. You know [Clarence]. He has put all his kids through school [college]. Now that's amazing. Most straight people don't do that. They don't do that at all. And not with their gay children. If you see a gay man who's educated then you can know that he has paid for his education himself.

While all of these features of their cultural lives also encapsulate the values of mainstream America (Ehrenreich 1990), these gay men feel that they more often demonstrate the values that they are taught non-gay men espouse. They are very quick to point out that straight men, white or black, do not always maintain homes, cook and clean, cater and entertain. Many of them do not maintain close contact with their families or friends, let alone seek higher education or the advancement of careers.

SHERMAN: All this shit about the American dream. What is that? I mean we [black folks] are taught at school, and in church, and on television that we should have these jobs; we should look like this; have a car like this, and have a wife and children like this, and go to church. OK, so we buy it. We get caught up in the shit. The rat race. But if you tell me, we get there. We achieve those things. Well, maybe not the wife and children. You know, we gay men. But generally, you look around and you'll see that the ones in this society that make it, according to the dream, we're the gay ones.

Louis reinforces this idea, noting his achievements and the "jealousy" of his non-gay acquaintances.

LOUIS: [Paul] and I have been saving for this car, right? So, we've got the money together in a year. All these women in my office go on. "Oh, you're so lucky. You have a house in Manhattan, and do all these trips around the country, and go to the gym, and buy all these expensive clothes." You know they're dying to say it's 'cause you're gay and you ain't got no kids. But they don't realize it's just as hard. [Paul] and I are like two big kids. It costs a lot to keep us fed and housed and goin' to school. But they're jealous. They just can't make it on their salaries. And they're married and can't go out. . . . I do not want children. Thank God I didn't have any when I was young. 'Cause it is a burden.

While inequality of pay and other economic issues, as well as familial concerns, differentiate the experiences of Louis and his female co-workers, he clearly shares their aspirations and values and has, in his own opinion as well as in theirs, gone a long way toward achieving those goals. His successes may be a result of his "single lifestyle,"[22] but gay men in Harlem are part of extensive social networks to which they contribute financially. That is, they have economic obligations to "family" as well. In some cases this striving may be the result of a sense of insecurity vis-à-vis the individual's position in society, but most of these men agree it's because they are gay and black.

## Gay History

---

The achievements of gay men in Harlem are as much the issue of folklore and "tea" as they are of fact. Gradually a consciousness of a historic presence of gays in Harlem is emerging, not only among gays themselves but in the broader black community as well. Knowledge of gay history[23] and significant gay individuals and participation in major gay memorial events are important features of being gay. While the lack of archival documentation indicates that a record of such people, places, and events has not been well maintained, especially in Harlem, oral history contributes to the maintenance of a proud sense of achievement.

RICHMOND: We know all those grand divas were gay. Honey, just open thine eyes and see the glory of the word! Any of Langston Hughes's poems will tell you she's gay. I mean any of her work. Now, Miss Countee Cullen and her friends, they were a different story. They were well known. And then there were all those boys that used to hang out with them. And Gladys Bentley and all the bulldaggers [lesbians]! They were famous in Harlem for twenty or thirty years. Everyone knew them. And then later, there was Stormé and Octavia and all the drag girls. In the Jewel Box Theater. The whole gay thing has been around forever in Harlem, and everyone knew about it. And, what's more, honey, they loved it![24]

The most important event in the gay social calendar in Harlem is the annual drag ball (see chap. 4). As each year's ball slides into history, it becomes a memory embellished with legends about the queens in attendance and the activities that took place.

DONNY: I wouldn't miss that ball for anything, child. It's *the* event of the year. Everybody goes. All of Harlem society goes. An' I makes sure I'm there.... [Colin] be sellin' tickets back in December and January. An' the ball ain't till April!.... I believe it's been goin' for fifty years.

COLIN: The girls [drag queens] are fierce. They spend months getting their gowns ready. And the [hair]dos, child. The makeup. They're truly grand.

WILBERT: They give a prize to the best "Queen of the Ball." I think they get a trip to the Caribbean. All expenses paid.... That's where vogueing started here in Harlem. 'Cause they have a big parade, like models on a walkway.

The girls come out and pose and carry on. And the judges judge them. That's where those young children get the vogue thing from. But these old queens are divas. Truly fabulous.

In 1988 a few gay men at the Schomburg Center for Research in Black Culture began compiling a "gay catalog." They are assembling a library of books, articles, and news clippings that refer to gay black culture. As news of this effort has filtered through the gay community in Harlem, gay black men have begun to contribute materials. In time, these librarians hope to produce a written record of the involvement of gay people in the history of Harlem. Their efforts are regarded by many informants as important to the development of a gay society within Harlem and to the maintenance of the gay black identity.

## Gay Folklore

Gay people have pursued the justification of their position in American society through the establishment, recording, and presentation of a long history.[25] Where such a record is missing, myth or information of dubious validity has emerged to claim the famous as "one of us." The sexual preference of political and religious leaders, film stars, singers, and other "greats" has been discussed and embellished. Marlene Dietrich, Joan Crawford, John Wayne, and Burt Reynolds are among many Hollywood stars about whom rumors persist. Rock Hudson's homosexuality was revealed toward the end of his life, much to the surprise of the straight media.[26] The gay press retorted by saying, "What's news?" However, some stars do admit their sexual preference, for example, Marlon Brando, who admitted his bisexuality.[27]

This is also true, of course, of the black gay world. While gay historians have claimed significant black Americans as part of the gay tradition, in the name of diversity or racial equality, gay blacks have also incorporated the sex lives of prominent artists and politicians into their lore. The following are examples.

GERARD: Now we all know that [a prominent black actor] liked his white women. We all know that. But I've heard he liked his boys too. I heard he liked fair-skinned black boys. He had quite a reputation as a sex machine.[28]

ROMAN: She's [a prominent male R&B singer] in here all the time. Not so much now like before. She used to sit at that end of the bar [near the entrance] and cruise all the children when they came in.

GARVEY: I spooked Miss [same singer as above] on Fifth Avenue with her beau. He was a fine man. Tall and light-skinned. And you could tell he had the last body. He was fine, honey. Just fine. I give [her] points for that!

GILBERT: He [a prominent married singer] used to go to [Pete's Paradise] all the time. He used to come for the drugs. You know, it was easy for him to come in and do some stuff in the bathroom, or make contacts here for him to get some stuff. But I've seen him cruising the children too. I've seen him socializing with intent! He likes his men too. I believe that he's had several of them [hustlers].

Other stories about gay men in the past abound in the bars in Harlem. Many of my informants were able to recite a tale or two about some legendary gay figure. There was the famous choreographer who was evicted in the 1960s for fighting too much with his lover and vandalizing their apartment; the television star who could not refrain from having sex in Marcus Garvey Park through the 1960s and 1970s; and the male half of a popular married singing duo who frequented the most notorious of the bars, to buy drugs and sex, in the 1980s. One prominent married politician in the 1940s was believed to maintain a separate lodging near 125th Street so that he had somewhere to take his "trade" for quick sex. Many stories abound about the legendary figures of the Harlem Renaissance. There is the "Langston Hughes chair" in one gay bar, the apartment where Countee Cullen and Harold Jackman played out their long-term affair, the solicitation of young college students by the eminent Alain Locke, and tales of the restroom and park sex of Richard Bruce Nugent and Wallace Thurman.

While the sexual orientation of some famous black men (and women) has not been questioned—for instance, police records indicate the sexual preference of Countee Cullen, his father, and Wallace Thurman (Lewis 1989)—those whose sexual identity remains a mystery are often claimed as "one of the children" (members of the gay community). What is significant is that these people, whether or not "gay" or "homosexual," have been elevated to the status of cultural icons in gay lore through the creation of legend within the gay black community. (For example, in Isaac Julien's movie *Looking for Langston*, the search for a cultural identity by contemporary black gay men is symbolized by the search for the true sexual identity of Langston Hughes.[29] Thus the creativity of the gay black sensibility has incorporated these members of gay black society into "the Life" and the process to legitimate the social identity of being gay.

## Homophobia

Anti-gay actions have been experienced and witnessed by many gay men in Harlem. Both of the instances of verbal abuse that I witnessed during my fieldwork were perpetrated by teen-agers.[30] Experience of some form of anti-gay discrimination is as much a part of gay black culture as are many of the elements discussed above. If all of the members of a community share or are at least aware of this sense of rejection, then it becomes important to the social construction of their identity.

PAUL: Part of bein' gay is bein' ridiculed. They just don't realize that's what makes us more stronger. Whenever I encounter that bullshit, I come away angry. Not scared, but angry. And that's when I feel the most gay.

Thus discrimination is often turned around to reassert the positive attributes of being gay.

JEVON: Any queen can tell you about that homophobia shit. I mean, all of us has experienced that shit at some time or another. Like in school, or on the street. Even nowadays some of these kids will call at you on the street. Especially if they see you goin' in and out of the bars. They know what the bars are for. They know who and what you are. They just too young yet. Wait and see. If they're that interested to say something now, wait till they're eighteen or nineteen. Then we'll see who's the faggot. Wait and see. They'll be runnin' up in there lookin' for some stuff![31]

Fear of discrimination also has its roots in the church. The church, as an important social institution in Harlem, appears contradictory in its dealings with homosexuality.

EPHRAIM: Then there was the church. You know how those girls can get upset. As long as we not makin' any fuss or protestin' or shoutin' about it they leave us alone. But all of a sudden this thing comes from nowhere, and all the preachers start sayin' how bad we are, and how it was God's way of punishing us. . . . You can see what effect it would have here. I mean all those church girls goin' back into the community and tellin' folks that the gay children are evil and its their own fault for doin' all this nonsense. I can just imagine. . . . We were very lucky, I do honestly believe that. I mean most of us are known in the community. Most people can tell if you're gay or not. They can tell. We were lucky they didn't come after us. I often wonder about that.

Some churches, renowned for their sermons against homosexuality, condemned homosexuals and their "God-given punishment" earlier on in the AIDS epidemic. The Pentecostal and fundamentalist branches of the Protestant churches seem to be the most entrenched with homo- and AIDS-phobia, a strange situation given the fact that most of the congregation who became ill were not gay men.

LUTHER: I used to go to C. Baptist Church [a small fundamentalist church]. The Reverend H—— was pastor. I was sure he was gay. I really liked him. Then when AIDS hit us, he started on about homosexuals this and homosexuals that. I thought to myself, "This man can't be for real. What's he sayin'?" I don't go to church no more. It ain't right to be treatin' people like that.... Anyways, all the people gettin' AIDS at his church was the women.

However, most gay men in Harlem will be quick to note that experiences of homophobia are few and far between and that they feel more "at home" in their own neighborhood than in gay society where they are confronted with issues of race. Generally they feel that gays are more tolerated and better accepted in Harlem then they are in mainstream America.

CLYDE: I think it's because we are everywhere. We're in the schools, in the stores, in the bars, on the street, in the churches. We're everywhere. And everybody knows that. So they don't be startin' no shit.

When pressed to explain why they felt more accepted at home, most of these men mentioned that their success in surviving, maintaining jobs, and obtaining worthwhile educations owes to their social and cultural visibility as role models who attend church regularly.

BYRON: I know that my family, you know, my mother and sisters. I know they accept me. They have me and my lovers up in their homes. That's acceptance. And you know where it's from? It's from goin' to church. If l didn't sing in that choir, then they wouldn't know me.

Such men also attribute their acceptance to sexual issues not being especially significant in the black urban ghetto when compared to the more pressing issues of poverty, unemployment, poor education, teenage pregnancy, the production, distribution, and consumption of illicit narcotics, AIDS, and other health concerns.

## Racism

Racism does not intrude into the daily lives of most of the informants in this study. It may have been an unconscious force in the determination of some to reside and socialize in a black community, although all of them said they live in Harlem because they prefer black men as friends and lovers and because they prefer to live closer to family and other relatives. Thus they avoid prolonged contact with whites. Their interaction with white society is sufficiently limited so that they experience discrimination along color lines infrequently. When it does happen outside Harlem, however, it serves to reinforce their primary identity as black men, for it is more often along this color line that they experience bigotry in mainstream society than alone the line of sexual preference.

Some have experienced overt displays of racism outside Harlem in mainstream New York society and at work. Not getting promoted, being followed in stores and "served attitude" by white store clerks, and being stopped in their cars by police are examples.

Within the mainstream gay scene, racism happens quite frequently, according to these men. Many informants recounted instances of racism experienced in the predominantly white gay scene downtown. This is one of the reasons they do not like to socialize downtown. Attitudes of bar staff and other gay men on the streets are others. Not only are they followed on the street, treated rudely, ignored, or barred from certain premises, they witness or hear of physical abuse against black men in the gay scene on Christopher Street.

Also, some white gay men mistakenly maintain the image that all black men are sexually aggressive and well endowed.

BASIL: Most gay men I know have been treated that way. You know it. Whenever you walk down [Christopher] Street or into a bar. All the white boys be lookin' at your crotch. Even if you're a real sissy. They be thinkin' how much of a man you are. And that's just because you black.

While many gay black men enjoy the attention they receive, they believe that it is premised on inherently racist reasoning. As Garvey said, "I feel exploited sometimes. Demands are made. Sometimes in just the way white men look at you perform. You're typecaste." The myth of the black man as a surperstud, the "great walking phallus" (Hernton 1965), has been absorbed into white gay culture through the gay press and especially in gay pornography. The myth of the black stud as the ideal sex partner is even present in the culture of gay Harlem. However, for many of my informants who have direct experience with white gay society, this myth persists as a racist stereotype.[32]

The choice of my informants to live and socialize within the black community comes about in large part from a desire to "subtract" issues of racism from their daily lives.

## Summary

Various elements of gay culture are internalized by gay men as integral aspects of their gay identity. In Harlem, having gay friends and socializing with them, participating in the gay scene, and utilizing the expressive means of gay culture figure as important influences on the adoption and maintenance of a gay identity. Other important factors bearing on gay black identity are knowledge of gay history and folklore and the experience of homophobia and racism. These social and cultural factors complicate the merely psychosexual models of gay identity development that tend to dominate literature on homosexuality.

# 7

## "Different to Other Men": The Meaning of Sexuality for Gay Black Men

In the gay black community, sexuality is explored in many ways. Besides their variety of sexual experiences, gay men frequently discuss the topic of sexuality, not only sexual performances, conquests, partners, and preferences but the more philosophical issues at the heart of gay sexuality as well. In reflective moments, many gay men ponder why they are gay, what is special about being gay, and what it all means.

When a gay black man refers to himself or someone else as being "gay," we can assume that he is at least homosexual—that is, engages in same-sex behavior.[1]

GERARD: Now you take J——. He been carryin' on in the [Mt. Morris] park since I been alive. Everyone knows he's gay. He's an old queen. But he don't be comin' in the bars and all that. Some of the children been askin' him to come to parties and things. But he ain't havin' any o' that. He just goes up in the park and carries on.

However, additional information is needed to determine whether the individual is indeed "gay"—that is, not only homosexual but a participant in the social life of the gay community around him.

Gay black men are especially concerned with their homosexuality, as they perceive their sexuality as a distinguishing feature not only of their individual personalities but as a point of differentiation from other types of black men in the black community. Just as race distinguishes them on one level from white gay men, their sexuality distinguishes them from other black men.

## Into the Life: Gay Socialization

During the socialization of many gay black men, one major influence is that of the love relationships of their parents. Most gay men are raised in heterosexual two-parent households, and whether or not parents are in fact exclusively heterosexual, their children perceive them as such. Furthermore, since heterosexuality is the dominant image portrayed in public, gay men tend to be socialized according to heterosexual norms. If a gay man is attracted to other males as a child, consciously or not, his earliest model for interacting with men, emotionally, socially, and sexually, may be female. From watching and interacting with his mother, sisters, grandmothers, aunts, female cousins, and female friends, the gay black male may be less inclined than a non-gay male to reject feminine traits. This was the case among several of my informants.

LEE: I was always hangin' out wit' the girls. They'd be cussin' and carryin' on because Mama told them to take me with them. All they wanted to do was follow them boys around. That's where I got that from. I guess it came from them.... They were much older than me. Maybe ten years older. Or more. And whenever they went on a date I had to go to chaperone them. I used to watch them kissin' and carryin' on. Sometimes they'd be sittin' outside talkin' 'bout their boys, and tellin' each other what they'd be doin'. Now I was a young child. Highly impressionable. So I took it all in. I watched how they dealt with the boys. Their father [speaker's uncle] was very wealthy so there was always boys hangin' around. Those girls were a good catch. And the boys knew it.

These gay men may not only observe their female relatives interacting with men, they may also imitate them.

LOUIS: I remember my aunt tellin' my older sister to take her time with [Willie]. I remember her tellin' her that those kind of men only wanted one thing. And that was to have as many children as possible. And she'd say, "And you know what that means." But she knew what she was talkin' about. It wasn't just the babies. Or the sex. It was the fact that so many of those boys weren't around to take care of the young ones. They couldn't get themselves a job. So she was tellin' the girls to pick and choose. Not that any of them did. They got stuck in. I just [copied them].

In order to imitate the behavior of sisters and other female relatives, some gay men adopt an interest in things feminine—for example, dressing up in women's clothes or playing with dolls.

COLIN: I always been interested in dresses, child. Ever since I was a little girl! My mother used to catch me carryin' on in her clothes and into her makeup. She used to go off on me. But later on I think she just gave up. I remember when she was older that she'd always come and see me before I did a show or some thing, like the Ball, and she'd be givin' me advice about my makeup and shit. It was fun.

Some gay men may also empathize with the emotional responses they hear female contacts recounting in their relations with men; hence the tradition of strong affinity for the divas of torch songs—Garland, Dietrich, Piaf, and Billie Holiday. To quote Shawn, "Billie's ma girl. The way she sings about her men. Mm, mm. That's my life she's singin' about. Now that's the truth."

For some gay men, their parents' heterosexual, monogamous marriage is the only example of a devoted couple. One of my informants expressed his frustration with trying to maintain this idealized model of a loving relationship.

CECIL: I don't know why I let that motherfucker get to me that way. I love him. The only way I know how. My mother taught me that. So I know it's right. But he just upsets me all the time. He's always messin' up. Shit. Or around. And it's easy for him. 'Cause these bitches [other gay men] see he's loyal to me. But they don't understand that that takes hard work. They just throw themselves at him and he just takes what he's offered. But it hurts me. I was raised proper. My Mama and my Daddy were always close and lovin'. They had a lovin' relationship. Now that ain't too much to ask for, is it? I just wish these other bitches would appreciate that he's spoken for.

Gay men are often perceived as being effeminate socially and passive sexually. Some men who are overtly effeminate in their gay social lives may in fact be modeling their behavior on that of females who played important roles in their socialization. They may feel they have to act effeminately to entice a man, regardless of what they might actually want to do with him sexually. Effeminate gay black men, "sissies" in Harlem, may also be acting on stereotypical models of gay men prescribed for them during their socialization by heterosexuals. Such models are undoubtedly reinforced during schooling years, as effeminate men are usually harassed by peers at that age, regardless of their role preferences in sexual encounters.[2]

While women provide early models of behavior for some, further socialization into gay life for most gay men takes place within the gay scene itself. Language, nonverbal expression, clothing styles, a sense of history and community, as well as details of sexual and other associated behaviors are all learned by talking with or observing other gay men.

DEMOND: I learnt everything I know from Miss [Francis]. She taught me everything I know about bein' gay. She knew it all. I mean there were some things I knew about myself. But she taught me so much. About dressin' up and how to carry myself. How to pick up men. How to act once I got one. She even taught me a few tricks I didn't think anyone could do.... When I first heard that she liked to [be active with her] men, I screamed. I said, "No you don't, Miss Thing." I always remember her. She fell out. She could hardly tell me about all those men she'd [been active with sexually]. I mean could you imagine her. She's a big woman. All dressed up in one o' her dresses, and being the top man!

The evidence thus suggests that the process of socialization for some gay black men begins in the home with non-gay family members as early role models and continues into the gay scene itself. Most gay men have been subjected to the stereotype that they are not really men. As boys, they are pressured to live up to prescribed standards of masculinity. If they sense at an early age that they are really different from other boys, some may realize that female examples of behavior are no less valid than the ones prescribed for them. For most gay men, socialization into a gay identity occurs among peers, where old stereoypes of homosexuality are challenged by new models of masculinity.

## Sexual Behavior

The significance of collecting data on sexual activities is that it enables the anthropologist to deconstruct received notions concerning traditional sex typologies and to provide an insider's perspective on sex and the meaning of sexuality.

In the gay black population, two types of men are clearly defined.

This is a generalization, for, as in gay populations anywhere, a continuum is present of types of men, whether defined by social behavior or sexual activity. These types are "sissies" and "men," that is, effeminate and masculine gay men, who usually partner each other in sexual intercourse but whose difference is displayed socially in a variety of expressive media, including clothing, language, nonverbal gestures, and types of drinks.

My data on sexual behavior include both hustlers and non-hustlers (the "boys").[3] Despite their intentionally traditional masculine social behavior, hustlers are experiencing gay culture in their daily lives and they are establishing gay identities by participating in certain sexual behaviors usually defined as "gay" or "homosexual." The "boys" give all the appearance of being heterosexual men. They dress, walk, talk, and otherwise enact a butch persona. They are presumed to be exclusively dominant in the sexual ecounter; they certainly maintain that image in public. Yet according to their personal accounts and those of their sex partners, they often assume a receptive role in the sexual encounter.[4]

LOUIS: I had him. He's a big whore. Big ass on him. I really got lost in all that stuff.

HARRY: He [Darryl] is flexible. You know. He goes both ways. But from what I know, and, honey, I know, he always bendin' over. Ask any of the boys. And the girls. He done had everybody.

The "butch" persona presented to the gay community, and indeed to the surrounding mainstream black community in Harlem, counteracts the "sissy" image presented by some gay men in the scene who are their prospective partners. Yet the presentation of gender roles in public does not necessarily follow into ensuing sexual encounters.

Likewise, data on sexual behavior were collected from the fifty-seven respondents involved in the life history collection for this study. Living an openly gay lifestyle in the environs of their hometown, many of these men are regarded as "sissies" (not altogether pejoratively) by the surrounding community. Their adoption of female gender-role traits in the gay scene not only contrasts with the expressed masculinity of the "boys" and other "men" but also confirms the presumption that gay men imitate and manipulate the gender roles that have been established in heterosexual society. Here, then, gay men are playing with ideal male and female roles. But in the sexual encounter, sexual behavior does not follow the expectations usually assigned to gender types. In other words, sexual role playing is not a reliable indicator of gender.

In Harlem we have a population of gay black men who have no problem reconciling their sexuality with their male identity. Through socialization and social experiences among peers, they fully accept their "gay" identity. In their sexual encounters, where private acts may contradict public appearances, they challenge the ideas of what gay men are supposed to do sexually and assert that they are still "men."

## Challenging Sexual Typologies

By collecting data on the actual sexual activities of individuals, we are able to redefine some of the received notions of homosexual and bisexual men and their sexual behavior and question the lines drawn between the sexual types: "heterosexual," "homosexual," and "bisexual."[5] In fact, most of my informants' sexual behavior over their lifetimes appears to have been quite fluid in terms of the received sexual topology. During their sexually active lives, they have practiced all types of sexual behavior.

Willis, who is thirty-four, is a good example. His first sexual experience was with a woman when he was fourteen. Shortly after this, he experienced his first same-sex encounter. While walking his dog in Marcus Garvey Park, he engaged in oral sex with an older man. Throughout his high school years, Willis would visit the park several times a week. Some years after school, when he was working downtown, he met up with some other gay men and began frequenting some of the gay discos of that era, especially the Loft and the Flamingo, popular with gays and blacks. At the age of twenty-eight, tired of "running around" and of several failed attempts at settling down with a male lover, Willis befriended a long-standing neighborhood girlfriend. After a few months their relationship became sexual, and his son was born in 1984. Shortly afterward, his "wife" left him to follow her newfound junkie friends, and Willis was left alone to raise his child. He has since attempted to find himself a male lover. During the period of the research, he was dating a slightly older black man and planned to move in with him. He describes himself best.

WILLIS: I'm gay. That's all. I'm just a gay man.... Most of the gay men I know have had sex with women. Lots of us have children to prove it. But that's just part of growing up. Or wanting to have children, and doing something about it. We're still gay.... I'll always be gay. That's how I see myself.

To categorize Willis as exclusively homosexual or bisexual, or to say he made a choice to be gay, would indeed be incorrect. We need to break down the rigid sexual typologies that have caused so much inaccurate reporting and labeling of people, especially homosexuals and bisexuals. Such typologies have also encouraged ideas of deviancy and promoted oppression by those who think they are in the majority.

## Sexuality and Social Status

Gay black men include homosexual behavior as an integral part of their being gay,[6] but the construction of their gay identity, as well as an understanding of what homosexuality means for them, can only be extrapolated from data on sexual behavior, socialization experiences, and an analysis of the social context of the development of these experiences.

Most of the gay black men who participated in this study are well known in the black community. They have an important niche in black society as a distinctive type of black man, although this is not necessarily a result of their sexuality alone. It is more often than not a result of their contributions to the social life of their respective communities. However, this distinction is usually expressed in terms of their sexuality.

NICHOLAS: I don't see myself as different to other men. Except, of course, I have sex with other men. And of course, I'm a different color to some other men. But it's not that important, is it? You have shown me that. You're just you, and I'm just me. The fact we're different colors doesn't matter. So it really doesn't matter if we sleep with men or women. It just doesn't matter.... But, of course, society thinks it matters. That's why you have prejudice. That's why folks don't be likin' white folks. That's why they has to have something to say about us gays. If you ask me, it's jealousy. Because they see the gay children being gay, even in the face of this epidemic, they're, how do they say it, they're "fabulous"! The gay children are doing just fine. So, they're different to other black folks, they're different to other black men. So, I guess there is a difference. You know, a difference between us and them, you know, the other black men. We're gay and they're not!

CLEVELAND: We're different from other men. There's all kinds of men. And we're one kind. We're different to other men.

LOUIS: You see we are different. We have a different consciousness about what's going on in our lives. We've lived as black men too. We know it ain't easy. But we have something else that's driving us to make an effort to survive, as best we can. I thank that drive comes from the fact that we're gay. Whether it's happened to us or not, the fear of being abandoned by your friends, or family, or job, because you're gay, it makes you want to work that much harder to survive. So in the end we come out doin' OK. It ain't easy. It's like being insecure I suppose. But there you have it. We're different.

Louis distinguishes himself most emphatically from the black men "that you white folks talk about." Having read Liebow (1967), Hannerz (1969), and Stack (1974), he distinguishes between social science's rendition of black men (that is, the white idea of black men) as "street corner men"—an image constantly reinforced by both the white and black media[7]—and his own idea of gay and straight black men.

LOUIS: Nothin' pisses me off like when the white folks talk about the dying race of black men. I'm livin' proof, baby. Here I am and I'm doin' just fine. We [gay black men] may not be the kind of man you were lookin' for, but we are men nonetheless. And we're doin' fine. In fact most of the men, gay or straight, most of the men that I know are doin' OK. Some may be struggling to keep those kids in school, but we're makin' it.... I really don't know, Bill. I don't know where those reporters and those other writers are gettin' their stories from. Well, that's not true. You see if you come to Harlem, and walk around the street, of course you're gonna see all these hustlers and bums. That's all that's around any neighborhood. Day and night. Just hangin' out. Most of the real men are at work! Day and night. We all need two jobs to live in New York. You know that! No matter what color or class you from. So if you come snooping around the neighborhood, what do you expect to find? What kind of men would you expect to find in the middle of the daytime in any neighborhood?

Louis sees himself first as a man, then as a black man, and then as a black man who also happens to be gay.

LOUIS: Look. The only way I know to distinguish myself from other men is by sayin' I'm gay. Most of the men I know have jobs and nice homes and families and so on. OK there are the bums. Well. I hope you can see I'm different to them! But from a point of view that compares me with other men of my age and education and class, the only difference is that I'm gay.... Yes, that's right. Being gay is the difference between me and other men. Other things like job and that may distinguish me from other types of men, but being gay crosses all those things. You know, it's like a brotherhood between us gay men. Then there's a brotherhood between all of us black men. Say, as opposed to white men. Or Spanish men. Then, we're all men together.... I'm a man, who is black and gay. That's how I describe myself. In that order: man, black, gay. But it's all one person. I'm all o' those together.

One of the reasons gay black men in Harlem openly express their gayness, especially to outsiders, is to distinguish themselves from more marginalized types of black men in the black community.

JEVON: I make sure of that, honey. I make sure of that. I don't want to attract unnecessary trouble, as you can imagine. But I sure as hell let them know that I'm gay. And that they better not mess with me unless they know what the story is. I mean really know. Don't go countin' me in with the numbers on the street. Just because I know them or hang out with them. [Don't think] I'm always on the street. No sir. Not me. I'm different. And I lets people know.

SHERMAN: Most of my family know. So it doesn't matter if Mrs. Jones or Mrs. Black sees me goin' and comin' from the [gay] bars. They all know. And they know that makes me different to the other guys runnin' out on the street. They know I'm different. Respect me different.

"Being gay" and openly expressing that in the black community brings this distinction home to other blacks. And it is reinforced by other things gay men do, such as buy homes, educate themselves, hold down good jobs, attend church, and contribute to the well-being of their extended families. Along with the open expression of their sexual orientation, their social behavior in the black community reinforces the distinction between them and other black men, whether "street corner men" or members of the black middle class. For most people in Harlem, issues of survival—getting food, paying for shelter, providing for dependent relatives, schooling children, and maintaining health—are more important than concern about people's sexuality. Thus simply being sexually different in Harlem does not generally provoke antagonism or being categorized as deviant.

## Summary

In this chapter I have described the adopted sexual and gender roles of gay black men in Harlem through the study of sexual behavior. A social-interactionist perspective has enabled me to offer alternative theories on socialization and the meaning of sexuality for this population. Being gay in Harlem means more than simply engaging in same-sex behavior. But it certainly includes that basic ingredient. Being openly gay is a significant social statement concerning one's status in society. Being a gay black man in Harlem means that one is different, but not less than other black men in the community. By coming out and being openly gay, gay black men are able to assert their identity in order to affirm their difference as a positive attribute.

# 8

## "This Epidemic Thing": Gay Black Men and AIDS in Harlem

> The saddest thing about being gay? I guess it's this
> epidemic thing. It's changed our lives. People we
> know have died. All kinds of people. Men, women,
> children, gays, straights, old people, young people,
> friends, family, neighbors, school friends, church
> friends. It's everywhere. It's frightening. It's really
> scary.
>
> —Willis

In the memories of most of my informants, intravenous (IV) drug
users, male and female, gay and non-gay, were the first to become ill
and die of "this epidemic thing." Thus, at first at least, my informants
considered AIDS an IV drug user issue[1] and by extension, because IV
drug users in Harlem tend to be poor, an issue of class and poverty.
The gay black men who are the focus of this study are connected socially to this IV drug user population through their extended social
networks, which reach across all social classes.

The next group of people my informants saw become infected were
gay black men who had regular sexual contact with "the white gay
scene" (that is, mainstream gay society downtown). Their observation fits with the information, available to my informant population,
in the press in New York City. This particular population of gay black
men, who come from Harlem but do not include any of my informants, has been devastated by the current AIDS epidemic. In New

York City they make up almost 25 percent of the total number of gay males diagnosed as having AIDS (New York City Department of Health 1989). For this reason, the importance of measuring the impact of the AIDS epidemic on the black gay population has become urgent.[2] This is all the more important because much of the research into the sociological impact of the epidemic on the gay community in New York has focused on the white mainstream gay community.[3] The ratio of black and white respondents in these surveys does not proportionately represent the "people of color" of either the city or the gay community.

Even though some concern is now expressed for the disproportionate occurrence of HIV-AIDS in black and Hispanic populations in New York City,[4] it is still perceived as a disease of IV drug users and gay white men.[5] However, in Harlem, the nature of IV drug use has meant that HIV has been transmitted to women and children. As the AIDS epidemic caught the attention of mainstream America, particular groups of people (gay men, initially) were identified as being more "at risk" of contracting the disease. By shifting attention away from the virus itself, and onto particular people as agents of the illness, AIDS quickly became a disease that "other" people got. By singling out gay men as carriers of the disease, non-gay people could comfort themselves with the mistaken notion that difference was the cause of illness. My informants have seen that the spread of AIDS does not discriminate according to sexual identity. These gay men are not creating a scapegoatable "other." They fully expect that HIV will arrive in their midst.

This is not to say that gay men in Harlem have not died from AIDS or been diagnosed with the disease. According to my informants, the gay men who have died or are ill all had or have social and sexual connections with the mainstream gay community downtown or with gay friends and sex partners in other areas of the city that have been affected by the epidemic—for example, Spanish Harlem and the Bronx. But the discrete gay population upon which I have stumbled in Harlem limit their social and sexual lives within Harlem, and within an exclusive population of black men who seemingly have been able to remain AIDS-free even as family members and acquaintances have contracted the disease. This is not because they practice "safer sex," because they do not. Nor is it because they have refrained from certain immune system–suppressive behaviors, such as cigarette smoking, alcohol consumption, narcotic use, or poor dietary and sleep habits. They have simply been lucky. By avoiding sexual contact with the IV drug user community (which for many has in fact been a conscious effort) and by selecting sexual partners out of a neighborhood pool of potential men, they have been protected so far from the onslaught of this epidemic.[6]

In the face of the epidemic, gay black men in Harlem have reinforced an earlier commitment to their community, their families, and to each other in their extensive and resilient social networks. Moving closer to kith and kin is but one of their many social responses to the AIDS epidemic. The social networks of gay black men have provided them with the emotional support to withstand the psychological impact of the epidemic as they witness the havoc the disease wreaks on their non-gay relatives and friends. At the same time, the gay acquaintances in these social networks have provided them with a discrete circle of potential sexual partners that may have spared them from, or at least delayed, the actual arrival of HIV in their midst. Nevertheless, the epidemic has an impact on the identity of these gay men. Repression of sexual freedom, the modification of social and sexual behavior, and the fear of increased discrimination have all influenced what it means to be gay.

## Knowledge and Belief about AIDS

Forty-nine percent of the men in this study first heard about AIDS from gay friends and 46 percent from television or the written media. The remainder heard about the illness from lovers or family members. All admitted feeling shock and dismay at the news. All heard about the disease between 1979 and 1984 but most in 1981 (when it was known as GRID) or in 1982, when the illness was first given the acronym AIDS.[7]

Following on the heels of early media headlines of AIDS as a "gay cancer," the belief that this illness was a gay men's disease became well established not only among gay black men but in the black community at large.[8] Ninety-eight percent of the respondents in this study believed AIDS "largely" or "mainly" affected the gay population[8] (complemented by male and female IV drug users). A third of the informants indicated that they believed the disease to be predominantly a white gay men's issue.[9] Also, the media persist in portraying AIDS as a disease of white gays and IV drug users (Albert 1986; Baker 1986). Reinforcing this view is the fact that in the large gay social scene in Harlem, only a few of the 156 gay black men I spoke with have known members of the gay community to have died with an AIDS-related condition since 1984.[10] Thus if they consider AIDS a "gay-related illness," they also consider it primarily "white."[11]

## AIDS in Harlem

Confusion reigns when informants reflect on the disease and its origins. Although the media during the period of study did indicate that gay men were still the one category of people at highest risk for the disease in New York City,[12] the reality of the epidemic in Harlem tells another story.

The epidemiology of AIDS in Harlem and many other poor black and Hispanic neighborhoods in the inner city is vastly different from that elsewhere in the United States, save Miami, Atlanta, and Washington, D.C. Gay black men have known mainstream gay men of all races to die from AIDS. They have seen male and female IV drug users in Harlem die from AIDS. Now they see women and children ill and dying with AIDS. My informants expressed disbelief that many saw AIDS as only a gay issue. "Let them come to Harlem. It's straight men and straight women.... They be the ones getting the AIDS," Kevin remarked. In Harlem, AIDS is a "disease" any black person can fall victim to, not just gay black men. In fact, straight men and women and children are more likely than gay men to become ill, mainly from IV drug use or from sex with infected men (New York City Department of Health 1989:5–6, 15–16). In Harlem, knowledge of this is based on observation of the situation; residents are well aware that the most common routes of transmission in their community are shared needles, heterosexual behavior, and births.

Yet popular beliefs that AIDS is only a gay disease have instilled fear in many gay men in Harlem, fear not only of the disease itself but also of irrational discrimination against those considered to be responsible for the spread of the virus.

TERRY: I remember us joking that we'd have to move outta town. Nobody'd be wantin' to deal with us. I honestly thought they'd close all the bars. Especially when they started to downtown. You know, close all the baths. But they didn't do that up here. It was very confusing, really. You didn't know what to expect. It was a bit unnerving. Especially being gay.

The churches in Harlem were originally reluctant to attend to the AIDS community (Greaves 1987; Quimby and Friedman 1989), but the established Baptist and Methodist churches have shown more compassion in recent years.[13] The strong presence of gay men in these churches may well have played a major role in their change of heart. Some have now established soup kitchens and other social services for people living with AIDS.

Many social variables need to be considered when measuring the effects of AIDS on different populations. In the black community, all ages, socioeconomic groups, genders, sexual orientations, and religious and political persuasions have been affected. The fact that the condition appears to be fatal more rapidly among blacks and Hispanics could be the result of a variety of resource constraints, not the least of which is lack of access to health care.[14] And the stresses and poor nutrition related to poverty undoubtedly complicate the health issues confronting people whose immune systems have been compromised by the HIV virus (Carillo 1988).

## "Risky Business"

All gay black men in Harlem with whom I spoke were well informed of the risks involved in certain behaviors with regard to contracting AIDS.

COREY: Of course, I know that shit. I know you're supposed to wear condoms, or pull out before you cum. I know that. You know, having sex is risky business. But it always has been. You just gotta do what ya gotta do.

Generally, gay men in Harlem understand the routes of transmission of AIDS and the ramifications of persisting with unsafe sex practices (May, Anderson, and Blower 1989). Yet when interviewed, none of the respondents had used condoms in their sexual encounters specifically because of AIDS. Some had used them in the past to avoid mess, in situations where other sexually transmitted diseases may have been an issue, or as contraceptives in a heterosexual encounter. Most refused to use them because they thought condoms were uncomfortable or difficult to use or interfered with the spontaneity of the sexual encounter or because they believed their partners were not infected.[15] Moreover, their sexual encounters were often unplanned and they were not always carrying condoms. None raised the issue of risk associated with drug or alcohol use, yet most of their sexual encounters, even with lovers, occurred after drinking or drug use in bars, at parties, or at home.[16]

The continuation of unsafe sex practices may in fact reflect a supposition voiced by Merrill Singer and colleagues with regard to Latinos in Connecticut.

The Northeast Hispanic AIDS Consortium study in Hartford found that individuals who complain of receiving too much AIDS information are more likely to engage in risky behavior than those who say they get about the right amount of information. It may be that individuals who are tired of hearing about AIDS stop listening to AIDS prevention messages and are thus more likely to engage in risky behaviors. Conversely, individuals who have decided to engage in risky behaviors may be resistant to AIDS information because they do not want to hear about the potential consequences of their actions. (Singer et al. 1990)

This "overload" theory may help explain the presumed return to unsafe sex that is capturing the headlines of both the mainstream and the gay presses across the country.[17] Lack of safe sex practices in Harlem may also reflect the lack of HIV-prevention education in the neighborhood, the refusal of the churches to become engaged in such efforts for many years (*The Body Positive*, 1989), and existing organizations' (such as Gay Men's Health Crisis and the Minority Task Force on AIDS) inability to reach successfully into this gay community.[18] At no time during my fieldwork did flyers, posters, pamphlets, or condoms become available to members of the community in their social gathering places. Such places are regarded by researchers as vitally important loci of education (Stall, Huertin-Roberts et al. 1990). At one time a single condom was distributed to each incoming client at the local bathhouse (Bronstein 1987). By 1987 the practice had ceased. This pathetic gesture was ridiculed by clients who usually had several partners on a visit.[19]

## AIDS and Discrimination

Given the increased discrimination against gay men in the United States resulting from the emergence of the AIDS epidemic in their population,[20] it could be expected that anti-gay behavior would also increase in the black community at large. Generally, this does not appear to be the case (Greaves 1987). In Harlem, only rarely did instances of verbal abuse convey anti-AIDS sentiment.

TIMOTHY: The only time I ever heard anybody say anything was on a street one afternoon. These kids called out, "Faggot!" as I walked by. And one of them shouted afterwards, "Yeah, and AIDS gonna get you!" ... It upset me. I was a little scared, 'cause you dunno what these boys will get up to, especially when they run in gangs like that. You know they won't do it if they're on their own. Or if their parents are there. It's too much. But that's the only time I ever heard anything.

Although they fear increased stigmatization because of AIDS, gay men in Harlem do not view such discrimination as a major issue. However, AIDS has increased the black community's awareness of the presence of homosexuality and of the presence of gay men on the streets. According to my informants, AIDS has not led to increased "gay bashing" in Harlem, although they fear this may yet happen.

## AIDS and the Gay Black Community

Although these gay black men are not becoming ill with and dying from AIDS, they are being affected by the epidemic. They are losing non-gay and gay friends, neighbors, and even kin to the disease.

Louis is well acquainted with the AIDS epidemic. He has known ten gay men who have died from AIDS and five people who are currently ill with the disease. Eight of the deaths had occurred before my fieldwork commenced in 1987. Six of these deaths were in Washington, D.C., where Louis had lived for ten years in the 1970s. Five of them were acquaintances; only one was a close friend. That friend was a former lover of one of his Washington roommates. Although he had not seen him during his illness, Louis returned to D.C. for his friend's funeral in 1985. The two deaths in New York were acquaintances from his neighborhood in Harlem. Both were men about his own age. Their deaths brought home the reality of the epidemic, especially as he watched them deteriorate.

LOUIS: Their deaths really affected me. I mean every time we saw them they looked worse. Just a long gradual thing. It was so sad to watch them die. It certainly affected me. I don't play around as much now. I think I'm just happy to be alive. And that [Paul's] alive. And I want to keep it that way.

During the period of my fieldwork, Louis attended the funerals of two more friends who had died in New York. One was an old school friend who passed away in New Rochelle. The other was the roommate of a close friend in Harlem. Neither was involved in the gay social scene in Harlem. In fact, the friend who lived in Harlem had a lover in Brooklyn, where Louis said he had socialized most often. That lover also has AIDS. Although he saw neither of these men during their illness, the fact that they are no longer alive has troubled him deeply: "I'm finally getting a sense of what it must have been like for those guys in the Village. They had all their friends die. Finally, it's coming uptown. I feel like it's arrived. Here in Harlem."

Currently, Louis knows one gay man in Harlem with AIDS. He is a twenty-four-year-old "brother" who has lived on Louis's block for some years. Louis has never seen him in the scene in Harlem and has only known him to socialize downtown. The fact that this man is so young upsets Louis, yet the epidemic is still at arm's length. Not one of Louis's close friends in Harlem has died from AIDS, let alone been diagnosed, nor have any of his relatives. The two women and two children he knows of who have AIDS are friends of his sisters and reside in Mt. Vernon, north of New York City.

Cleveland knows of four people who have died from AIDS and three people who have been diagnosed recently. A close non-gay friend from his church and a close gay friend, who was both a hustler and an IV drug user, both died in 1984. (The latter is the only member of this community of study whom I have heard about dying from AIDS). Cleveland also knew another acquaintance from church who had died, a gay man who had socialized elsewhere. He also knew a woman from his neighborhood who had died from AIDS. She was known to have been an IV drug user. The three current cases of people living with AIDS are gay men not known to him personally. One is an IV drug user, and one lives in the Bronx. None of them participate in the gay social scene in Harlem.

Of the five people whom Byron knows to have died from AIDS, two were also known by Cleveland. The other two men lived outside the neighborhood—one in Queens, and one in Spanish Harlem with his Puerto Rican lover. The woman Byron knew was an acquaintance from public school days. The four men Byron knows who are currently ill are all acquaintances he knows by sight through his church connections. (Two of them actually live in New Jersey.) He presumes that one or two of them may be gay, but he's not sure. He also presumes that IV drug use was the mode of transmission of HIV to the two women in his neighborhood whom he knows are now ill.

Hamilton's experiences with the dance world have not been all positive. He knows five dancers who have died from AIDS, but only one in New York City. The one local man, who was not gay, and a neighborhood woman and her child who died from AIDS acquired the disease from IV drug use. The one man he knows who is ill now was an IV drug user, as are the two women from his street who have AIDS. None of the gay men living with AIDS in Harlem are members of the gay social scene in Harlem.[21]

Although all of my informants know someone who has or has died from AIDS, none of them know anyone with AIDS in this discrete gay community within Harlem. Gay friends who are sick or who have died are acquaintances who socialized elsewhere in the city. However, my informants are losing friends out of their social networks. Non-gay relatives and neighbors and mainstream gay friends have become ill or have died. Only a handful are close enough to the respondents that they feel obligated to render some sort of care.

## Caregiving

As a result of much illness in the black community around them, especially in their own extended social networks, many gay black men have been affected by the caregiving and bereavement processes associated with AIDS. Only a few of my informants, however, are actively caring for people living with AIDS. Although some did express initial nervousness about their duties, none of my informants believed that the HIV virus could be contracted through casual contact.[22]

Willis travels to the Bronx once every two weeks to visit a friend who is living with AIDS. The friend has Kaposi's sarcoma and has had one visit to the hospital with pneumonia. He is constantly tired, very thin, and housebound. His mother, an elderly welfare recipient who lives in Harlem, visits once every two weeks. A couple other friends deliver food, but basically Willis's friend is alone. Because of this, Willis takes the time out of his hectic schedule of raising his son and trying to maintain a job to lend a hand. He cleans house for his friend, cooks a meal, and runs errands. He spends four to six hours each visit.

The young man whom Hamilton helps out is a non-gay neighbor who lives on the block. Shortly after he was diagnosed, one of his roommates died (at twenty-four) and the other moved out. He manages to pay rent from his savings (from his former employ as a bouncer at a disco in Harlem) and from his disability checks. Friends, including Hamilton and his sister, bring him food. He spends his days at home watching television because he is too ashamed to see friends and neighbors on the street. His girlfriend has also been diagnosed, and she has moved home to Queens to her parents'. His own family has abandoned him. Between them, Hamilton and his sister feed their friend five or six nights a week. Hamilton's sister helps him clean house and does his laundry on the weekends.

The twenty-one-year-old gay son of Leonard's first cousin was diagnosed with AIDS in 1988. He suffered a bad bout of pneumonia and was hospitalized for some weeks. His parents learned at that time that he was gay. Their reaction was to ignore his existence.[23] When he left the hospital he moved into the apartment of two friends in Brooklyn, only blocks from his parents' home. His parents have not visited him since. Leonard travels to Brooklyn almost every weekend to visit his cousin. He takes him walking and shopping, gives him "some cash dollars," and brings him some "home cooking." Often Leonard will also call on the young man's parents, in the hope that one day he will convince them to visit their son at least. Their religious beliefs and close attachment to the local Seventh Day Adventist Church prevent their acceptance of a gay son. Leonard says, "Their church produces more gay men than God hisself!"

Most of the respondents in this study do not have close friends, family members, or close neighbors who are living with HIV; these examples of caregiving are exceptions. The issue of caregiving is not that significant for most gay black men in Harlem.

## Bereavement

Garvey lost his roommate to AIDS in 1984, and he is still affected by it. They had been close friends for twelve years and had lived together for about five. His friend had rarely seen a doctor and just gradually "faded away." He died in Garvey's arms early one morning—a morning that still brings tears to Garvey's eyes.

GARVEY: He was so young, you know. So young. I knew that it would happen. For some time. He had been running around too much. I knew he was gonna get it. I prayed hard for him to recover, but nobody knew anything. There was nothing we could do. His doctor told us he should just stay home and be peaceful. . . . J—— was an artist. He made a lot of money.

Garvey's friend had had a succession of lovers, all white men, and was well known in the Christopher Street scene downtown. He lived in the discos and had been a heavy user of cocaine.

Garvey's roommate's family lives out west. When he called his friend's parents, they were very matter of fact about his death and asked Garvey to "take care of everything." Garvey organized a funeral—a wake in a funeral home on Lenox Avenue and a burial on Staten Island. He had the help of two very good friends who stayed with him, cooked for the wake, and helped him financially. The funeral arrangements cost him about $5,000—all of his savings. His friend's sister attended the funeral. She was the only member of a large family to fly in for the services. Garvey's friend had not made a will, so his sister automatically collected his money. When she left, she took the money from his friend's bank account and a life insurance policy worth "tens of thousands of dollars." She never visited the apartment, so Garvey had to go through the task of clearing out his friend's belongings. She gave Garvey no financial assistance.

GARVEY: I'm still sore about that. At least I had the money to do what I could for him. At least he had friends that came and made his farewell such a beautiful occasion. You can always rely on the children for that. They always pull through. Every time. You can rely on that. I'm happy that I did what I did. I just hope they feel satisfied when they get to spend his money.

Cleveland's buddy from the bar scene passed away from AIDS in 1984 as well. He had been a hustler and, Cleveland suspects, an IV drug user.

CLEVELAND: In those days they were dropping like flies. Even way earlier than that. Even before they said it was a gay cancer these boys [IV drug users] were dropping like flies. Your could see them deteriorate. You know, just wither up and die. When E—— passed, I really missed him. I mean he wasn't that close.

Like he never came home with me. But he would always come in the bar and keep me company. I missed him for a long time.

Cleveland attended his friend's funeral. He had come from a well-known family in Harlem, and the church was filled to overflowing. Cleveland presented his friend's mother with a "big" check (Hamilton said it was for $3,000) to cover the funeral expenses. She was a retired woman and did not have the resources for the lavish funeral that the community expected.

Of the fifty-seven respondents in the study, six had organized funerals or memorial services for non-gay family members who had died from AIDS. A further forty-one had attended funerals of acquaintances, family members, or neighbors who had passed away. Nineteen had contributed financially to their friends' funerals, and sixteen had performed at the services, singing or playing music.

WILBERT: I've played for two friends at home [Birmingham]. Now that was expected. But here, I've played for hundreds.... Well, not really. About forty or fifty. Most of them are people I don't know, but some of them were. You know, people I'd seen in the neighborhood. On the street. If I know it was one of the girls, child, I'd play my heart out. 'Cause I know they'll be sittin' up there lookin' down and sayin', "Play that box, girlfriend! Play it well, 'cause this is my last show!" After all, I'll have to face them up there one day. Lord willing! So I make sure I do right by them on their way out.

Wilbert related some of the typical incidents surrounding the services. He recalled that families often kept the gay friends away from the funeral, especially if the family was from out of town. Sometimes "scenes" would occur outside the church.

WILBERT: I remember one funeral. It was a sad day. I mean it was cold and wet, and a big crowd turned out. Girlfriend was a lawyer, with a white lover. So you know, she knew some people. A whole lotta white folks came uptown. Well, outside the church the mother arrives in this limo. She lives in a wealthy part of Detroit. You'd think it was *her* party! She served you fashions for your nerves. She carried on like Alexis Carrington! And when [the deceased man's] lover arrived, she turned her back. I heard that she sent some nephew over and asked if he would stay outside until the service was over. Apparently there was a commotion and the Reverend G—— had to step outside and calm everybody down.... Of course, they all came in. [The man's lover] and his friends just sat at the back. But that bitch carried on! She hadn't even seen her son in ten years![24]

Not one of my informants have been left an inheritance from family or friends who have died from AIDS. Only three had received some sort of memento, but that had been expected in each case. According to Louis, "Our society thrives on memories. And oral history. We pass on stories about friends and things we may have done together. And the memories. That's what's most important."

## The Impact

The effects of the AIDS epidemic in Harlem can be differentiated on the basis of psychological impact (Forstein 1989) and sociological impact (Patton 1985).

All of my fifty-seven respondents knew somebody who had died from AIDS. Roommates, friends, former school friends, acquaintances, neighbors, co-workers, and family members are missing from people's lives. In a section of town where death is a frequent caller, these losses add to many others.[25] For every friend who has died from AIDS, my informants could list two or three others who had died from other causes, notably from drug abuse or violence. Thus while AIDS has definitely made a profound sociological impact, the losses it has brought are regarded as another very sad fact of life.

In terms of the gay social scene, the impact of AIDS has been far-reaching according to my informants. Two or three respondents have ceased drinking and drugging; bathroom sex has disappeared; park sex has all but gone; and the frequency of sexual partners has dropped off dramatically. Although safer sex practices were not an issue for many of my respondents, three have admitted they tried using condoms after the end of the study, and several who frequented the bathhouse reported that much of the unsafe sexual behavior had "calmed down." People were even using condoms there too. Many have abstained from anal intercourse altogether, although none had stopped practicing fellatio.

As a result of AIDS, five of the hustlers, who were formerly IV drug users, had kicked their habits before the study commenced. Since then, all five have taken up "crack" or "ice," since, in Larry's words, "you can't get AIDS from smoking crack."[26] Although few of the hustlers are engaging in safer sex practices, some had abstained from anal intercourse by the end of the study period.

Psychologically, the epidemic has proved very disturbing to this community. Apart from the fear of becoming ill, concern exists that anti-gay discrimination may develop specifically because of AIDS and its presumed association with gays. The confusion surrounding the social construction of AIDS as a "gay disease,"[27] the experience of caring for persons with a terminal illness, and other bereavement issues place a psychological burden on members of this gay community. What is especially significant about the data on these issues is that they reflect the horrific impact of AIDS on Harlem. Not only has the disease itself reached women and children, gay and straight men, of all ages, classes, and neighborhoods, but it has psychologically damaged the survivors. Such damage continues to diffuse through the community as AIDS reaches more and more people.

## Issues for Identity

For some in Harlem, as elsewhere, AIDS has repressed freedom of sexual expression. Modification of sexual and social behavior has also influenced gay men's sexuality and identity. For many, the importance of particular sexual acts to being gay has declined. For these men, sex is no longer the primary element of being gay.

Fear of increased discrimination expressed in the rise of homophobic "gay bashing" in the mainstream gay community has returned many gay men to the "closet." We do not know what the impact on the next generation of gay men will be, although several researchers are working currently with gay men who have come to maturity during the AIDS era.[28] It is presumed that many will not come out into gay society at all for fear of retribution due to the association of AIDS with the gay population.

Some studies suggest that the gay population in New York, and in Harlem especially, are heavier users of illicit substances than most in the general population.[29] All of my informants consume alcohol or drugs on a daily basis. While no one volunteered that AIDS and its emotional effects had caused such behavior, several could see that it may have spurred "use" on to "abuse." At the same time, the epidemic is responsible for some of the men quitting alcohol and drugs. Both Gregory and Louis have stopped drinking because of their fear of contracting the HIV virus.

ROGER: All this shit has changed things. Man, there's no more gay in being gay.

THURMAN: All the gay things have gone. The discos, the parties, the clothes, the drugs. All the good times have gone. Even the drugs. The ludes and the poppers. It's all gone.

Fundamental aspects of the identities of these gay men have been influenced, if not altered, by the presence of the AIDS epidemic in their lives.

## Summary

CICERO: I have a sister and a sister-in-law with AIDS. I have a niece [age three] and a nephew [age four] with AIDS. How come? I'm a thirty-four-year-old gay man. I've done it all. I've been everywhere. I'm supposed to be the one who's sick. It's me that should be dead.

In this remark of Cicero's lies the impact of the epidemic on my informants. This discrete gay black community of Harlem has suffered little loss from the disease per se. Yet the social networks of its members have been affected; everyone knows someone who has died from AIDS or is currently living with the disease. Only a few have lost close gay friends, and always some years ago. The strongest impact on this particular community of gay black men has been psychological. The losses that have been close to many of these men have been female relatives and friends and their children.

Apart from the bereavement related to these losses, which I do not mean to belittle, there are many other side effects to this epidemic. As Cicero points out, it doesn't make sense that women and children are ill or dying, especially when compared to received knowledge about the epidemic in New York City. Information available to this population of gay men continues to portray AIDS as an issue for gay men, yet it is not directly affecting this particular population of gay men. This fact probably causes much confusion. Nevertheless, the epidemic is affecting them indirectly. And their anxiety that the epidemic can eventually strike *them* down has caused them to change sexual and social behaviors they normally considered important to being gay and black.[30]

# 9

## "One of the Children": Being a Gay Black Man in Harlem

This ethnography is about gay black identity: its expression in the lifestyle, social organization, and family life of men in Harlem. Its findings provide broader contextualization of gay black experience and challenge received wisdom concerning black men, sexuality, and AIDS.

### Being Gay and Black

Respondents included in this study reside in Harlem, conduct their gay social lives in Harlem, and prefer other black men as sexual partners. The fact that these men reside in a black community rather than a gay community is significant, especially when one of the world's most famous "gay ghettos" is located minutes away and when most of them have the means to make the move. The respondents socialize almost exclusively with other black people in their residential neighborhoods in Harlem. Members of their social networks include gay and non-gay friends and kin, who by and large also live in Harlem. Because family and friends are black and live in Harlem, and because social institutions central to being black are in Harlem, these gay black men choose to stay "close to home." In doing so, they are often choosing to avoid direct confrontation with issues of race and racism and to be with those who love and nurture them. Thus individual preference is reinforced by racial and social constraints.

Family and church remain the most significant aspects of the lives of these black men, much the same way that they are important to most black people, especially in Harlem. Ties among kin and fellow churchgoers are close and constantly pursued. The social networks of informants, which include kin and fictive kin, become important means of economic, social, and emotional survival.

But being black means more than this. It is more than just an issue of color. In other words, while race or skin color may be a defining or limiting factor, being black is a cultural identity. Some knowledge of black folklore and history and of contemporary cultural traits, including an interest in things African and an ability to participate in black "styles" of clothing, hair, speech, and dance, are also important aspects of being black.

All of these factors allow for the conclusion that these gay men perceive themselves first as black men. Their gayness is of secondary importance to their identity, even though, I argue, they express their different status in the black community through their sexuality. They overcome both the stereotypical exaggeration of the masculinity of black men and the assumed passivity of being "sissy" and become a different kind of black man. They express this difference both openly through their publicly gay social lives and privately in their assumption of the masculine role in the sexual encounter.

At the intersection of gay and black cultures, gay black men have constructed a culture of their own by drawing on distinctive elements of both. For many men in this study, sexuality is the only aspect of their identity that is different from other black men. For other gay men in Harlem, however, being gay means more than just being homosexual. Being gay means being involved in a community in which identity is expressed through membership in specific social institutions and through ways of living.

Because they feel tolerated, close to kin and other people in church, and secure in their hometown, these men are open about their sexuality and gayness. This open expression allows them to maintain their own status and niche in black society. A gay black man in Harlem is still a black man, just different from other black men in the community.

Reinforcing this sense of difference within the black community is a growing consciousness of gay black participation in the history of Harlem. Knowledge of gay life in earlier times in Harlem seems scant among my informants, mainly because the history of gay life in Harlem has not been recorded. This lack of attention to the gay past is being remedied through the collation of a catalog under the auspices of the Schomburg Center for Research in Black Culture.[1] Researchers are reading early editions of newspapers and magazines published in or about black society in New York and are extracting the very rare references to gay black life from police records.

The Harlem Renaissance is increasingly regarded as an important era in gay black history.[2] Some references to "homosexuality" and a "homosexual scene" are made in the novels and poetry of the time. During the 1920s and 1930s, Harlem saw the blossoming of the arts in black society. Many artists, writers, painters, and musicians were drawn from all over the country to this newly established arts mecca. Not only did black arts flourish but the artistry of black Americans reached into general American society, attracting the support of many wealthy white patrons and establishing the value of black artistry to American culture.

Many of the Renaissance writers were overtly gay. Richard Bruce Nugent and Countee Cullen had reputations widely publicized yet publicly ignored (Garber 1983:14–16, 1989:327; Lewis 1989:76–77, 196). Wallace Thurman has been described as "effeminate" and his police record of public lewdness has been exposed (Lewis 1989: 236, 279). His novel *Infants of the Spring* is perhaps the most openly "homosexual" of all the works of this period. Also, many of these artists, including Claude McKay and Raymond Barthé, were known as bisexuals (Garber 1989:327).

Much controversy exists concerning the sexuality of some of these heroes, as black society is trying to establish the significance of this artistic period in the history of American letters and black culture. For example, the sexuality of Langston Hughes remains the subject of debate,[3] yet his work obviously raises gay issues (see "Cafe: 3 A.M." and "Poem for F.S.").[4] What is most significant is not the rumors of the presence of these men in gay establishments during their lifetime, nor indeed that they may have been homosexual or gay, but that gay black men today, in their attempts to create and validate a cultural identity uniquely their own, have made cultural icons of these artists.

This was the thrust of Isaac Julien's extraordinary black-and-white docudrama on gay black life in the 1920s, *Looking for Langston*.[5] This movie sought to compare the ambiguity surrounding Hughes's sexual identity with the ambiguity surrounding gay black identity today, as gay black men seek a place and a voice for themselves within the emerging gay culture of the Western world. That Julien, basing the storyline on Nugent's short story "Smoke, Lilies and Jade" (1926),[6] invokes Hughes's name and sexuality is significant for extending the legend of this and other historic figures in gay folklore.

Many other significant gay men, black and white, were important to the Harlem Renaissance as intellectual mentors and fundraisers. Alexander Gumby, Alain Locke, Harold Jackman, and Carl Van Vechten[7] were well-known homosexuals who promoted the literary effervescence of the Renaissance (Garber 1983:14, 1989:327–328; Lewis 1989:288). They too have become important legends in gay folklore in Harlem.

On a day-to-day basis, differences today between gay black men and other black men are expressed in Harlem through a distinctive style—a style that draws on both black and gay cultures and finds its expression on the streets of Harlem and in the bars and clubs of the gay social scene. This fusion of black and gay cultures offers a rare glimpse at the social construction of a new cultural identity.

LOUIS: You learn all that on the street. And especially in the Life. You know. The children will give you fashion: clothes, hairstyles, jewelry, makeup, shoes, music, dance. They'll give you pose. Talk. No one can read you like a queen! No one can serve [wear] fashion like a queen! No one can dance like a queen! Now, you learn all this on the street.

One current example of original gay black expression is the "Gumby hairdo"—a razor-cut hairstyle, flat-topped and curving upward at the front. First appearing in black gay discos in 1986–1987, these haircuts, created by gay hairdressers in salons throughout Harlem, are now worn by black and Hispanic men everywhere. At the same time, gay black men brought bicycle clothing into the disco scene. Spandex shorts, bicycle caps, and bicycle pouches (waist or "fanny" bags) became de rigueur in black gay clubs in 1986. By 1987 white gays were wearing them, and in the summer of 1988, non-gay Hispanic and black and white men and women were wearing these items like a uniform. In 1989 the idea of rolling up an extra inch or two of leg length in blue jeans made an appearance in the gay black scene. In 1990 the style was absorbed by white gays and even by non-gay black men.

While much of this creativity in "style" has its roots in the gay black community, often these men will take an idea from black culture, change it, expand it, or simply use it in an innovative manner.

This transformational process is typical of many American subcultures that are socially constructed and develop in opposition to mainstream society. Various expressions and gestures among gay black men have their roots in black society. "Editing," for example, is a dramatic demonstration of conversational wit that has its roots in the black church. It assimilates the behavior of "shouters" who call out a word or sound of approval in response to the preacher's urgings during a sermon. Much of this verbal behavior, as well as the use of such female kin terminology as "sister," "mother," "daughter," and especially "girlfriend," has come from playing with gender roles that have been observed in frequent interaction with women in their families and churches.

At the time of this writing, "snapping" is still a gay black phenomenon. A single finger snap means approval or adds emphasis to a point being made verbally. A series of three snaps, or a single snap executed in an archlike wave of the hand above the head, indicates exceptional approval or agreement. While "reading," or redressing another for errant behavior or gossip, my informants often snapped directly in front of the face of the addressee or executed a series of snaps from head to toe in front and behind the addressee to stress the strength of their objections.[8]

"Vogueing," a particularly energetic and skillful dance performance, was introduced to New York's gay black community by gay black men from Atlanta in 1986.[9] As Jackie Goldsby (1989:34) notes, "As a dance, it's unorthodox. Kids use classical movements— some aerials, spins, and splits—but it looks untrained, natural. Vogueing shows that blacks and Latins can produce an art form that's our own." Originally appearing at Tracks, a gay disco in Chelsea, voguers struck fashion-model poses in time to the music. A large following ensured their popularity as they performed on the stage adjacent to the dance floor. Their success is due in part to a tradition in black and gay black dance halls and discos of individual members of the audience standing apart from the general crowd and performing dance routines. In some clubs, low platforms around the main dance floor serve as stages for these performers. Some such dancers earn reputations that lead to large followings. The Paradise Garage, one of New York's most famous black gay clubs in the 1980s, encouraged such performances.[10]

LIONEL: The place I learnt everything about myself was at the Garage. That's where you saw everything. I mean everything. Everything you could ever imagine. It was a powerful place. Any style of music or clothes or drugs or dance, especially dance. That's where it come from.... The Garage? It was a club to die for. We lived in the Garage. All weekend. It was a party for life. I have never seen so many fierce-looking men in one place at one time. It was over! I miss that place so much. I miss the people. I don't know where they've all gone now. I often wonder that.

By 1989 many gay men had adopted the practice of vogueing, then created a faster and more vigorous version. Their performances have even reached the monthly gay dances at Columbia University. As news spread throughout campus of the voguers' presence at the dances, many people turned up to watch their extraordinary gymnastic feats.

RICHMOND: Honey, let me tell you. They are too much. I mean, when we were doing it [in Atlanta], it was all about Miss Thing. Carrying on giving the children great fashions. And posing. Elegantly. Now these children have taken it to the limit, do you hear me. I mean I can vogue, honey, but not like that. Those children are crazy. All flyin' around the dance floor. They gonna hurt themselves.

At several nightclubs in the city, voguers have developed dance competitions, often held in concert with other significant gay events, fashion shows, or drag balls. Groups of young black and now Hispanic gay men organize themselves into "houses."[11] They often become affiliated with a particular gay bar in the South Bronx, midtown Manhattan, or in one instance Harlem. The "House of Xtravaganza" is one of the originals and the one with the most notorious reputation in Harlem. By 1989 several vogueing competitions were being held for trophies, and various nightclubs around Manhattan sought different "houses" to perform. The houses are named for fashion houses and goddesses—for example, the "House of Chanel," the "House of St. Laurent," and the "House of Labeija." They are renowned for clothing styles as much as for dance capabilities: the "House of Africa," for example, has "the fiercest voguers," and the "House of Fields" is sponsored by a Greenwich Village clothing retailer.

The music that developed at this time, to which the voguers perform their distinctive style of dance, is called "house music." It is now the preferred disco music at most clubs in New York, Washington, D.C., and Chicago, where it is touted as original. "Like its predecessors, disco and club, house is a scene as well as a music, black as well as gay.... House, disco, and club are not the only black music that gays have been involved in producing.... Still, the sound, the beat, and the rhythm have risen up from the dancing sensibilities of urban gay Afro-Americans" (Thomas 1989:25).

All of the expressive elements of gay black culture mentioned so far in this chapter are found in the gay black community and on the streets of Harlem. Gradually they diffuse into mainstream gay culture, but all of my informants insist that these elements have their roots in black society.

Because the gay black community exists within black society, much of what is expressively gay draws on elements of black culture, especially family and church. Gay black men frequent many of the cultural events and institutions of mainstream black society. One significant example is the Jazzmobile Festival in Riverside Park and the Harlem Day Parade every fall. In 1989 a group of gay blacks marched under their own banner in the parade for the first time. Although none of the informants in this study participated, almost all of them saw the group in the parade and cheered them on. Also, some of these men are jazz singers of some reputation in Harlem and sing in many non-gay jazz clubs. Gay black men also strongly support Harlem Week and the Studio Museum on 125th Street, and they actively participate in community programs such as after-school sports programs at churches in Harlem, arts programs at the YMCA, and fund-raising with groups like Men Who Cook.[12] It is through such participation that these men are exposed to black culture, contribute to it, and construct their own culture.

Community for most black people in Harlem comprises individual social networks of kinfolk and neighbors. Based on this model, gay black men have created a community consisting of their social networks of other gay black men. While this community also includes non-gay kin and friends, it is the core group of gay friends, who refer to each other by kin terms, that forms its backbone. Gay black men symbolically refer to this community they have constructed as "family," as in "We are family," "He's family," or "He's one of the children." Gay black men depend on these networks for emotional, physical, and economic survival. Members of the networks exchange money and other commodities, as well as child care services if they are raising children. Their interdependence fits well with the model of a support system that Stack (1974) has described for women in "the flats."

Commitment to these networks has increased during the years of the AIDS epidemic. Their networks have provided them both with the emotional support necessary to withstand the psychological impact of the epidemic as they witness its effects on their non-gay relatives and friends and with a discrete circle of potential sexual partners that, it appears, has spared them from, or at least delayed, the actual arrival of HIV in their midst.

The sociological impact of the AIDS epidemic is somewhat obvious. Primarily, this group of gay men has responded by regulating membership in their specific social networks and, therefore, the gay black community as a whole. This has meant that the pool of potential sex partners has been restricted. While gay black men have not necessarily pursued safer sex, the social construction of barriers around the community seems to have helped them avoid contracting the HIV virus.

Yet friends and acquaintances have been dying from AIDS for a long time in Harlem. The image of AIDS as a "gay disease" has been challenged by the reality of its epidemiology in the broader black community. In Harlem, heterosexuals die from AIDS. While gay black men, who read that AIDS is a gay disease, are somewhat confused, they are able to see that AIDS is indeed an issue not only for them but also for intravenous drug users and their sex partners.

Some members of this discrete gay black population are involved with caregiving and organizing and participating in the funerals of people who have died from AIDS. However, the epidemic has remained at arm's length for many and has not taken any of the gay "family" members. The psychological impact, however, has been quite devastating. Apart from the effects of bereavement and the stress associated with caring for the terminally ill, gay black men worry about the possibility of contracting HIV and the possible upsurge of anti-gay sentiment in the neighborhood as a result of the general misperception of AIDS as a gay disease.

## Conclusion

This initial ethnographic foray has revealed a distinct gay black culture within mainstream black society. By describing the social lives of these men and analyzing significant factors in their socialization, we can see that they take an active role in forming their identities. This is an important consideration when existing theories of identity development present socialization as a passive process for the individual. Assumptions surrounding issues of their sexuality have been challenged as well. These men are very much aware of their difference in black society, and they manipulate and negotiate that difference to distinguish themselves from other types of more marginalized men.

The impact of the AIDS epidemic on the members of the community has been measured, showing how pockets of at-risk individuals have thus far managed to avoid contact with HIV. Nevertheless, this population exists in an extremely vulnerable situation in New York City. It would be hoped that, in the rush to study, reach out, and rescue the IV drug user, and in the vitally important thrust to educate women about AIDS in Harlem, time is found to reach out and educate this special community of gay men. The need for such education has become especially urgent since two gay bars around 125th Street in Harlem have recently closed due to gentrification. Some of these gay men may enter the mainstream gay community to pursue their gay social lives. In fact, several of them attended the Gay Pride Parade in 1990. Participation in mainstream gay society in New York City may eventually increase their risk of exposure to HIV.

The minority outreach programs of the Gay Men's Health Crisis and the Minority Task Force on AIDS are the best avenues for intervention programs.[13] They should reach into the gay community through its social institutions, such as the remaining bars and bathhouse (Stall et al. 1990), as well as the churches, the central organizing institutions in the black community, since that is where the largest population of gay black men can be found (Greaves 1987; Quimby and Friedman 1989).

Perhaps one of the most effective ways to reach into the gay black population would be to "snowball" the social networks of selected gay men. These networks have been portrayed above as the essence of gay social organization in Harlem. Such networks of support would facilitate the education, intervention, and prevention efforts of outreach programs (Greaves 1987; Schinke, Holden, and Moncher 1989).

Black politicians should also be encouraged to speak out about AIDS, to support education efforts among their constituents, and to lobby for improved health services in the community (Tauer 1989). Yet when they spoke out against a needle-exchange program being established in and by the city and state of New York (Dalton 1989), it became evident that they too needed to become educated about AIDS in the black community. In fact, they need also to lobby for improved access to drug rehabilitation programs and for health care facilities designed to engage in the treatment and care of people living with AIDS (Williams and Hopps 1988).

I only hope that I have been able to capture some of the complexity and extraordinary vitality of a vibrant, colorful, and expressive culture and to convey the importance of social networks and personal relationships to the survival of a population of men often neglected not only by social science but by American society at large. A more comprehensive historical study could highlight the extraordinary contribution to black and American culture made by gay black men (and women). This focus would undoubtedly be supported by the collection of life histories of prominent gay black men and women and the people who shared their lives. Fortunately, some record of the lives of Richard Bruce Nugent and Bayard Rustin was established before they passed in 1987 (Garber 1983; Chauncey and Kennedy 1987; Jeanmarie 1988).

Comparison with the gay populations of other black communities, such as Brooklyn's Fort Greene and East New York's Brownsville, and parts of other major cities that are reputed to support large gay black populations (e.g., Newark, Philadelphia, Baltimore, Washington, D.C., Atlanta, Birmingham, Cleveland, Detroit, Chicago, St. Louis, New Orleans, Oakland, and Los Angeles) would further our understanding of the extraordinary status of these men in their own communities.

Within black society, these gay black men exist as a close-knit community. In a series of socially constructed, interconnected social networks, they think of, talk about, and refer to themselves as a "family." As a member of this "family," each individual can lay claim to being "one of the children."

GILBERT: Honey, they all family. Miss [Cleveland], Miss [Sherman]. But you know, my closest sisters are [Harry, Barry, and Donny]. Them three are my blood, honey. They my closest family. But all these girls are family, honey. All these children.

By so defining themselves, they establish their niche in black society while asserting a sense of dignity about their dual identities as gay black men. In a larger society divided by racism and homophobia, this "family" is a powerful symbol of the degree to which gay black men acknowledge that they all have a place in the community and are all connected by a space they share and lives that intertwine.

# Glossary

| | |
|---|---|
| *ain't all that* | is not that good |
| *ain't usin' it* | is not doing (something); not attending (a place or an event); not dealing with (a person) |
| *bidwiss* | card game (similar to gin rummy) |
| *boys* | hustlers |
| *bulldagger* | lesbian |
| *bump on up* | to enter |
| *camp* | in American English, refers to the culture of the drag world; in British English, it applies to gay culture in general |
| *carry on* | to perform; to party |
| *child* | gay friend; lover; gay man |
| *church girls* | gay men who frequent church |
| *coins* | money; wages |
| *cut up* | to laugh and joke |
| *data* | gossip; news |
| *deep* | serious; sincere; thorough; through and through |
| *diction* | speech |
| *to die for* | the best |
| *dishing* | to sarcastically insult; to gossip; to send up (the non-gay black equivalent is "dissing") |
| *down* | well done; well prepared; plenty |
| *drag* | cross-gender dressing |
| *edit* | to interrupt speech with grunts, words, phrases of approval |

194

| | |
|---|---|
| *family* | gay community; members of gay clique, such as the "church girls" |
| *fashions* | clothes |
| *feature* | to turn up; to appear; to put in an appearance |
| *feeling it* | in the mood |
| *festive* | gay (in the traditional sense), but excessive |
| *fierce* | fine; the best |
| *friendgirl* | gay friend |
| *garments* | clothes |
| *get down* | to have fun; to party; to dance |
| *get over* | to get the better of; to trick |
| *girlfriend* | gay friend; any fellow gay man |
| *hijra* | homosexual; eunuch; transsexual; transvestite; hermaphradite (from *hijra*, a third sex and gender in Indian society) |
| *ho* | whore |
| *husband* | lover; sex partner |
| *hustler* | man who sells sex, among other commodities, to other men |
| *kente* | woven cloth of West African origins (see Cole 1990) |
| *kufi* | Afro-Muslim cap, popularized by Black Muslim and "back to Africa" movements in the African-American community |
| *last* | best; finest |
| *the Life* | being gay |
| *Miss Thing* | title for gay man (especially if the man's name is unknown), used out of respect or jokingly |
| *for your nerves* | the best |
| *one of the children* | a member of the gay community |
| *only* | the best |
| *outing* | exposing a gay person to non-gays |
| *over* | the best |
| *perch* | to sit |
| *punk* | southern black prison expression for a gay man (pejorative) |
| *read* | to reprimand; to reproach (usually comically) |
| *real man* | potential husband, lover, or sex partner |
| *rock* | to surprise; to shock (often used in the expression "rock my world") |
| *the scene* | the social institutions frequented by members of the gay community |

| | |
|---|---|
| *serve* | to tell; to express (usually nonverbally); to deliver |
| *shade* | attitude |
| *shady* | sly |
| *sissy* | gay man (not necessarily pejorative) |
| *sister* | best gay friend |
| *snap* | to click fingers as emphasis to verbal monologue |
| *spook* | to expose |
| *stuff* | sex; sex partner |
| *tea* | gossip |
| *through* | angry; had enough |
| *tired* | not worthy of attention; all used up; trashy |
| *toast* | folk poem |
| *tough* | very good |
| *trade* | sex partner; hustler; man |
| *trash* | to put down; to gossip about |
| *twirl* | sashay |
| *use* | to do; to attend; to deal with |
| *vogue* | to dance imitating typical poses of models in *Vogue* |
| *work* | to cruise |

# Notes

## Chapter 1. "He's Family"

1. To ensure anonymity, the names of my informants and the institutions where they socialize have been concealed by the use of pseudonyms throughout the book.

2. Explanations of gay black slang and African terms appear in the glossary.

3. Dr. John Martin of the Sociomedical Sciences Division of the School of Public Health at Columbia University directed a seven-year study of the psychological and sociological effects of the AIDS epidemic on the gay communities of New York City. The project was funded by National Institute of Mental Health grant number MH 39557. Initially we networked 850 gay men into the project during 1985 and 1986. Each year we interview these men for approximately three hours, questioning them about changes in their lives, their homes, their work, their religious, alcohol, drug, and sexual activities, and their social networks, and about AIDS losses and their coping strategies.

4. For example, Hannerz (1969), Keiser (1969), Lefever (1988), Liebow (1967), MacLeod (1987), Schulz (1969), Sullivan (1989), and Wilkinson and Taylor (1977).

5. For example, *The Black Scholar* 18, no. 3 (1987) and *Essence* 20, no. 7 (1989).

6. See the novels of Chester B. Himes and Donald Goines, for example.

7. For example, Baldwin (1965), Brown (1965), Ellison (1972), and Wright (1966a, 1966b).

8. For example, Brink and Harris (1967), Connolly (1977), Engerman and Genovese (1975), Farley and Allen (1987), Killian (1964), Newman (1978), and the New York Urban League (1984).

9. Rarely is Suttles's work ethnographic (descriptive or contextualized), and he tends to neglect the individual people themselves, their perceptions of their lifestyles, their roles, and their relationships.

10. Inevitably, a well-written ethnography on the gay black community will also find an ordered structure. But a different picture of black men emerges—that is, different from received descriptions.

11. According to Hannerz, issues of economy and race prevent more people from achieving "mainstream" status. He defines "mainstreamers" as "those who conform most closely to mainstream American assumptions about the 'normal' life" (Hannerz 1969:38). Although he addresses the characteristics of "mainstream" families, he does not focus on the roles of "mainstreamer" men.

12. See Moynihan (1965) and Rainwater and Yancey (1967).

13. See Gutman (1976), Hill (1971), Ladner (1971), Martin and Martin (1978), Schultz (1969), Stack (1974), and Staples (1971).

14. For some excellent discussions of the "poor" in America, and in black society in particular, see Howell (1973), Piven and Cloward (1972, 1979), Susser (1982), and Valentine (1968).

15. Nowhere in the literature on black society are black gay men (or gay black men) studied in depth. Anderson (1978) refers to black gays as "sissies" in passing, but they are marginal to the group of men he is studying.

16. The psychological studies of Bell and Weinberg (1978) and Julius Johnson (1981) do include black gay men in their samples.

17. Only passing references to black gay men appear in some works—for example, D. Altman (1986), Jay and Young (1972, 1978), and Levine (1979). More commonly, black gay men appear in fiction—for example, Beam (1986), Duplechan (1985, 1986), and Smith (1983).

18. Gilbert Herdt's (1981, 1982, 1984) works deal with ritualized homosexuality in Papua New Guinea. Male initiation and male cults, rich in symbolism, are shown to express a philosophy that views growth into manhood not as predetermined by nature but as presided over by men. The Sambia, among other Melanesian peoples, define the separation of men and women as both a biological and a social imperative, so they transform young boys of the female realm into warriors and adult men of the male realm by insemination. The works inform us about the social construction of gender; they do not inform us about "being gay." However, their importance to the study of sexuality, and homosexuality in particular, cannot be denied. In fact, as a result of this work, Herdt questions the validity of sexual typologies created and utilized by earlier sex researchers (see Kinsey, Pomeroy, and Martin 1948, Karlen 1971) and in much the way that more recent works attempt (Callender and Kochems 1985, De Cecco and Shively 1984, Nanda 1990). Nanda's work on the *hijra* is an excellent ethnographic example of a society's (here India) cultural construction of a third sex or gender, for which we have no term in English.

An interesting collection of papers on the anthropology of gay society and homosexuality is Evelyn Blackwood's *The Many Faces of Homosexuality* (1986). Some of the papers deal with methodological issues: the ethnographic pieces deal with the *berdache* (ritualized Native American drag performances), Mexican bathhouses, and gender roles in Brazil. No particular theme links this collection of papers, but they do present the cross-cultural existence of homosexuality and portray a variety of expressions of the "gay lifestyle." The best example of an ethnographic description of homosexual behavior comes from the work of Joseph Carrier, an example of which is included in Blackwood. He contextualizes homosexual behavior in the Mexican-American community and shows how it is accepted, at one level, as an extension of male machismo (Carrier 1976a, 1976b, 1977, 1985, 1989).

19. Humphreys's is a groundbreaking work in sociology and followed closely on the heels of the extensive psychological literature of the 1960s. The lasting controversy concerning issues of ethics surrounding Humphreys's methodology have somewhat marred an otherwise important work. While one or two of his informants are black, he does not discuss the issue of race in relation to this setting.

20. The issue of racism is taken up by John Victor Soares (1979). The author states that the gay population in the United States apes non-gay America in its treatment of people of color. The article briefly mentions different types of black gay men, without investigating the types or analyzing their roles in society. It really acts as a guide to travels in black gay America.

21. The only other published source of information on black gay men (and gay black men) appears in the fictional writings of black gay men themselves (Beam 1986; Duplechan 1985, 1986; Johnson, Robinson, and Taylor 1988; Smith 1983). These works are mainly autobiographical and provide an interesting record of what it feels like to be black and gay. While they are important and informative background reading, they lack the sociological analysis necessary to make them significant contributions to our comprehension of gay black identity.

22. This was in contradiction to the interest-group theory of Glazer and Moynihan (1963), which stressed the psychological dimensions of ethnic affiliation.

23. It is "affect" that gives identity its psychological power, not only to inform individual values and attitudes (which we see manifested in "intimate" situations) but also to unite people into groups and to maintain group boundaries.

24. While Cass (1985) Richardson (1984), and Shively et al. (1985) all bemoan the lack of definition in the terminology employed in the study of homosexuality, they discuss the importance of homosexual behavior as a significant aspect or stage in the process or development of the homosexual and, therefore, the gay identity: "Sexual fantasy and practice, however, is inevitably the major, if not the sole, criterion by which sexual orientation might be inferred" (Richardson 1984:85).

Richardson explains that the behavioral aspects of homosexual identity were raised to significance by the behavioral determinists of the 1940s (see Kinsey, Pomeroy, and Martin 1948). Later, Hart and Richardson distinguished homosexual behavior from homosexual identity: "Many people engage in same-sex acts without necessarily identifying as homosexual. Alternatively, a person may not have actually engaged in same-sex sexual acts, although they would define themselves as homosexual" (Hart and Richardson 1981:73).

Today, some social constructionists apply "homosexual" just to sexual activity between members of the same sex, while using "gay" to describe a whole identity that incorporates other sociocultural attributes (Richardson 1984:83–85).

25. For example, see Cass (1985), Hart and Richardson (1981), and Minton and McDonald (1985).

26. Prior to 1970 most of the literature on homosexual men dealt with psychological issues, reinforcing the labeling of homosexuality as a mental illness. See Bieber et al. (1962), Cass (1985), Richardson (1984), and Westwood (1953).

27. See Rainwater's definition of a "valid identity" as "one in which the individual finds congruence between who he feels he is, who he announces himself to be, and where he feels his society places him" (Rainwater 1970:375). In other words, not only are an individual's psychological needs satisfied but he or she utilizes the cultural material available to him or her to validate his or her chosen identity and make it socially acceptable.

28. Unfortunately, Humphreys does not follow through on a discussion of the intersection of race and the gay identity, even though he lists ethnicity as a sociological variable that may influence the degree of acceptance of a gay identity. He does provide data on the socioeconomic standing of some of his informants and discusses the significance of different religious teachings to the development of a gay identity, even providing "Negro" examples.

29. While Dank and Humphreys agree that sexual orientation is an overriding factor in the construction of a gay identity, many other culturally definable attributes are incorporated: socioeconomic status, occupation, education, and a host of expressive traits, for example, dress, language, and nonverbal behavior.

30. Much of the recent approach to the study of homosexuality and the development of a gay community by the social constructionists has resulted in comprehensive historical accounts of the evolution of the concept "homosexuality" and its predecessors, for example, "inversion" and "uranism" (Karlen 1971, Lauritsen and Thorstad 1974, Symonds 1901). The production of such historical accounts is a significant feat in its own right and ought to be pursued, not only to set the record straight but also to instill a sense of pride in a scattered, diverse, and often disillusioned population (Duberman et al. 1989, Greenberg 1988, Weeks 1977).

31. This is not to deny the fact that all fifty-seven respondents to the life history interviews for this project declared their homosexuality "natural." To believe that sexuality is indeed an integral part of one's essence is to accept oneself in the face of constant denial by the society around one and many of the individuals with whom one interacts socially. Here one could aptly argue that this essentialist belief itself is the product of social construction.

32. See Goffman (1963), Plummer (1975), and Weinberg (1983).

33. The best examples of this theoretical approach in relationship to gay communities are Goffman (1961, 1963) and Weinberg (1983).

34. See Banton (1987), Becker (1963), Cory (1951), Polsky (1969), and Reiss (1961).

35. Sources include Bott (1957), Buchler and Selby (1968), Fox (1967), Lévi-Strauss (1969), Schneider (1968), and Young and Willmott (1957).

36. See Cohen (1985) and Varenne (1986).

37. See Barnes (1969), Epstein (1961), Stack (1974), and Weston (1991).

38. In Harlem the gay black community refers to itself as "family" and to its members as "mothers," "aunts," "brothers," "sisters," "cousins," "uncles," "husbands," or "children." For examples of structuralist analyses of gender roles, see MacCormack and Strathern (1980), Ortner and Whitehead (1981), and Strathern (1987).

39. See Weeks (1985, 1986).

40. See D'Emilio (1983:231), Musto (1987), and Salholz (1989).

41. See Adam (1987:79).

42. Five gay bars have closed on Christopher Street since 1987. Several others in the surrounding Greenwich Village neighborhood have also closed. The East Village community has been even more devastated with the closure of several bars, bathhouses, sex clubs, movie theaters, and discos (McFadden 1988). But the most noticeable changes in the mainstream gay scene appear on Christopher Street itself. Not only are the current patrons younger (teenagers and young men in their twenties, as another generation takes over) but they are also by and large non-white: one bar formerly catering to a mixed clientele is now exclusively black, one white neighborhood bar has become a black and Hispanic disco bar, and three white bars now serve a mixed clientele. As well, five gay bars on Christopher Street now employ black barmen, and black players feature prominently on the bars' pool and gay softball league teams. These changes not only reflect the arrival of another generation on the scene but also the dramatic effects of the AIDS epidemic. The middle-aged generation of gay men, say, from thirty to fifty, predominantly white and from out of town, are now absent. Many have succumbed to the disease, many others have moved away from the epidemic (often to the towns and states of their origin), and those who remain have withdrawn from the social scene. The residents of Greenwich Village have also changed: white non-gay couples, often with children in tow, who would have been a rare sight on the streets just ten years ago, are most visible in the daytime and during the weekends. At night they stay indoors, and the vacant social scene becomes replete with young gay New Yorkers, probably reflecting the true gay population of New York itself in its racial makeup.

43. This "snowball" method of making contact with potential informants is what Roger Sanjek employed in his study of network serials. He saw it as "an explicit urban ethnographic research strategy" by which "the problem of urban dispersal which arises once a unit of study has been selected can be overcome" (Sanjek 1978:266–267).

44. For example, regulations concerning the participation of gays in the U.S. armed forces.

45. This contradiction between perception and experience runs through

all the accounts of gay life in Harlem recorded by my informants. It is most obvious when they discuss AIDS.

46. In 1968 Columbia University resolved to erect a gymnasium in the neighboring Morningside Park. The local black community in Harlem protested. The student body at Columbia sided with the black community, an act that is regarded as crucial in the ensuing student uprising at Columbia. For further opinions of black Americans on the white power structure in the United States, see Gwaltney (1980).

47. When and where it did, I decided to leave up to my informants. After all, I expected any impact and resulting changes in social behavior would mirror those found in other AIDS studies on other gay communities around the country.

## Chapter 2. "A Host of Different Men"

1. See "Brothers from Georgia" section and Berry and Blassingame (1982).

2. See Aschenbrenner (1983) and Martin and Martin (1978).

3. Figures from the 1980 national census (Farley and Allen 1987) show that 2.5 percent of all black men counted completed college (compared to 7.4 percent of white men) and 2.2 percent of black men go on to graduate school (compared to 7.3 percent of white men). While this may imply that my sample is skewed, Farley and Allen's statistics are based on figures that do not include the whole black population, let alone Harlemites in particular (78 percent of the informants in my study did not participate in the 1990 census).

4. Prices paid for brownstones and apartments range from $60,000 to more than $200,000.

5. See Gary (1983), Hannerz (1969), Landry (1987), Liebow (1967), and Meister (1972).

6. See Anderson (1978), Gary (1983), Keiser (1979), Landry (1987), and Liebow (1967).

7. Here I sometimes refer to these men as "hustlers," as do some of the gay black men who help support them. However, these men differ in terms of background, employment, and gay community participation from hustlers in communities elsewhere, as described by other social scientists (Boyer 1986; Kamel 1983; Panajian 1983). Because these men are not (exclusively) sexual laborers, neither exploiting nor being exploited by their contacts in the gay community, whom they refer to as their "family," I use the gay black men's term "boys" to distinguish them from other types of hustlers.

8. While some of these men do choose to hustle, it is understood that the choice is made under severe racial, socioeconomic, and class constraints. Although many of them do not need to live a life of hustling, it is a vocation that is appealing to gay men who may have intermittent employment problems or who do not want to work a 9:00 A.M. to 5:00 P.M. job for low wages.

9. See Boyer (1986), Erickson (1986), Kamel (1983), Panajian (1983), and Wright (1988).

10. See, for example, Hannerz (1969), Schulz (1969), and Stack (1974).

11. See Cone (1991).

12. There are plans to "gentrify" 125th Street. In preparation, several businesses have closed (including two bars where gay men socialized) and several buildings have been razed. During the period of research, no new construction had commenced, although the city was in the process of reconstructing the sidewalks.

13. The "rent party" is a rare phenomenon today in Harlem. Historians of Harlem in the 1920s and 1930s (Anderson 1987, Garber 1989, Johnson 1968, Lewis 1989, Ottley 1968) describe them well. Essentially, a host would invite people to come to a party where they would pay for the liquor and food they would consume. Alternatively, guests could donate a gift of money. The profit from the sales and the money collected by donation helped to pay the rent. In the 1920s these parties were the main avenue for social contact between gay people (Garber 1989). At that time, hosts opened their doors to the public. Nowadays, for security reasons, rent parties are by invitation only.

## Chapter 3.  "One Big Family"

1. Only two acknowledged that they socialized elsewhere than Harlem. Their workmates downtown often take them out in SoHo or midtown, or they meet friends from Brooklyn halfway and go out drinking or dancing in the Village or Chelsea. Invariably, though, they "hang out" in Harlem, especially if they go out from home.

2. See Gans (1962) and Stack (1974).

3. See Martin et al. (1989) and Martin and Dean (1990).

4. Compare Stack (1974:32–34, 42–43).

5. This is a classic example of Radcliffe-Brown's (1952) "mother's brother."

6. See White (1987).

7. See Gans (1962), Park (1982), and Weston (1991).

8. See Grahn (1984).

9. These uses of fictive kinship are also found in Britain, Australia, New Zealand, Fiji, and in the white gay population in the United States (Rodgers 1972).

10. These fictive kin terms are further defined in White (1987), who provides an interesting discussion of solidarity and unity among black people, a unity that is reflected in the use of fictive kinship terms as a result of their common experience in the United States.

11. See Cohen (1985).

## Chapter 4. "Close to Home"

1. Theater is a popular pastime in Harlem. The YMCA, schools, and some established theaters, such as the Apollo, provide constant live entertainment that is well supported by the local population. Many gay men participate in the theater, but none of the theaters is exclusively gay.

2. Two of the gay bars employ four women (in their fifties and sixties) during the daytime hours. All are married with families and have been bartending all their adult lives. Two have since retired.

3. A distinction is drawn by many informants between having sex with someone and dating another man. To be "seeing" someone, or having sex with them, refers to the act of sexual intercourse or sexual gratification. To "date" someone means to be socializing with someone with the intention of entering into a long-term monogamous relationship. Dating may or may not include having sex.

4. Joking relationships have been the focus of much anthropological attention, from Radcliffe-Brown (1952) on. They are also discussed within the bar setting by Cavan (1966) and Spradley and Mann (1975). Among gay men, where kinship rules do not restrict interpersonal relations, a joking relationship may evolve as a social sanction of sexual relations between close gay friends. The joking overcomes the inherent tension that may result from the relationship. In fact, the closer the friends, the deeper the sexually explicit, joking insult may be.

5. The use of the feminine pronouns here reflects the siblinglike nature of the relationship between these two men. They regard each other as and call each other "sisters." With other friends, called "girlfriend" or "friendgirl," the feminine pronouns are also used. Nicholas informed me that the inverted "friendgirl" was created by black gays "just to be different." Now that mainstream, white gays are referring to their friends as "girlfriends," gay black men have taken their display of affection one step further.

6. "Finish it up" means to terminate the relationship, and "in trouble deep" means physical violence.

It is important to note that one of the main areas in Harlem where gay bars are located is also a section that is marginal to mainstream black life. Here immigrant Hispanic communities are developing. For example, the full length of Broadway from 125th Street to 168th Street, as it passes through Harlem, is lined with Hispanic residences and stores. Some "interethnic tension" has resulted as the two populations meet.

7. This atmosphere contrasts sharply with the feeling of alienation in lesbian bars described in Wolf's *The Lesbian Community* (1980). Here gay black men's bars more closely resemble the sociability of the English pub.

8. Mainstream American culture promotes an ambiguous attitude toward drinking and bar culture (Cavan 1966).

9. Pete's Paradise fronts 125th Street. It has a narrow entranceway, no awning, but a sign painted above. There is a small window, which is often barred.

10. Like almost all the bars and clubs in Harlem (and many elsewhere in Manhattan), the doors are locked for security purposes. Entry is gained by a buzzer to the bar staff or by a bouncer.

11. "Moonwalking" is a dance step created and popularized by the singer Michael Jackson.

12. The "meat rack" at Pete's Paradise was a shelf that ran down one side of the barroom at elbow height. Drinks and ashtrays were placed on top of it, and patrons frequently leaned against it. From here individuals could cruise the other patrons sitting in the bar, dancing, or walking up and down the length of the barroom.

13. None of the informants in this study participates in the national political process. They do not vote. Some admitted they would probably support the Democratic party, but they were not registered. Most had no party affiliation. Local, city, and state politics were of conversational interest, but again no one voted. The attitude seemed to be captured by Sue: "Ain't nothin' different he [Charles Rangel] can do."

14. For example, see Johnson (1990) and McKay (1928).

15. In most of the bars in Harlem, books and magazines, videos, cassettes, furniture items from chairs to televisions, groceries (especially meat), and clothing were sold by street hustlers. These vendors, both male and female, were of all ages. Money earned was often the sole income of the individual seller, but sometimes such an income supplemented welfare checks or other irregular income.

16. Most of these men have high-paying jobs ($40,000 to $100,000 per year), and several own their apartments. Moses is probably a millionaire.

17. Staying out till dawn means remaining inside a bar after its 4:00 A.M. closing time until the bar staff decides to turn everyone out, or it means that after 4:00 A.M. everyone moves on to an "after-hours" club. Such private social clubs exist all over Harlem. From Mickey's Place, the gay crowd has only one block to walk to a gay after-hours club. There, in dimly lit rooms, drinks can be purchased and conversations continued, and dancing to the jukebox is permitted. This particular club, frequented by many of my informants, closes between 8:00 and 10:00 A.M. on Fridays, Saturdays, and Sundays. It is not open for business the other nights of the week.

18. The existing committee chooses its replacements. Applicants or nominees will be known to the incumbents. Character references, community service, and income are considered.

19. House music developed during the late 1980s in clubs in New York and Chicago. It is an R&B and disco fusion popularized by gay men who "vogue" to it as patrons or guest artists at the large, mixed dance clubs downtown.

20. These formal balls are not to be confused with the balls of the younger "house queens" occurring in Manhattan, the Bronx, and Newark in the 1990s. Although undoubtedly part of the inspiration for these smaller events, the large Harlem balls remain major annual social events in Harlem. They are attended by as many of Harlem's non-gay elite as its established drag celebrities.

21. Francis also liked gay men and had a reputation for being well hung. He preferred the active role in the sexual encounter, but with non-gay partners he frequently took a passive role sexually.

22. SoHar is the area of Harlem between 5th and Morningside avenues and 125th and 110th streets, directly north of Central Park.

23. This seems to be a different experience from that of other gay men, especially in Manhattan. Very few Manhattan gay men were born and raised in the borough. Martin and Dean (1990) note that about 80 percent are non–New Yorkers. Most come from the suburbs, other states, or abroad.

# Chapter 5. "Different from Other Colors"

1. Here I'm using *black* as a cultural adjective, not as a racial category. Admittedly, being black, as a political expression, may limit or dictate the adoption of black partners, but being black per se does not. Also, situational preference develops out of residence patterns.

2. Specifically, in anthropological writings that embrace the thesis of a black "culture of poverty." Works of that theoretical persuasion implied that cultural traits associated with poverty in the black community, such as single-parent families, were passed from generation to generation through socialization. See Lewis (1966) and Valentine (1968).

3. It is important to note that this study did not focus on race per se, or on interracial relationships (social or sexual). Also, most of the informants did not discuss race, as it is not an important issue for them in their daily social lives. Yet some social scientists, especially psychologists, would have it that the construction of a positive black identity is the result not only of interracial contact but also of black self-hatred. This may be the case for a few of these informants, but the majority do not and have not experienced any long-term interracial interaction. Moreover, they have been socialized by "black is beautiful" ideologies. Race and interracial conflict, then, are not big issues for these gay black men in their daily lives.

4. These men have a convenient supply of black male sex partners in the black community and rarely interact with men of other races. None rejected men of other races as potential partners, but they often noted that black-on-black relationships are an expression of pride. Gay Men of African Descent (GMAD) members, in particular, frequently stated that they actively sought such relationships as a pro-black statement. However, their choices are not meant as expressions of anti-white sentiment. It was evident from some informants' comments that blacks who have white or Hispanic partners are seen as "different" primarily because they tend to socialize outside of the community.

5. Incomes in this population range from $10,000 to $250,000. For example, Cleveland, with an $85,000 job, rents or leases apartments and land he owns down South, and he has other investments earning hundreds of thou-

sands of dollars per year. In contrast, Freddy depends on hustling (not just for sex) and the contributions (money, shelter, meals) of friends and family. His income was difficult to calculate and unreliable. Anyway, income is only one indicator of class. Education, residence, and social contacts, among other variables, need to be considered. Cleveland and Freddy are best friends.

6. Sometimes lesbian friends will accompany gay men to dances and on boat rides. But otherwise their presence in the gay social scene is minimal. It is presumed by these informants that lesbians in Harlem have their own social scene and are more likely to participate in mainstream lesbian and gay life.

7. Until comparable work is carried out with non-gay black men, we can not extend this finding beyond the black gay community. Evidence does exist in my data, however, that non-gay, unmarried black men are also involved in child care.

8. See Martin and Dean (1990).

9. Lewis (1975) stresses the importance given to interpersonal relationships, nurturance, and emotional expression (as well as idiosyncratic behavior and nonconformity) in the socialization of black children, as opposed to the independence, individualism, and conformity stressed in white children's socialization. For further examples of the cultural attributes instilled during socialization in the black community, see Kunkel and Kennard (1971), Lewis (1964), and Young (1970).

10. See Anderson (1987:3–7), Harris (1968:99, 103), Johnson (1968), Lewis (1989:27–28), McKay (1940:18–20), and Osofsky (1971:113–117).

11. For further information on the Nation of Islam, see Lincoln (1961) and Lomax (1963).

12. Kwanzaa is an annual festival celebrating the African roots of black Americans. Held over the Christmas and New Year's season, it features a different theme on each of the eight days of celebration (McClester 1985).

13. "It was inevitable that preachers who had played such an important role in the organized social life of Negroes should become political leaders during the Reconstruction period when the Negro enjoyed civil rights.... During the Reconstruction period a number of outstanding leaders in the Baptist and in the other Methodist denominations became outstanding leaders of Negroes in politics.... As a result of the elimination of Negroes from the political life of the American community, the Negro Church became the arena of their political activities.... The Negro church was not only an arena of political life for the leaders of Negroes, it had a political meaning for the masses. Although they were denied the right to vote in the American community, within their churches, especially the Methodist churches, they could vote and engage in electing their officers" (Frazier 1964:47–49). See also Du Bois (1989).

14. See Anderson (1987), Huggins (1971), Lewis (1989), and Naison (1985).

15. For further information, see Ottley (1968) and Schiffman (1984).

16. See Berry and Blassingame (1982); Breitman, Porter, and Smith (1976); and Harris and Wicker (1988).

17. A "toast" is a "folk poem" usually associated with black hustler culture (Wepman, Newman, and Binderman 1976).

18. Such separatist ideological expression can best explain the racial attitudes statistically accounted for by Schuman, Steeh, and Bobo (1985).

19. See Cromartie and Stack (1990).

20. See Garcia-Barrio (1988).

21. "These hero figures were important. They symbolized the strength, dignity, and courage many Negroes were able to manifest in spite of their confined situation. . . . After slavery Afro-American folklore began to feature other types of heroes as well: secular, human heroes who were not to be contained by the limits of the actual" (Levine 1978:400).

22. John Henry was a black laborer, a big, powerful man of slave ancestry who worked in the mines and on the railroads. He worked harder and faster than any other laborer but was finally defeated in a race against a train, or, in some accounts, from overexertion while steel-driving in competition against a steam drill. The white man's machine finally crushed the honest labor of the black man. The events of John Henry's life have been much embellished over the years, and different storytellers emphasize different attributes of the man and his deeds. Here, many gay informants emphasized the refrains concerning the man's physical strength, his masculine attributes, and his sexual prowess.

23. See Hannerz (1969:94–104); Schulz (1969); and Wepman, Newman, and Binderman (1976:3–4).

24. This may reflect a "negative" respect—that is, respect out of fear. Undoubtedly, many do not respect the church, reflecting a resentment born of the churches' teachings on homosexuality.

25. For an explication of "expressive culture" and its application to aspects of black culture, see Gay and Baber (1987). In their anthology, they have collected papers that discuss the sociocultural aspects of black expressiveness, an "Afro-American ethos" that derives as much from Africa as from slavery, economic deprivation, and inner-city living: "[African-Americans have] created an ethos of expressiveness which was (and is) at once pragmatic and aesthetic, poetic and paradoxical, sustaining and enriching, ironic and incredibly imaginative. Of great importance to this ethos were an aesthetic of style, the spirituality of communal participation, and the power of performance in conveying the essence and vitality of life and culture" (Gay 1987a:2–3).

26. See Anderson (1978), Hannerz (1969), Keiser (1969), Liebow (1967), Stack (1974), and Williams (1981).

## Chapter 6. "Gay Is Lovin' Men"

1. See Goffman (1963) and Goode and Troiden (1975).

2. It is important to note as the ensuing chapters unfold that there is some anti-gay discrimination in Harlem. It appears on the street (verbally) and in

the churches. Informants here who have experienced such discrimination in Harlem brush off the incidents. Thus some apparent contradiction exists between these men's experiences and their belief that people in Harlem are more tolerant than people elsewhere in the city.

3. For a discussion of the development of this distinction between "gay" and "homosexual," see Chesebro (1981), Harry and DeVall (1978), Humphreys and Miller (1980), Taylor (1978), and Warren (1974).

4. Such experiential foundations for acceptance of a homosexual identity have been confirmed in other reports: "The evidence now available suggests that, at least for some individuals, childhood and adolescent experiences may serve as the basis for the adult homosexual identity" (Minton and McDonald 1985:97). However, such experiences are only a stepping-stone in the achievement of a gay identity. Most researchers of homosexual and gay identities, who incorporate a variety of theoretical approaches, have produced models comprising a linear progression toward the achievement of a homosexual identity and the management of a gay identity. Homosexual experiences are but a stage in that development. See, for example, Cass (1979), Coleman (1981/82), Dank (1979), Hart and Richardson (1981), Lee (1977), Minton and McDonald (1985), Plummer (1975), and Troiden (1979).

5. See Coffman (1963), Gagnon and Simon (1967, 1973), and Minton and McDonald (1985), and Plummer (1975). Hoult (1985) emphasizes a "social learning model."

6. This is comparable to the manner in which "being black" is learned (see chap. 5).

7. See especially Minton and McDonald (1985:100) but also Coleman (1981/82), Lee (1977), and Plummer (1975).

8. This finding is corroborated by the works of Coleman (1981/82), Gagnon and Simon (1973), and Troiden (1979).

9. See de Monteflores and Schultz (1978).

10. These men challenge the arguments of some researchers, for example, Cass (1979), Ross (1978), and Weinberg and Williams (1974), who insist that a gay identity can only be achieved when both the private and public selves of an individual are one. This stage of the developmental process of achieving a gay identity, called "identity synthesis" by Cass (1979), requires a unified self-image. Yet many gay men in Harlem, it would appear, are able to function being gay without achieving this "final stage."

11. See D. Altman (1971), Humphreys (1972), Jay and Young (1972, 1975), and Muchmore and Hanson (1982, 1986).

12. Verbal and nonverbal behavior among gays is the topic of an anthology edited by James Chesebro (1981). The writers' "communication perspective" elucidates such behavior by analyzing its functions and contextualizing its performance. Two papers by Hayes and one each by Darsey and Chesebro are especially good examples.

13. Kenneth Read (1980), in his symbolic analysis of a white West Coast bar, provides many interesting examples of cruising gestures.

14. Compare white mainstream America. Writing in 1971, Altman noted

in his lucid analysis of coming out that gays had to emulate heterosexual role models anyway, because there was, at that time at least, no gay role model available for young gay people: "It is in the playing of social roles that the gay world seems best to mirror the straight. Because there is, as yet, no genuine homosexual community, homosexuals take their cues from the straight world" (D. Altman 1971:35). See also Wolf's *The Lesbian Community* (1980) for a similar view.

15. The fact that these positions become inverted in actual sexual activity is another matter (see chap. 7).

16. In fact, Grahn (1984) has produced an interesting commentary on the development of a gay "tongue," presenting a well-researched etiology of gay slang terms. Hayes's article "Gayspeak" (1981) analyzes the social function of gay terminology on the basis of three types of social setting: the secret, the social, and the radical-activist, where "gayspeak" is found. Such contextualization enhances the comprehension of different meanings for familiar words. Rodgers's (1972) lexicon remains the definitive dictionary of gay slang. In it he refers to some words and expressions that are rooted in the gay black community, including "tea." See also Chesebro (1981) and the fiction of Mordden (1985, 1986).

17. "Fierce" has its origins in black diction, according to my informants. Black gays have used the expression for twenty years or more, especially in reference to men or clothing. By 1989 mainstream gays were using the expression, and in 1990, *New York* magazine noted that a fashion house in New York had brought a new expression to the fashion world by using "fierce" in its fall window display. The article noted, incorrectly, that the expression "started about two years ago with the black kids who vogue every day in front of McDonald's" (Walls 1990:28).

18. Rodgers (1972) refers to "tea" only in reference to the usage "have some tea," meaning to engage in small talk. Three southern-born informants explained "tea" as "gossip," such as that exchanged between "girls" taking tea in the afternoon. They indicated that the expression was black and originally southern.

19. I use the term "sensibility" in the same manner that Bronski does, almost equating it with "culture" but incorporating a psychological dimension that allows for individual expression: "Homosexuals have created a separate culture that reflects their attitudes, moods, thoughts, and emotions as an oppressed group" (Bronski 1984:11–12). It is because gay society is separate from but dependent on mainstream American society that Bronski labels it the "gay subculture."

20. Many gay men live in Harlem but socialize in gay areas elsewhere in New York City, in Westchester County, or in New Jersey. They may be openly gay in their daily lives in Harlem, but they do not socialize within the gay community there. (This factor precluded their participation as respondents in this study.) Also, many gay men in Harlem who prefer other black men as lovers do not socialize in gay bars. They socialize with other gays at church or in private homes in Harlem. Almost half of my informants fit this description.

21. These men would fall into a category of the immigrant or the educated

"native son" in an urban black community, men whom Gwaltney (1981) defines as of the ghetto or of black culture but not of "core black culture." These are men who are raised black but are unfamiliar with many of the finer stylistic attributes of the expressive culture that is found at the "heart" of the black community—that is, in the urban "ghetto" environment. This is probably because they have been raised in the suburbs or have attended private schools out of town and thus have not shared experiences with peers who run the streets and who are the creators and diffusers of urban black culture. Arthur Spears, a black linguist and anthropologist, suggested this explanation to me in a conversation on 27 February 1990, during which he discussed similar experiences in his own life.

22. What is being implied here is double-income males with no children.

23. The written record of gay history has been slow to evolve. Many of the historians reiterate the claim of repression as the cause for the absence of gays in the historical record and indicate their intent to correct that record. Katz (1976) remains the "Bible" of gay American history, although Greenberg's (1988) thoughtful reconstruction of the history of homosexuality provides the most comprehensive international perspective. Boughner (1988) and Rowse (1977) seek to produce a more general account of gay involvement in the history of Western Civilization. Lauritsen and Thorstad (1974) provide an interesting account of the rise of homosexual consciousness over the turn of the last century, especially in Europe. And Altman (1971), D'Emilio (1983), and Adam (1987) document the rise of the gay liberation movement in the United States in the 1970s. These works and others, including academic treatises about particular individuals and events (see Bérubé [1990] on gay servicemen and women in World War II, for example), culminated in the large collection of papers on gays in history by Duberman, Vicinus, and Chauncey (1989). Such increased enthusiasm for "setting the record straight" involves an attempt not only to justify gays' rightful place in history but also to validate their presence in society at large.

24. For further information about the role of "bulldaggers" (lesbians) in the Harlem Renaissance and the Jazz Age, see Garber (1983) and Lewis (1989). For further information on Gladys Bentley, see Garber (1988). This article contains an interesting map of Jazz Age Harlem and a brief but excellent bibliography. Also, Parkerson (1987) writes about the Jewel Box Revue, a drag theater, and its master of ceremonies, Stormé, a lesbian in drag. The Harlem Renaissance is discussed further in chapter 9.

25. Gay folklore has become a significant feature of gay life. Joseph Goodwin, in his comprehensive study of gay folklore, has noted,

Being forced to form a secret system for interacting [with] and meeting people similar to themselves meant that gays also had to develop a private means of communication, which in turn fostered a heightened sense of community. Rejected by the larger culture, gay people turned to their subculture, which—especially through its folklore—could serve as a source of strength and as a way of developing a surrogate system of social support. (Goodwin 1989:2)

Goodwin goes on to embellish his analysis of gay folklore with examples of gossip, repartee, and jokes. His theoretical construct—including concepts of humor, ambiguity, and inversion—enables him to explain the power and significance of folklore to gay people and to the maintenance of their gay community.

With these points in mind, we can examine folklore as a multifaceted process that functions in many ways. Traditions help to hold the subculture together and in many cases express the gay community's differences from the straight culture, defining the in-group based on an understanding of its folklore and a sharing and acceptance of subcultural attitudes. (Goodwin 1989:4–5)

26. See Clark and Kleiner (1989).

27. See Bronski (1984:104–106).

28. In this and the following quotes, names have been omitted to protect the identity of the individuals referred to and because no documentation to validate the claims was located.

29. For a good example of noncommitment on the issue of Hughes's sexuality, see Rampersad (1988). Rampersad leaves the question of Hughes's homosexuality unresolved, yet he provides some interesting evidence that is frequently referred to in gay folklore.

30. This does not exonerate their behavior in any way but should at least be understood as a typically teenage attitude toward nonconformity, whether a matter of sexual orientation, color, ethnicity, religious belief, age, or whatever. Also, teenagers are less inhibited when expressing society's intolerances.

31. While all of my informants have related instances of name-calling, and one or two instances of physical abuse were reported during the period of research, but not among the informant population, I believe that gay black men are more widely accepted in their residential neighborhoods, in their churches, and within the gay scene than comparable communities in the mainstream gay areas of the city. Verbal abuse, especially from teenagers, is common in New York; you do not have to be black and gay to experience that! For further reading on homophobia, see Larsen, Cate, and Reed (1983), *Journal of Homosexuality* 10(1/2), and Hooks (1988). Gomez and Smith (1989) deal with homophobia in the black community in particular.

32. This stereotype does not take into consideration yet another symptom of racism in the gay scene outside of Harlem, in which gay white men express no interest, at all, in black men as sexual partners and potential lovers. See De Marco (1983), Icard (1986), and Loiacano (1989).

## Chapter 7. "Different from Other Men"

1. For example, closeted men are also labeled "gay," although they are regarded as being different because they are still in the closet. Their gayness is assumed, usually as the result of a sexual encounter with another known gay man. Gay black men in Harlem did not verbally distinguish between these different types of gay men; they considered all of them "gay."

2. The popular image of the femininity of gay men's behavior includes

a desire to act passively in the sexual encounter with other men; that is, to assume the passive or receptive role in sexual intercourse. This assumption smacks of earlier psychological analyses of homosexuality, in that the "condition" (homosexuality) is assumed to be the result of an overbearing mother, hence the "sissification" of the boy child. See Bieber et al. (1962), Green (1987), Litten, Griffen, and Johnson (1956), Socarides (1968), and Westwood (1953). It is important to note the peculiarly skewed samples with which these researchers worked. No doubt psychological dimensions of the gay identity exist, but ideas of homosexuality as a mental illness are currently out of favor, not only within the gay population at large, which has struggled so long to shrug off the mantle of mental illness placed over it by psychologists, psychoanalysts, and psychiatrists, but also in the growing social-scientific literature on gay culture. See D. Altman (1971), Greenberg (1988), Hooker (1969, 1972), Humphreys (1972), McCaffrey (1972), Marmor (1965, 1980), and Szasz (1972).

Some of the earliest works questioning the concept of homosexuality as a disease or mental illness were Kinsey et al. (1948) and Ford and Beach (1951). Some of the key players in the development of psychological theory concerning homosexuality are Freud (1905), who introduced the psychological dimensions to his consideration of the etiology of sexuality (along with the social and the biological); Bieber et al. (1962), who found heterophobia (my term) as the root cause of homosexuality; Ovesey (1954), who described homosexuality as a neurosis; and Kolb and Johnson (1955) and Litten, Griffen, and Johnson (1956), who raise the issue of parental relationships in their theory on the development of homosexuality.

3. Data were collected from a total of 91 men. Sixty-one were anally passive, 54 anally active, 75 orally passive, and 75 orally active. Since the arrival of the AIDS epidemic, 8 men have desisted from active anal intercourse, 4 from anally passive intercourse, 2 from orally passive intercourse, but none from orally active intercourse.

4. This contradicts the received wisdom on hustlers in the gay community. Most reports describe how hustlers view their active sexual role in the homosexual encounter as an extension of their masculinity, thus conforming to the "machismo" model. See Boyer (1986), Kamel (1983), and Panajian (1983).

5. See Greenberg (1988:2–3, 483–493) and Halperin (1990:4–9).

6. Deconstructing stereotypes, popular or academic, lays bare the scene for those who would piece the evidence together and reconstruct the notion of gay identity and the emergence of gay culture from the experiences, feelings, and opinions of individuals. Some social scientists would prefer to label gay sexual behavior "same-sex behavior" in an attempt to eradicate "homosexual" as too restrictive a term (Vance 1989). I would agree, given the broad range of behavior and the changes in sexual object preference over time that I encountered in this population of gay men.

7. For examples of the white media, see Wilkerson (1988), Barbanel (1989), Kolata (1989), and Terry (1990), all in the *New York Times*. For examples of the black media, see *Black Scholar* (May/June 1987), *Essence* (November 1989), and *Emerge* (February 1990).

## Chapter 8. "This Epidemic Thing"

1. See Goldsmith (1989) and S. Altman (1986).
2. See chap. 9 for suggestions for further research.
3. See Coimbra and Torabi (1987), Davies (1986), Martin and Dean (1990), Schreiner (1986), Siegel et al. (1988), and Turner, Miller, and Moses (1989).
4. See Bakeman, Lumb, and Smith (1986), Friedman et al. (1987), Quimby and Friedman (1989), Rogers and Williams (1987), and Selik, Castro, and Pappaioanou (1988).
5. There is, of course, much literature within anthropology and other disciplines on the social creation of the "other." This construction is especially common when those who are suffering with AIDS are blamed for their own illness. Patton's (1985) groundbreaking work on the sociological impact of AIDS not only explains why we create an "other" category when threatened but also carefully exposes the social construction of AIDS by the gay community. Gilman (1988) shows how AIDS was constructed by media images as a disease of the "other." Sontag (1989) applied her model of illness as metaphor to AIDS in much the same manner as she had for cancer in *Illness as Metaphor* (1979). Clatts, an anthropologist who works with adolescents and AIDS, and Mutchler (1989) unravel nonmedical representations of AIDS. And Murray, a medical sociologist, and Payne, a sociologist who recently died from AIDS, explain how the creation of risk groups helps deflect attention, by blaming the victim as "other," from the inability of science and medicine to cope with AIDS (Murray and Payne 1989).
6. None of my informants had been tested for antibodies to HIV by the conclusion of this study. Since that time (1989), approximately 20 to 30 percent have, but all have tested negative.
7. GRID (gay-related immunodeficiency) is believed by Murray and Payne (1989) to be a 1981 gay press term for the illness. AIDS (Acquired Immune Deficiency Syndrome, the same acronym for Autoimmune Deficiency Syndrome) made its first appearance in print in *Science* (13 August 1982).
8. That AIDS may have its origins in the African continent was either ignored by my informants or, if acknowledged as a possible theory, always discussed within the context of racism: another attempt by the white power structure to blame blacks for something wrong in society and to further stigmatize African-Americans (Dalton 1989). For discussion of the theory of African origins of AIDS, see Barnes (1987), Dickson (1987), Doolittle (1989), Feldman (1986), Greaves (1987), Newmark (1986), Palca (1988), Penny (1988), Piot and Plummer et al. (1988), Sharp (1988), and Schmidt (1984).
9. Compare Rogers and Williams (1987), who state that AIDS is regarded in the "public consciousness" as a disease of white, middle-class, gay men. See also Senak (1987). For black perspectives, see Greaves (1987) and Porter (1989).
10. During the course of the fieldwork for the study, five informants

passed away: key informant Cletuh died during an epileptic seizure in April 1988; Ralph and Bailey suffered fatal heart attacks in December 1987 and October 1988, respectively; Franklin passed from pneumonia after surgery in April 1989; and Todd, a hustler, died from a brain aneurism in March 1988. After completion of the data collection, Francis, a diabetic and another key informant, passed away after surgery in July 1990. None of these men had been diagnosed with HIV.

11. Centers for Disease Control statistics reported in the gay press (*Outlines,* February 1990, 43; Brinkley [1989]) and elsewhere (Quimby and Friedman 1989:405) show that black gay men comprise 10 percent of the total AIDS diagnoses and 16 percent of the "male gay/bisexual contacts" category. Blacks total 27 percent of reported AIDS cases to date. This percentage is the same as reported a year earlier (*BLK*, March 1989, 17). For New York City, the percentages are higher; for example, at least 19 percent of gay diagnoses are black men, and a further 37 percent are men who engage in homosexual practices and use IV drugs (Quimby and Friedman 1989:406).

12. Some of the significant New York City and national press examples are L. Altman (1981, 1986, 1987), Brand (1988), Collins (1985), Johnson (1988), Lambert (1988), Shilts (1988), Stone (1987), and Sullivan (1986).

13. Quimby and Friedman list organizations and individuals in the black community who have assisted in their respective communities' mobilization against AIDS. All of the churches noted are in Brooklyn (Quimby and Friedman 1989:408). Since that time at least three churches in Harlem have offered some type of assistance to people living with AIDS.

14. The availability of drugs and a lack of sex education allow for the transmission of HIV in Harlem. See Friedman et al. (1987), Greaves (1987), and *BLK* (1990).

15. These reasons for and against condom use compare favorably with the responses of male clients of female street prostitutes in Camden, New Jersey (Leonard 1990), and with the responses of patrons of singles bars in San Francisco (Stall, Huertin-Roberts et al. 1990). See Martin et al. (1989) on changes in sexual behavior.

16. Increased risk-taking associated with drug and alcohol consumption has been the focus of other research (Hasin and Martin 1988). It has been found that sexual risk-taking among drinkers, especially regular bar patrons, gay and non-gay, is substantially enhanced by substance abuse (Stall, Huertin-Roberts et al. 1990).

17. See De Stefano (1990), Hardy (1990), and *Au Courant* (1990).

18. This is not to denigrate the Minority Task Force on AIDS. It is composed of a group of hardworking gay men (and others) who are devoted to this cause.

19. During 1989, condoms and nonoxynol-9 lubricant were once again made available to whoever wanted them in the bathhouse.

20. See Greer (1986), Voelcker (1990), and Zuckerman (1988).

21. Altogether, the 57 respondents in this study identified 86 different people who had died from AIDS (57 men, 23 women, and 6 children). Of the 57 men who had died, 27 were presumed to be gay, 7 of whom were

also reputed to have been IV drug users. Currently, these respondents know a total of 62 different people who are living with AIDS (31 men, 26 women, and 5 children). Of the 31 men with AIDS, at least 20 are believed to be gay. Most of the gay men who died from AIDS passed away early in the epidemic: 1979 to 1984. The 6 who died later were not members of this community.

22. Compare the findings of Singer et al. (1990:81–83), who found the opposite in the "Latino community."

23. This is an example of homophobia. It's happening in Brooklyn, not Harlem, and is being perpetrated by staunch church members.

24. Several reports of funerals have emerged in the gay literature on AIDS. A similar example from Harlem is Harris (1986).

25. As an aside, one of the most startling impressions made on me in Harlem was the ubiquity of the funeral parlors. Every block seemed to have a funeral home tucked away in a basement. On main thoroughfares like Lenox Avenue, some blocks sported two or three. I wondered if the surrounding neighborhoods had the population to support such a need. For reports on morbidity in Harlem, see Kristal (1986) and Terry (1990).

26. The press reports otherwise (Lazare 1990). It is suspected that the trade in (and the addiction to) crack have enhanced a sex-for-crack exchange, which may in fact lead to an increase in the spread of the HIV virus to other addicts and dealers (Des Jarlais et al. 1986, Hamid 1990).

27. See D. Altman (1986), Clatts and Mutchler (1989), Fabian (1983), Ingstad (1990), and Sabatier (1988).

28. See Herdt (1988/89) and Schinke, Holden, and Moncher (1989).

29. See Gagnon (1989), Kus (1988), Martin et al. (1989), Sandoval (1977), Zehner and Lewis (1983/84), and Ziebold and Mongeon (1982).

30. Lack of safer sex practices and forays outside of this community will endanger the entire community. Recommendations have been made to outreach workers at the Gay Men's Health Crisis and the Minority Task Force on AIDS to educate these men.

## Chapter 9. "One of the Children"

1. The Schomburg Center for Research in Black Culture has become the most significant repository of black American artifacts in the United States. It is based on the collection by Arthur Alfonso Schomburg of over ten thousand books, newspapers, and other materials, which the black Puerto Rican bibliophile amassed during a thirty-five-year period. This collection was purchased in 1926 by the Carnegie Corporation for the New York Public Library. For further information, see the Schomburg's publications "The Legacy of Arthur Alfonso Schomburg: A Celebration of the Past, a Vision of the Future" (1986) and "Remaking the Past to Make the Future" (1986).

2. The Harlem Renaissance was originally named by the *New York Herald*

*Tribune* in "A Negro Renaissance" (7 May 1925). (Also, see Lewis [1989: 116]). It is used today to refer to a period of artistic production in many fields, including literature, poetry, drama, journalism, music, composition and performance, dance, Broadway productions, painting, sculpture, and the academic and business support of the artists involved. Those artists were perceived to represent the "Talented Tenth" of their generation by such black leaders as W. E. B. Du Bois and Charles S. Johnson. Most agree that the Renaissance began in 1919 with the return of black troops from Europe and World War I; they differ, however, with respect to the date of its demise. Some would have the 1929 Wall Street collapse as the final blow, others 1934 or 1935, with the deaths of writers Fisher and Thurman and the persistence of the depression. See Lewis (1989), as well as Ottley (1968), Anderson (1987), and Campbell (1987).

3. Further reading on the ambiguity of Hughes's sexuality should include Berry (1983), Rampersad (1988), and Smith (1983).

4. Reprinted in Smith (1983).

5. Isaac Julien is a young gay black British film director well known in Europe for his documentaries and television commercials on AIDS. At the time of writing, his full-length feature on Langston Hughes has had only two screenings in New York City, restricted by legal proceedings pursued by the Hughes Estate. Even at those screenings the censor cut much of Hughes reading his own poetry.

6. Reprinted in Smith (1983).

7. Gumby owned the Bookstore, a book-lined studio on 5th Avenue at 131st Street which hosted parties for literati and readings. "White author Samuel Steward remembers being taken to Gumby's one evening by a lesbian friend and enjoying a delightful evening of 'reefer,' bathtub gin, a game of truth, and homosexual exploits" (Garber 1989:322). Locke, a Harvard Ph.D., was a professor of philosophy at Howard University who negotiated much financial support for Renaissance writers, especially Toomer, McKay, Cullen, and Hughes. He acted as a go-between for the white wealth invested in Harlem at that time and the Talented Tenth. He was as well known for his predilection for young men as for his essays about the Harlem Renaissance. Jackman, Countee Cullen's lover, was a West Indian–born Harlem schoolteacher and friend of the Renaissance artists. He was painted by Reiss and sculpted by Barthé. Van Vechten is the most famous of Harlem's white entrepreneurs during the Renaissance period. A *New York Times* music critic, he spent much time in the speakeasies and parties of 1920s Harlem, acting as a go-between for publishers like Knopf and the Renaissance writers. He is most famous in Harlem for his controversial novel on the times, *Nigger Heaven*. For further information on these men and others, and their roles in the Renaissance, see Garber (1983, 1989) and Lewis (1989).

8. In the winter of 1990, white gay men on Christopher Street were "snapping." Marlon Riggs makes delightful reference to different types of snaps in a scene from his 1989 videodocumentary *Tongues United*. He has also recorded young gay black men vogueing at the Christopher Street piers. Also, during 1990, Fox Television's Emmy Award–winning comedy series *In*

*Living Color* featured a skit in which gay black men snapped. On television now, snapping will probably diffuse into American culture at large.

9. Some debate exists as to the actual origin of vogueing. Some informants believe the younger dancers got their posing moves from the large Harlem drag balls, where contestants pose on a runway in competition for the title Queen of the Ball. See chap. 4.

10. The Paradise Garage was located downtown and catered to a large black gay crowd. It offered R&B and other popular black music—for example, "house." It was open Friday and Saturday from midnight to noon, and several thousand gay men danced the night away. No alcohol was served, but a movie room and a roof garden provided space for imbibing other substances. Whitney Houston, Colonel Abrams, and Gwen Guthrie, among many other pop stars, performed on a large stage in the dance area. Grace Jones always started her show at 6:00 A.M. on Sunday.

11. These "houses" are described as "gay street gangs" in the documentary film *Paris Is Burning,* directed by Jennie Livingston.

12. Men Who Cook is an organization of black artists, many of whom are gay, that holds a cookout to raise funds for a children's art festival held each summer in Harlem.

13. Compare Gorman and Mallon's (1989) report on the success of community-based efforts at AIDS education in Los Angeles.

# References

Abrahams, Roger D. 1963. *Deep Down in the Jungle.* Chicago: Aldine.
———. 1970. *Positively Black.* Englewood Cliffs, N.J.: Prentice-Hall.
Adam, Barry D. 1987. *The Rise of a Gay and Lesbian Movement.* Boston: Twayne.
Albert, Edward. 1986. "Illness and Deviance: The Response of the Press to AIDS." In *The Social Dimensions of AIDS*, ed. Douglas Feldman and Thomas Johnson, pp. 163–178. New York: Praeger.
Altman, Dennis. 1971. *Homosexual: Oppression and Liberation.* London: Allen Lane.
———. 1986. *AIDS in the Mind of America: The Social, Political, and Psychological Impact of a New Epidemic.* Garden City, N.Y.: Anchor Press/ Doubleday.
Altman, Lawrence K. 1981. "Rare Cancer Seen in 41 Homosexuals." *New York Times,* July 3:A20, 1.
———. 1986. "AIDS May Spread Outside the Blood." *New York Times,* December 13:I10, 1.
———. 1987. AIDS Mystery: Why Do Some Infected Men Stay Healthy? *New York Times,* June 30:C1, 4.
Altman, Stan. 1986. "AIDS and the Substance Abuser: Service Needs and Policy Issues." Paper presented at Conference on AIDS and the Substance Abuser, Veterans Administration Medical Center, New York, June 12.
Anderson, Elijah. 1978. *A Place on the Corner.* Chicago: University of Chicago Press.
Anderson, Jervis. 1987. *This Was Harlem: 1990–1950, A Cultural Portrait.* New York: Farrar, Straus, Giroux.
———. 1989. "Harlem Clergy Pray for AIDS Awareness." *The Body Postive* 2(8):11.
Aschenbrenner, Joyce. 1983. *Lifelines: Black Families in Chicago.* Prospect Heights. Ill.: Waveland Press.

Associated Press, Hilton Head Island, South Carolina. 1990. "Black PWAs Survive Half as Long as White PWAs." *BLK* 2(4):29.

Baber, Ceola Ross. 1987. "The Artistry and Artifice of Black Communication." In *Expressively Black: The Cultural Basis of Ethnic Identity*, ed. Geneva Gay and Willie L. Baber, pp. 75–108. New York: Praeger.

Baim, Tracy. 1990. "AIDS Cases Reflect Disproportionate Rates Among Gays, Blacks, Latinos, Asians, Native Americans, and Others." *Outlines* 3(9):43.

Bakeman, R., J. R. Lumb, and D. W. Smith. 1986. "AIDS Statistics and the Risk for Minorities." *AIDS Research* 2:249–252.

Baker, Andrea. 1986. "The Portrayal of AIDS in the Media: An Analysis of Articles in the *New York Times*." In *The Social Dimensions of AIDS*, ed. Douglas Feldman and Thomas Johnson, pp. 179–194. New York: Praeger.

Baldwin, James. 1965. *Going to Meet the Man*. New York: Dial Press.

Banton, Michael. 1987. *Racial Theories*. Cambridge: Cambridge University Press.

Barbanel, Josh. 1989. "How Despair Is Engulfing a Generation in New York." *New York Times*, April 2:E6.

Barnes, Deborah M. 1987. "AIDS: Statistics But Few Answers." *Science* 236:1423–1425.

Barnes, John A. 1969. "Networks and Political Processes." In *Social Networks in Urban Situations*, ed. J. Clyde Mitchell. Manchester: Manchester University Press.

Barth, Fredrik, ed. 1969. *Ethnic Groups and Boundaries: The Social Organization of Culture Difference*. Boston: Little, Brown.

Baugh, John. 1983. *Black Street Speech: Its History, Structure, and Survival*. Austin: University of Texas Press.

Beam, Joseph, ed. 1986. *In the Life: A Black Gay Anthology*. Boston: Alyson Publications.

Becker, Howard S. 1963. *Outsiders: Studies in the Sociology of Deviance*. New York: Free Press.

Bell, Alan P., and Martin S. Weinberg. 1978. *Homosexualities: A Study of Diversity Among Men and Women*. New York: Simon & Schuster.

Berry, Faith. 1983. *Langston Hughes: Before and Beyond Harlem*. Westport, Conn.: Lawrence Hill.

Berry, Mary F., and John W. Blassingame. 1982. *Long Memory: The Black Experience in America*. New York: Oxford University Press.

Bérubé, Allan. 1990. *Coming Out Under Fire: The History of Gay Men and Women in World War Two*. New York: Free Press.

Bieber, Irving, et al. 1962. *Homosexuality: A Psychoanalytic Study*. New York: Basic Books.

Billingsley, Andrew. 1968. *Black Families in White America*. Englewood Cliffs, N.J.: Prentice-Hall.

Blackwood, Evelyn, ed. 1986. *The Many Faces of Homosexuality: Anthropological Approaches to Homosexual Behavior*. New York: Harrington Park Press.

Bosworth, Patricia. 1978. *Montgomery Clift: A Biography*. New York: Limelight Editions.

Bott, Elizabeth. 1957. *Family and Social Network: Roles, Norms and External Relationships in Ordinary Urban Families*. London: Tavistock.

Boughner, Terry. 1988. *Out of All Time: A Gay and Lesbian History*. Boston: Alyson Publications.

Boyer, Debra, K. 1986. "Male Prostitution: A Cultural Expression of Male Homosexuality." Ph.D. dissertation, University of Washington.

Brand, David. 1988. "Surviving Is What I Do." *Time*, May 2:62–63.

Breitman, George, Herman Porter, and Baxter Smith. 1976. *The Assassination of Malcolm X*. New York: Pathfinder Press.

Brink, William, and Louis Harris. 1967. *Black and White*. New York: Simon & Schuster.

Brinkley, Sidney. 1989. "AIDS and Men of Color." *BGM* 4:14–17.

Bronski, Michael. 1984. *Culture Clash: The Making of Gay Sensibility*. Boston: South End Press.

Bronstein, Scott. 1987. "4 New York Bathhouses Still Operate Under City's Program of Inspections." *New York Times*, May 3:A58,1.

Brown, Claude. 1965. *Manchild in the Promised Land*. New York: Signet Books.

———. 1972. "The Language of Soul." In *Rappin' and Stylin' Out: Communication in Urban Black America*, ed. Thomas Kochman, pp. 134–139. Urbana: University of Illinois Press.

Buchler, Ira R., and Henry A. Selby. 1968. *Kinship and Social Organization: An Introduction to Theory and Method*. New York: Macmillan.

Callender, Charles, and Lee M. Kochems. 1985. "Men and Not-Men: Male Gender Mixing Statuses and Homosexuality." *Journal of Homosexuality* 11:165–178.

Campbell, Mary S. 1987. *Harlem Renaissance Art of Black America*. New York: Harry N. Abrams.

Canavan, Peter. 1984. "The Gay Community at Jacob Riis Park." In *The Apple Sliced: Sociological Studies of New York City*, ed. Vernon Boggs, Gerald Handel, and Sylvia F. Fava, pp. 67–82. South Hadley, Mass.: Bergin & Garvey.

Carillo, Emilio. 1988. "AIDS and the Latino Community." *Centro de Estudios Puertoriqueños* 2(4):7–14.

Carrier, Joseph M. 1976a. "Cultural Factors Affecting Urban Mexican Male Homosexual Behavior." *Archives of Sexual Behavior* 5(2):103–124.

———. 1976b. "Family Attitudes and Mexican Male Homosexuality." *Urban Life* 5(3):359–375.

———. 1977. " 'Sex-Role Preference' as an Explanatory Variable in Homosexual Behavior." *Archives of Sexual Behavior* 6(1):53–65.

———. 1985. "Mexican Male Bisexuality." In *Bisexualities: Theory and Research*, ed. Fritz Klein and Timothy J. Wolf, pp. 75–85. New York: Haworth Press.

———. 1989. "Sexual Behavior and Spread of AIDS in Mexico." *Medical Anthropology* 10:129–142.

Cass, Vivienne C. 1979. "Homosexual Identity Formation: A Theoretical Model." *Journal of Homosexuality* 4:219–235.

————. 1985. "Homosexual Identity: A Concept in Need of Definition." In *Origins of Sexuality and Homosexuality*, ed. John P. DeCecco and Michael G. Shively, pp. 105–126. New York: Harrington Park Press.

Cavan, Sheri. 1966. *Liquor License: Ethnography of Bar Behavior*. Chicago: Aldine.

Chauncey, George, Jr., and Lisa Kennedy. 1987. "Time on Two Crosses: An Interview with Bayard Rustin." *The Village Voice*, June 30:27–29.

Chesebro, James W., ed. 1981. *Gayspeak: Gay Male and Lesbian Communication*. New York: Pilgrim Press.

Clark, Tom, and Dick Kleiner. 1989. *Rock Hudson: Friend of Mine*. New York: Pharos Books.

Clatts, Michael C., and Kevin M. Mutchler. 1989. "AIDS and the Dangerous Other: Metaphors of Sex and Deviance in the Representation of Disease." In *The AIDS Pandemic: A Global Emergency*, ed. Ralph Bolton, pp. 13–22. New York: Gordon and Breach.

Cohen, Anthony P. 1985. *The Symbolic Construction of Community*. New York: Tavistock Publications.

Coimbra, Carlos, and Mohammad Torabi. 1987. "Sexual Behavior and AIDS in Sociocultural Perspectives: Commentary." *International Quarterly of Community Health Education* 7(3):269–275.

Cole, Herbert M. 1990. "Kente: A Meaningful Tradition in Cloth." *American Visions* 5(5):18–22.

Coleman, E. 1981/2. "Developmental Stages of the Coming Out Process." *Journal of Homosexuality* 7(2/3):31–43.

Collins, Glenn. 1985. "Impact of AIDS: Patterns of Homosexual Life Changing." *New York Times*, July 22:B4.

Cone, James H. 1991. *Martin & Malcolm & America: A Dream or a Nightmare*. Maryknoll, N.Y.: Orbis Books.

Connolly, Harold X. 1977. *A Ghetto Grows in Brooklyn*. New York: New York University Press.

Cooke, Benjamin G. 1972. "Non-verbal Communication Among Afro-Americans: An Initial Classification." In *Rappin' and Stylin' Out: Communication in Urban Black America*, ed. Thomas Kochman, pp. 32–64. Urbana: University of Illinois Press.

Cory, Donald Webster. 1951. *The Homosexual in America: A Subjective Approach*. New York: Greenberg.

Crimp, Douglas, ed. 1988. *AIDS: Cultural Analysis of Cultural Activism*. Cambridge, Mass.: MIT Press.

Crimp, Douglas, and Adam Rolston. 1990. *AIDS Demo Graphics*. Seattle: Bay Press.

Cromartie, John, and Carol Stack. 1990. "Who Counts? A Reinterpretation of Black Return and Non-return Migration to the South, 1975–1980." *Geographical Review*.

Curtis, Wayne. 1988. *Revelations: A Collection of Gay Male Coming Out Stories*. Boston: Alyson Publications.

Dalton, Harlon L. 1989. "AIDS in Blackface." *Daedalus* 118(3):205–227.

Dalton, Harlon L., Scott Burris, and the Yale AIDS Law Project, eds. 1987.

*AIDS and the Law: A Guide for the Public.* New Haven: Yale University Press.

Dank, Barry M. 1979. "Coming Out in the Gay World." In *Gay Men: The Sociology of Male Homosexuality,* ed. Martin P. Levine, pp. 103–133. New York: Harper and Row.

Davies, P. M. 1986. "Some Problems in Defining and Sampling Non-Heterosexual Males." *Working Paper* no. 21. Social Research Unit, University College, Cardiff, Wales.

De Cecco, John P., and Michael G. Shively. 1984. "From Sexual Identity to Sexual Relationships: A Contextual Shift." *Journal of Homosexuality* 9(2/3):1–26.

Delph, Edward W. 1978. *The Silent Community: Public Homosexual Encounters.* Beverley Hills, Calif.: Sage Publications.

DeMarco, Joe. 1983. "Gay Racism." In *Black Men White Men: A Gay Anthology,* ed. Michael J. Smith, pp. 109–118. San Francisco: Gay Sunshine Press.

D'Emilio, John. 1983. *Sexual Politics, Sexual Communities: The Making of a Homosexual Minority in the United States, 1940–1970.* Chicago: University of Chicago Press.

———. 1989. "Gay Politics and Community in San Francisco Since World War II." In *Hidden from History: Reclaiming the Gay and Lesbian Past,* ed. Martin Bauml Duberman, Martha Vicinus, and George Chauncey, Jr., pp. 456–473. New York: New American Library.

de Monteflores, C., and S. J. Schultz. 1978. "Coming Out: Similarities and Differences for Lesbians and Gay Men." *Journal of Social Issues* 34(3):59–72.

Des Jarlais, Don C., Samuel R. Friedman, and David Strug. 1986. "AIDS among Intravenous Drug Users: A Sociocultural Perspective." In *The Social Dimensions of AIDS: Methods and Theory,* ed. Douglas A. Feldman and T. M. Johnson. New York: Praeger.

De Stefano, George. 1990. "Are Gay Men Having Safer Sex?" *Outweek* 34:38–43.

Dickson, David. 1987. "Africa Begins to Face Up to AIDS." *Science* 238:605–607.

Dillard, Joey Lee. 1973. *Black English: Its History and Usage in the United States.* New York: Vintage Books.

Doolittle, Russell F. 1989. "The Simian-Human Connection." *Nature* 339: 338–339.

Drake, St. Clair. 1987. Preface. In *Expressively Black: The Cultural Basis of Ethnic Identity,* ed. Geneva Gay and Willie L. Baber, pp. ix–xiv. New York: Praeger.

Drimmer, Melvin. 1987. *Issues in Black History: Reflections and Commentaries on the Black Historical Experience.* Dubuque, Iowa: Kendall-Hunt.

Duberman. Martin B., Martha Vicinus, and George Chauncey Jr., eds. 1989. *Hidden from History: Reclaiming the Gay and Lesbian Past.* New York: New American Library.

Du Bois, W. E. B. 1989. *The Souls of Black Folk.* New York: Bantam Books.

Duplechan, Larry. 1985. *Eight Days a Week.* Boston: Alyson Publications.

———. 1986. *Blackbird*. New York: St. Martin's Press.

Ehrenreich, Barbara. 1990. *Fear of Falling: The Inner Life of the Middle Class*. New York: Harper Collins.

Ellison, Ralph. 1972. *Invisible Man*. New York: Vintage Books.

Engerman, Stanley L., and Eugene D. Genovese, eds. 1975. *Race and Slavery in the Western Hemisphere: Quantitative Studies*. Princeton: Princeton University Press.

Epstein, A. L. 1961. "The Network and Urban Social Organization." In *Social Networks in Urban Situations*, ed. J. Clycde Mitchell, pp. 77–116. Manchester: Manchester University Press.

———. 1978. *Ethos and Identity: Three Studies in Ethnicity*. London: Tavistock Publishing.

Erickson, Richard A. 1986. "Entrepreneurs of the Night: A Psychosocial Study of the Adolescent Male Prostitute." Ph.D. dissertation, Union for Experimenting Colleges and Universities, Cincinnati, Ohio.

Erikson, E. H. 1986. *Identity: Youth and Crisis*. New York: Norton.

Essien-Udom, E. U. 1962. *Black Nationalism: A Search for Identity in America*. Chicago: University of Chicago Press.

Evans-Pritchard, Edward E. 1940. *The Nuer: A Description of the Models of Livelihood and Political Institutions of a Nilotic People*. Oxford: Oxford University Press.

Fabian, Johannes. 1983. *Time and the Other: How Anthropology Makes Its Object*. New York: Columbia University Press.

Farley, Reynolds, and Walter R. Allen. 1987. *The Color Line and the Quality of Life in America*. New York: Russell Sage Foundation.

Fasold, Ralph W. 1969. "Tense and the Form *Be* in Black English." *Language* 45:763–776.

Fasold, Ralph W., and Roger W. Shuy, eds. 1970. *Teaching Standard English in the Inner City*. Washington, D.C.: Center for Applied Linguistics.

Fast, Julius. 1978. *Body Language*. London: Pan Books.

Feldman, Douglas A. 1986. "Anthropology, AIDS, and Africa." *Medical Anthropology Quarterly* 17(2):38–40.

Folb, Edith A. 1980. *Runnin' Down Some Lines: The Language and Culture of Black Teenagers*. Cambridge: Harvard University Press.

Ford, Clellan S., and Frank A. Beach. 1951. *Patterns of Sexual Behavior*. New York: Harper & Row.

Forstein, Marshall. 1989. "Understanding the Psychological Impact of AIDS: The Other Epidemic." In *The AIDS Epidemic: Private Rights and the Public Interest*, ed. Padraig O'Malley, pp. 159–171. Boston: Beacon Press.

Fox, Robin. 1967. *Kinship and Marriage*. Harmondsworth: Penguin Books.

Frazier, Franklin E. 1964. *The Negro Church in America*. Liverpool: University of Liverpool Press.

Friedman, Samuel, Jo L. Sotheran, et al. 1987. "The AIDS Epidemic Among Blacks and Hispanics." *The Milbank Memorial Fund Quarterly* 65(Supplement 2):455–499.

Freud, Sigmund. 1905. *Three Essays on the Theory of Sexuality*. London: Imago.

Gagnon, John H. 1989. "Disease and Desire." *Daedalus* 118(3):47–77.

Gagnon, John H., and William Simon. 1973. *Sexual Conduct: The Social Sources of Human Sexuality*. Chicago: Aldine.

Gagnon, John H., and William Simon, eds. 1967. *Sexual Deviance*. New York: Harper & Row.

Gans, Herbert. 1962. *The Urban Villagers: Group and Class in the Life of Italian-Americans*. New York: Free Press.

Garber, Eric. 1983. "T'ain't Nobody's Bizness: Homosexuality in 1920's Harlem." In *Black Men White Men: A Gay Anthology*, ed. Michael J. Smith, pp. 7–16. San Francisco: Gay Sunshine Press.

———. 1988. "Gladys Bentley: The Bulldagger Who Sang the Blues." *Out/ Look* 1(1):52–61.

———. 1989. "A Spectacle in Color: The Lesbian and Gay Subculture of Jazz Age Harlem." In *Hidden from History: Reclaiming the Gay and Lesbian Past*, ed. Martin Duberman, Martha Vicinus, and George Chauncey Jr., pp. 318–331. New York: New American Library.

Garcia-Barrio, Constance. 1988. "Telling Tales." *American Visions* 3(5):17–20.

Gary, Lawrence E., ed. 1983. *Black Men*. Beverly Hills: Sage Publications.

Gay, Geneva. 1987a. "Expressive Ethos of Afro-American Culture." In *Expressively Black: The Cultural Basis of Ethnic Identity*, ed. Geneva Gay and Willie L. Baber, pp. 1–16. New York: Praeger.

———. 1987b. "Ethnic Identity Development and Black Expressiveness." In *Expressively Black: The Cultural Basis of Ethnic Identity*, ed. Geneva Gay and Willie L. Baber, pp. 35–74. New York: Praeger.

Gay, Geneva, and Willie L. Baber, eds. 1987. *Expressively Black: The Cultural Basis of Ethnic Identity*. New York: Praeger.

Gayle, Addison, Jr., ed. 1971. *The Black Aesthetic*. Garden City, N.Y.: Doubleday & Company.

Gilman, Sander L. 1988. *Disease and Representation: Images of Illness from Madness to AIDS*. Ithaca, N.Y.: Cornell University Press.

Glazer, Nathan, and Daniel P. Moynihan. 1963. *Beyond the Melting Pot*. Cambridge: M.I.T. Press/Harvard University Press.

Goffman, Erving. 1961. *Asylums: Essays on the Social Situation of Mental Patients and Other Inmates*. New York: Doubleday.

———. 1963. *Stigma: Notes on the Management of Spoiled Identity*. Englewood Cliffs, N.J.: Prentice-Hall.

Goldsby, Jackie. 1989. "All About Yves." *Out/Look* 2(1):34–35.

Goldsmith, Douglas S., Douglas S. Lipton, and Edmundo Morales. 1989. "Drug Injection, HIV Concerns and Drug Treatment Entry in New York City." Paper presented at American Anthropological Association meetings, Washington, D.C., November 15.

Gomez, Jewelle, and Barbara Smith. 1989. "Taking the Home out of Homophobia: Black Lesbians Look in their Own Backyard." *Out/Look* 2(4):32–37.

Goode, Erich, and Richard R. Troiden, eds. 1975. *Sexual Deviance and Sexual Deviants*. New York: William Morrow.

Goodwin, Joseph P. 1989. *More Man Than You'll Ever Be: Gay Folklore and Acculturation in Middle America*. Bloomington: Indiana University Press.

Gorman, Michael, and David Mallon. 1989. "The Role of a Community-based Health Education Program in the Prevention of AIDS." In *The AIDS Pandemic: A Global Emergency*, ed. Ralph Bolton, pp. 67–74. New York: Gordon and Breach.

Grahn, Judy. 1984. *Another Mother Tongue: Gay Words, Gay Worlds*. Boston: Beacon Press.

Greaves, Wayne L. 1987. "The Black Community." In *AIDS and the Law: A Guide for the Public*, ed. Harlon L. Dalton and Scott Burris, pp. 281–289. New Haven: Yale University Press and the Yale AIDS Law Project.

Green, Richard. 1987. *The "Sissy Boy" Syndrome and the Development of Homosexuality*. New Haven: Yale University Press.

Greenberg, David F. 1988. *The Construction of Homosexuality*. Chicago: University of Chicago Press.

Greer, William R. 1986. "Violence Against Homosexuals Rising." *New York Times*, November 23:A36, 4.

Gutman, Herbert G. 1976. *The Black Family in Slavery and Freedom 1750–1925*. New York: Pantheon Books.

Gwaltney, John L. 1980. *Drylongso: A Self-Portrait of Black America*. New York: Vintage.

———. 1981. "Common Sense and Science: Urban Core Black Observations." In *Anthropology at Home in North America: Methods and Issues in the Study of One's Own Society*, ed. David A. Messerschmidt, pp. 46–61. Cambridge: Cambridge University Press.

Halperin, David M. 1990. *One Hundred Years of Homosexuality and Other Essays on Greek Love*. New York: Routledge.

Hamid, Ansley. 1990. "The Political Economy of Crack-related Violence." *Contemporary Drug Problems* Spring:31–78.

Hannerz, Ulf. 1969. *Soulside: Inquiries into Ghetto Culture and Community*. New York: Columbia University Press.

Hardy, Robin. 1990. "Risky Business: Confronting Unsafe Sex." *Village Voice* 35(26):35–38.

Harris, Craig G. 1986. "Cut Off from Among Their People." In *In the Life: A Black Gay Anthology*, ed. Joseph Beam, pp. 63–67. Boston: Alyson Publications.

Harris, Fred R., and Tom Wicker. 1988. *The Kerner Report: The 1968 Report of the National Advisory Commission on Civil Disorders*. New York: Pantheon Books.

Harris, M. A. 1968. *A Negro History Tour of Manhattan*. New York: Greenwood Publishing.

Harry, Joseph, and William B. DeVall. 1978. *The Social Organization of Gay Males*. New York: Praeger.

Hart, John, and Diane Richardson. 1981. *The Theory and Practice of Homosexuality*. London: Routledge & Kegan Paul.

Hasin, Deborah, and John L. Martin. 1988. "Alcohol, Alcoholism, and Risky Sexual Behavior in New York City Gay Men." Paper delivered at the

Annual Meeting of the American Public Heath Association, Boston, November.

Haugen, Einar. 1964. "Bilingualism and Bidialectalism." In *Social Dialects and Language Learning*, ed. Roger W. Shuy, pp. 8–9. Champaign, Ill.: National Council of Teachers of English.

Hayes, Joseph J. 1981. "Gayspeak." In *Gayspeak: Gay Male and Lesbian Communication*, ed. James W. Chesebro, pp. 45–57. New York: Pilgrim Press.

Henslin, James M., ed. 1971. *Studies in the Sociology of Sex*. New York: Meredith Corp.

Herdt, Gilbert H. 1981. *Guardians of the Flute: Idioms of Masculinity*. New York: Columbia University Press.

Herdt, Gilbert H., ed. 1982. *Rituals of Manhood: Male Initiation in Papua New Guinea*. Berkeley, Los Angeles, and London: University of California Press.

———. 1984. *Ritualized Homosexuality in Melanesia*. Berkeley, Los Angeles, and London: University of California Press.

———. 1988/89. "Gay Youth." *Journal of Homosexuality* 17(1/2):1–42.

Hernton, Calvin C. 1965. *Sex and Racism in America*. New York: Grove Press.

Hill, Robert. 1971. *The Strengths of Black Families*. New York: Emerson Hall Publishers.

Hoffman, Martin. 1968. *The Gay World: Male Homosexuality and the Social Creation of Evil*. New York: Basic Books.

Holt, Grace Sims. 1972. "Stylin' outta the Black Pulpit." In *Rappin' and Stylin' Out: Communication in Urban Black America*, ed. Thomas Kochman, pp. 152–159. Urbana: University of Illinois Press.

Hooker, Evelyn. 1969. "The Homosexual Community." In *The Same Sex: An Appraisal of Homosexuality*, ed. Ralph W. Weltge, pp. 25–39. Philadelphia: Pilgrim Press.

———. 1972. "Final Report of the Task Force on Homosexuality." In *The Homosexual Dialectic*, ed. Joseph A. McCaffrey, pp. 145–155. Englewood Cliffs, N.J.: Prentice-Hall.

Hooks, Bell. 1988. "Reflections on Homophobia and Black Communities." *Out/Look* 1(2):22–25.

Hoult, Thomas F. 1985. "Human Sexuality in Biological Perpective: Theoretical and Methodological Considerations." In *Origins of Sexuality and Homosexuality*, ed. John P. De Cecco and Michael G. Shively, pp. 137–155. New York: Harrington Park Press.

Howell, Joseph T. 1973. *Hard Living on Clay Street: Portraits of Blue Collar Families*. Garden City, N.Y.: Anchor Books.

Huggins, Nathan Irvin. 1971. *Harlem Renaissance*. New York: Oxford University Press.

Humphreys, Laud. 1972. "New Styles in Homosexual Manliness." In *The Homosexual Dialectic*, ed. Joseph A. McCaffrey, pp. 65–83. Englewood Cliffs, N.J.: Prentice-Hall.

———. 1975. *Tearoom Trade: Impersonal Sex in Public Places*. New York: Aldine.

———. 1979. "Exodus and Identity: The Emerging Gay Culture." In *Gay Men: The Sociology of Male Homosexuality*, ed. Martin P. Levine, pp. 134–147. New York: Harper & Row.

Humphreys, Laud, and Brian Miller. 1980. "Identities in the Emerging Gay Culture." In *Homosexual Behavior: A Modern Reappraisal*, ed. Judd Marmor, pp. 142–156. New York: Basic Books.

Icard, Larry. 1986. "Black Gay Men and Conflicting Social Identities: Sexual Orientation versus Racial Identity." *Journal of Social Work and Human Sexuality* 4(1/2):83–93.

Ingstad, Benedicte. 1990. "The Cultural Construction of AIDS and Its Consequences for Prevention in Botswana." *Medical Anthropology Quarterly* 4(1):28–40.

Jackson, Greg. 1986. "The Gay Ghetto." In *Gay Life: Leisure, Love, Living for the Contemporary Gay Male*, ed. Eric E. Rofes, pp. 87–91. Garden City, N.Y.: Doubleday.

Jay, Karla, and Allen Young. 1972. *Out of the Closets: Voices of Gay Liberation*. New York: Pyramid Books.

———. 1975. *After You're Out: Personal Experiences of Gay Men and Lesbian Women*. New York: Link Books.

———. 1978. *Lavender Culture*. New York: Jove Publications.

———. 1979. *The Gay Report: Lesbians and Gay Men Speak Out About Sexual Experiences and Lifestyles*. New York: Summit Books.

Jeanmarie, Redvers. 1988. "An Interview with Bayard Rustin (March 17, 1912–August 24, 1987)." In *Other Countries: Black Gay Voices*, ed. Carl A. Johnson et al., pp. 2–16. New York: Other Countries.

Johnson, Cary Alan, Colin Robinson, and Terence Taylor, eds. 1988. *Other Countries: Black Gay Voices*. New York: Other Countries.

Johnson, James Weldon. 1968. *Black Manhattan*. New York: Arno Press.

———. 1990. *The Autobiography of an Ex-Colored Man*. New York: Penguin Books.

Johnson, Julie. 1988. "Homosexual Groups and the Politics of AIDS." *New York Times*, October 6:B16, 3.

Johnson, Julius Maurice. 1981. "Influence of Assimilation of the Psychosocial Adjustment of Black Homosexual Men." Ph.D. dissertation, California School of Professional Psychology, Berkeley.

Jones-Jackson, Patricia. 1987. *When Roots Die: Endangered Traditions on the Sea Islands*. Athens: University of Georgia Press.

Kamel, G. W. Levi. 1983. "Downtown Street Hustlers: The Role of Dramaturgical Imagining Practices in the Social Construction of Male Prostitution." Ph.D. dissertation, University of California, San Diego.

Karlen, Arno. 1971. *Sexuality and Homosexuality: A New View*. New York: W. W. Norton.

Katz, Johnathan. 1976. *Gay American History: Lesbians and Gay Men in the U.S.A.* New York: Thomas Y. Crowell.

Keiser, R. Lincoln. 1969. *The Vice Lords: Warriors of the Streets*. New York: Holt, Rinehart and Winston.

Killian, Lewis, and Charles Grigg. 1964. *Racial Crisis in America: Leadership in Conflict.* Englewood Cliffs, N.J.: Prentice-Hall.

Kinsey, Alfred C., Wardell B. Pomeroy, and Clyde E. Martin. 1948. *Sexual Behavior in the Human Male.* Philadelphia: W. B. Saunders.

Knutson, Donald C., ed. 1979/80. "Homosexuality and the Law." *Journal of Homosexuality* 5(1/2):5–24.

Kochman, Thomas. 1972a. "The Kinetic Element in Black Idiom." In *Rappin' and Stylin' Out: Communication in Urban Black America,* ed. Thomas Kochman, pp. 160–169. Urbana: University of Illinois Press.

———. 1972b. "Toward an Ethnography of Black American Speech Behavior." In *Rappin' and Stylin' Out: Communication in Urban Black America,* ed. Thomas Kochman, pp. 241–264. Urbana: University of Illinois Press.

Kolata, Gina. 1989. "Grim Side of Park Rampage Found in East Harlem Streets." *New York Times,* May 2:C1, 13.

Kolb, L. C., and A. M. Johnson. 1955. "Etiology and Theory of Overt Homosexuality." *Psychoanalytical Quarterly* 24:506–515.

Kristal, Alan R. 1986. "The Impact of the Acquired Immunodeficiency Syndrome on Patterns of Premature Death in New York City." *Journal of the American Medical Association* 255(17):2306–2310.

Kunkel, Peter, and Sara Sue Kennard. 1971. *Spout Spring: A Black Community.* New York: Holt, Rinehart.

Kus, Robert J. 1988. "Alcoholism and Non-Acceptance of Gay Self: The Critical Link." *Journal of Homosexuality* 15(1/2):25–42.

Labov, William. 1972. *Language in the Inner City.* Philadelphia: University of Pennsylvania Press.

Lander, Joyce. 1971. *Tomorrow's Tomorrow.* New York: Anchor Books.

La Guardia, Robert. 1977. *Monty: A Biography of Montgomery Clift.* New York: Primus.

Lambert, Bruce. 1988. "Puzzling Questions Are Raised on Statistics on AIDS Epidemic." *New York Times,* July 22:B4.

Landry, Bart. 1987. *The New Black Middle Class.* Berkeley, Los Angeles, and London: University of California Press.

Langness, L. L., and Gelya Frank. 1981. *Lives: An Anthropological Approach to Biography.* Novato, Calif.: Chandler and Sharp.

Larsen, Knub, Rodney M. Cate, and Michael Reed. 1983. "Anti-Black Attitudes, Religious Orthodoxy, Permissiveness, and Sexual Information: A Study of the Attitudes of Heterosexuals toward Homosexuality." *Journal of Sex Research* 19(2):105–118.

Lauritsen, John, and David Thorstad. 1974. *The Early Homosexual Rights Movement, 1984–1935.* New York: Times Change Press.

Lazare, David. 1990. "Crack and AIDS: The Next Wave?" *Village Voice* 35(19):29–30.

Lee, John A. 1977. "Going Public: A Study in the Sociology of Homosexual Liberation." *Journal of Homosexuality* 3:49–78.

Lefever, Harry G. 1988. "'Deep Play': Rituals of Black Male Identity in

Urban Ghetto Communities." *Anthropology & Humanism Quarterly* 13(1):11–17.

Leonard, Terri L. 1990. "Male Clients of Female Street Prostitutes: Unseen Partners in Sexual Disease Transmission." *Medical Anthropology Quarterly* 4(1):41–55.

Levine, Lawrence W. 1978. *Black Culture and Black Consciousness: Afro-American Folk Thought from Slavery to Freedom.* New York: Oxford University Press.

Levine, Martin P., ed. 1979. *Gay Men: The Sociology of Male Homosexuality.* New York: Harper & Row.

Lévi-Strauss, Claude. 1963. *Structural Anthropology.* New York: Basic Books.

———. 1966. *The Savage Mind.* London: Weidenfeld and Nicolson.

———. 1969. *The Elementary Structures of Kinship.* Boston: Beacon Press.

Lewin, Ellen. 1991. "Writing Lesbian and Gay Culture: What the Natives Have to Say for Themselves." *American Ethnologist* 18(4):786–792.

Lewis, David Levering. 1989. *When Harlem Was In Vogue.* New York: Oxford University Press.

Lewis, Diane K. 1975. "The Black Family: Socialization and Sex Roles." *Phylon* 36(3):221–237.

Lewis, Hylan. 1964. *Blackways of Kent.* New Haven: Yale University Press.

Lewis, Oscar. 1966. "The Culture of Poverty." *Scientific American* 215(4):19–25.

Liebow, Elliott. 1967. *Tally's Corner: A Study of Negro Streetcorner Men.* Boston: Little, Brown.

Lincoln, C. Eric. 1961. *The Black Muslims in America.* Boston: Beacon Press.

———. 1974. *The Black Church Since Frazier.* New York: Schocken Books.

Litten, E. M., M. E. Griffen, and A. M. Johnson. 1956. "Parental Influence in Unusual Sexual Behavior in Children." *Psychoanalytical Quarterly* 25:1–15.

Loiacano, Darryl K. 1989. "Gay Identity Issues Among Black Americans: Racism, Homophobia, and the Need for Validation." *Journal of Counseling and Development* 68:21–25.

Lomax, Louis E. 1963. *When the Word is Given . . . A Report on Elijah Muhammad, Malcolm X, and the Black Muslim World.* Cleveland: World.

McCaffrey, Joseph A. 1972. "Homosexuality: The Stereotype, The Real." In *The Homosexual Dialectic,* ed. Joseph A. McCaffrey, pp. 137–144. Englewood Cliffs, N.J.: Prentice-Hall.

McClester, Cedric. 1985. *Kwanzaa.* New York: Gumbs and Thomas.

MacCormack, C., and M. Strathern, eds. 1980. *Nature, Culture and Gender.* Cambridge: Cambridge University Press.

McFadden, Robert D. 1988. "Health Officials Order Shutdown of Gay Cinema." *New York Times,* October 1:31, 6.

McKay, Claude. 1928. *Home to Harlem.* New York: Harper & Brothers.

———. 1940. *Harlem: Negro Metropolis.* New York: Harcourt Brace Jovanovich.

MacLeod, Jay. 1987. *Ain't No Makin' It: Leveled Aspirations in a Low-Income Neighborhood.* Boulder, Colo.: Westview Press.

Marmor, Judd. 1965. *Sexual Inversion: The Multiple Roots of Homosexuality.*
New York: Basic Books.

Marmor, Judd, ed. 1980. *Homosexual Behavior: A Modern Reappraisal.* New
York: Basic Books.

Martin, Elmer P., and Joanne M. Martin. 1978. *The Black Extended Family.*
Chicago: University of Chicago Press.

Martin, John L., and Laura Dean. 1990. "Development of a Community
Sample of Gay Men for an Epidemiologic Study of AIDS." *American Behavioral Scientist* 33:546–561.

Martin, John L., Laura Dean, Marc Garcia, and William Hall. 1989. "The
Impact of AIDS on a Gay Community: Change in Sexual Behavior, Substance Use, and Mental Health." *American Journal of Community Psychology* 17(3):269–293.

May, Robert M., Roy M. Anderson, and Sally M. Blower. 1989. "The Epidemiology and Transmission Dynamics of HIV-AIDS." *Daedalus* 118(2):
163–201.

Mazrui, Ali. 1986. *The Africans: A Triple Heritage.* Boston: Little, Brown.

Meier, August, and Elliott Rudwick. 1976. *From Plantation to Ghetto.* New
York: Hill and Wang.

Meister, Richard J., ed. 1972. *The Black Ghetto: Promised Land or Colony?* Lexington, Mass.: D. C. Heath.

Meltzer, Milton, ed. 1987. *The Black Americans: A History in Their Own
Words 1619–1983.* New York: Harper & Row.

Minton, Henry L., and Gary J. McDonald. 1985. "Homosexual Identity Formation as a Development Process." In *Origins of Sexuality and Homosexuality,* ed. John P. De Cecco and Michael G. Shively, pp. 91–104. New
York: Harrington Park Press.

Mohr, Richard D. 1988. *Gays/Justice: A Study of Ethics, Society, and Law.*
New York: Columbia University Press.

Mordden, Ethan. 1985. *I've a Feeling We're Not in Kansas Anymore: Tales
from Gay Manhattan.* New York: St. Martin's Press.

———. 1986. *Buddies.* New York: St. Martin's Press.

Moynihan, Daniel Patrick. 1965. *The Negro Family: The Case for National
Action.* Washington, D.C.: U.S. Department of Labor, Office of Planning
and Research.

———. 1986. *Family and Nation.* San Diego: Harcourt Brace Jovanovich.

Muchmore, Wes, and Willian Hanson. 1982. *Coming Out Right: A Handbook
for the Gay Male.* Boston: Alyson Publications.

———. 1986. *Coming Along Fine: Today's Gay Man and His World.* Boston:
Alyson Publications.

Murray, Stephen O., and Kenneth W. Payne. 1989. "The Social Classification
of AIDS in American Epidemiology." In *The AIDS Pandemic: A Global
Emergency,* ed. Ralph Bolton, pp. 23–36. New York: Gordon and Breach.

Musto, Michael. 1987. "Mandatory Macho: Butching Up Is Not a Liberated
Act." *Village Voice,* June 30:30.

Naison, Mark. 1985. *Communists in Harlem During the Depression.* New
York: Grove Press.

Nanda, Serena. 1990. *Neither Man Nor Woman: The Hijras of India*. Belmont, Calif.: Wadsworth.

Newman, Dorothy K., Nancy J. Amidei, et al. 1978. *Protest, Politics, and Prosperity: Black Americans and White Institutions, 1940–75*. New York: Pantheon Books.

Newman, Katherine S. 1988. *Falling from Grace: The Experience of Downward Mobility in the American Middle Class*. New York: Free Press.

Newmark, Peter. 1986. "AIDS in an African Context." *Nature* 324:611.

Newton, Esther. 1979. *Mother Camp: Female Impersonators in America*. Chicago: University of Chicago Press.

New York City Department of Health. 1989. *AIDS Surveillance Update (March–October)*. New York: New York City Department of Health.

New York Urban League. 1984. *Status of Black New York Report*. New York: New York Urban League.

Ortner, Sherry B., and Harriet Whitehead, eds. 1981. *Sexual Meanings*. New York: Cambridge University Press.

Osofsky, Gilbert. 1971. *Harlem: The Making of a Ghetto*. New York: Harper & Row.

Ottley, Roi. 1968. *New World A-Coming*. New York: Arno Press/New York Times.

Ovesey, Lionel. 1954. "The Homosexual Conflict." *Psychiatry* 17:243–250.

Palca, Joseph. 1988. "New Virus Lands in United States." *Nature* 331:381.

Panajian, Avedis Y. 1983. "A Psychological Study of Male Prostitutes." Ph.D. dissertation, United States International University, San Diego.

Park, Julie. 1982. "Doing Well: An Ethnography of Coping." *Working Papers in Anthropology* no. 61, Department of Anthropology, University of Auckland.

Parkerson, Michelle. 1987. "Beyond Chiffon." *Black/Out* 1(3/4):20–22.

Pasteur, Alfred B., and Ivory L. Toldson. 1982. *Roots of Soul: The Psychology of Black Expressiveness*. Garden City, N.Y.: Anchor Press/Doubleday.

Patton, Cindy. 1985. *Sex and Germs: The Politics of AIDS*. Boston: South End Press.

Penny, David. 1988. "Origins of the AIDS Virus." *Nature* 333:494–495.

Piot, Peter, Francis A. Plummer, et al. 1988. "AIDS: An International Perspective." *Science* 239:573–579.

Piven, Frances Fox, and Richard A. Cloward. 1972. *Regulating the Poor: The Functions of Public Welfare*. New York: Vintage Books.

——. 1979. *Poor People's Movements: Why They Succeed, How They Fail*. New York: Vintage Books.

Plummer, Kenneth. 1975. *Sexual Stigma: An Interactionist Account*. London: Routledge and Kegan Paul.

Polsky, Ned. 1969. *Hustlers, Beats, and Others*. Garden City, N.Y.: Doubleday.

Porter, Veneita. 1989. "Minorities and HIV Infection." In *The AIDS Epidemic: Private Rights and the Public Interest*, ed. Padraig O'Malley, pp. 371–379. Boston: Beacon Press.

Powdermarker, Hortense. 1939. *After Freedom: A Cultural Study in the Deep South*. New York: Viking Press.

Quadland, Michael C., and William D. Shattls. 1987. "AIDS, Sexuality, and Sexual Control." *Journal of Homosexuality* 14(1/2):277-298.

Quimby, Ernest, and Samuel R. Friedman. 1989. "Dynamics of Black Mobilization against AIDS in New York City." *Social Problems* 36(4):403-415.

Radcliffe-Brown, A. R. 1952. *Structure and Function in Primitive Society*. London: Cohen & West.

Rainwater, Lee. 1970. *Behind Ghetto Walls: Black Families in a Federal Slum*. Chicago: Aldine.

Rainwater, Lee, and William L. Yancey. 1967. *The Moynihan Report and the Politics of Controversy*. Cambridge: MIT Press.

Rampersad, Arnold. 1988. *The Life of Langston Hughes*. 2. vols. New York: Oxford University Press.

Read, Kenneth E. 1980. *Other Voices: The Style of a Male Homosexual Tavern*. Novato, Calif.: Chandler and Sharp.

Reiss, Albert J. 1961. "The Social Integration of Queers and Peers." *Social Problems* 9:102-119.

Richardson, Diane. 1984. "The Dilemma of Essentiality in Homosexual Theory." *Journal of Homosexuality* 9(2/3):79-90.

Rodgers, Bruce. 1972. *The Queens Vernacular: A Gay Lexicon*. San Francisco: Straight Arrow Books.

Rofes, Eric E., ed. 1986. *Gay Life: Leisure, Love, Living for the Contemporary Gay Male*. Garden City, N.Y.: Doubleday.

Rogers, Martha, and Walter Williams. 1987. "AIDS in Blacks and Hispanics: Implications for Prevention." *Issues in Science and Technology* 3:89-94.

Ross, Michael W. 1978. "The Relationship of Perceived Societal Hostility, Conformity, and Psychological Adjustment in Homosexual Males." *Journal of Homosexuality* 4:157-168.

Rowse, A. L. 1977. *Homosexuals in History: A Study of Ambivalence in Society, Literature and the Arts*. London: Dorset Press.

Ruitenbeek, Hendrik M., ed. 1963. *The Problem of Homosexuality*. New York: Dutton.

Sabatier, René. 1988. *Blaming Others: Prejudice, Race and Worldwide AIDS*. Washington, D.C.: Panos Institute.

Salholz, Eloise, et al. 1989. "Stonewall." *Newsweek*, July 3:56-57.

Sandoval, Mercedes C. 1977. "Patterns of Drug Abuse Among the Spanish-speaking Gay Bar Crowd." In *Drugs, Rituals and Altered States of Consciousness*, ed. Brian M. Du Toit, pp. 169-187. Rotterdam: A. A. Balkema.

San Francisco Department of Public Health. 1990. "Study: Gay Men Relapsing into Unsafe Sex." *Au Courant* 8(20):12.

Sanjek, Roger. 1978. "A Network Method and Its Uses in Urban Ethnography." *Human Organization* 37(3):257-268.

Schiffman, Jack. 1984. *Harlem Heyday: A Pictorial History of Modern Black Show Business and the Apollo Theatre*. Buffalo, N.Y.: Prometheus Books.

Schinke, Steven P., Gary W. Holden, and Michael S. Moncher. 1989. "Preventing HIV Infection Among Black and Hispanic Adolescents." *Journal of Social Work and Human Sexuality* 8(1):63-73.

Schmidt, Casper G. 1984. "The Group Fantasy Origins of AIDS." *Journal of Psychohistory* 12:37–78.

Schneider, David M. 1968. *American Kinship: A Cultural Account.* Englewood Cliffs, N.J.: Prentice-Hall.

Schomburg Center for Research in Black Culture. 1986. *Remaking the Past to Make the Future.* New York: New York Public Library.

Schomburg Exhibition Curatorial Committee. 1986. *The Legacy of Arthur Alfonso Schomburg: A Celebration of the Past, A Vision for the Future.* New York: Schomburg Center for Research in Black Culture.

Schreiner, J. 1986. *Measuring the Gay and Lesbian Population.* Chicago: National Orgainization of Gay and Lesbian Scientists and Technical Professionals.

Schulz, David A. 1969. *Coming Up Black: Patterns of Ghetto Socialization.* Englewood Cliffs, N.J.: Prentice-Hall.

Schuman, Howard, Charlotte Steeh, and Lawrence Bobo. 1985. *Racial Attitudes in America: Trends and Interpretations.* Cambridge: Harvard University Press.

Selik, R. M., K. G. Castro, and M. Pappaioanou. 1988. "Racial/Ethnic Differences in the Risk of AIDS in the United States." *American Journal of Public Health* 78:1539–1545.

Senak, Mark S. 1987. "The Lesbian and Gay Community." In *AIDS and the Law: A Guide for the Public,* ed. Harlon L. Dalton, Scott Burris, and the Yale AIDS Law Project, pp. 290–300. New Haven: Yale University Press.

Sharp, Paul M. 1988. "Understanding the Origins of AIDS Viruses." *Nature* 336:315.

Shilts, Randy. 1987. *And the Band Played On: Politics, People, and the AIDS Epidemic.* New York: St. Martin's Press.

———. 1988. "This Is Never Going to be a Middle-Class Heterosexual Disease." *Village Voice,* February 23:21, 23.

Shively, Michael G., Christopher Jones, and John P. De Cecco. 1985. "Research on Sexual Orientation: Definitions and Methods." In *Origins of Sexuality and Homosexuality.* ed. John P. De Cecco and Michael G. Shively, pp. 127–136. New York: Harrington Park Press.

Siegel, Karolynn, Laurie J. Bauman, Grace H. Christ, and Susan Krown. 1988. "Patterns of Change in Sexual Behavior Among Gay Men in New York City." *Archives of Sexual Behavior* 17(6):481–497.

Singer, Merrill, Cándida Flores, Lani Davison, Georgine Burke, Zaida Castillo, Kelley Scanlon, and Migdalia Rivera. 1990. "SIDA: The Economic, Social, and Cultural Context of AIDS among Latinos." *Medical Anthropology Quarterly* 4(1):72–114.

Smith, Michael J. 1983. *Black Men, White Men: A Gay Anthology.* San Francisco: Gay Sunshine Press.

Smitherman, Geneva. 1977. *Talkin' and Testifyin': The Language of Black America.* Boston: Houghton Mifflin.

Soares, John V. 1979. "Black and Gay." In *Gay Men: The Sociology of Male Homosexuality,* ed. Martin P. Levine, pp. 263–274. New York: Harper & Row.

Socarides, Charles W. 1968. *The Overt Homosexual.* New York: Grune and Stratton.

Sontag, Susan. 1979. *Illness as Metaphor.* New York: Vintage Books.

———. 1989. *AIDS and Its Metaphors.* New York: Farrar, Straus and Giroux.

Spears, Arthur. 1982. "The Black English Semi-Auxiliary *Come.*" *Language* 58:850–872.

Spradley, James P., and Brenda J. Mann. 1975. *The Cocktail Waitress: Woman's Work in a Man's World.* New York: John Wiley.

Stack, Carol B. 1974. *All Our Kin: Strategies for Survival in a Black Community.* New York: Harper & Row.

Stall, Ron, Suzanne Heurtin-Roberts, et al. 1990. "Sexual Risk for HIV Transmission among Singles' Bar Patrons in San Francisco." *Medical Anthropology Quarterly* 4(1):115–128.

Staples, Robert, ed. 1971. *The Black Family: Essays and Studies.* Belmont, Calif.: Wadsworth.

Stone, Michael. 1987. "Q and A on AIDS." *New York,* March 23:34–43.

Strathern, Marilyn, ed. 1987. *Dealing with Inequality: Analysing Gender Relations in Melanesia and Beyond.* Cambridge: Cambridge University Press.

Sullivan, Mercer L. 1989. *"Getting Paid": Youth, Crime and Work in the Inner City.* Ithaca, N.Y.: Cornell University Press.

Sullivan, Ronald. 1986. "City Data Show Reports of AIDS Leveling Off." *New York Times,* March 21:B1.

Susser, Ida. 1982. *Norman Street: Poverty and Politics in an Urban Neighborhood.* New York: Oxford University Press.

———. 1985. "Union Carbide and the Community Surrounding It: The Case of a Community in Puerto Rico." *International Journal of Health Services* 15:561–583.

Sutcliffe, D. 1982. *British Black English.* Oxford: Basil Blackwell.

Suttles, Gerald D. 1968. *The Social Order of the Slum: Ethnicity and Territory in the Inner City.* Chicago: University of Chicago Press.

Sutton, Edmund C. 1986. "A Guide to Urban Living." In *Gay Life: Leisure, Love, Living for the Contemporary Gay Male,* ed. Eric E. Rofes, pp. 75–86. Garden City, N.Y.: Doubleday.

Symonds, John Addington. 1901. *A Problem in Greek Ethics: Being an Inquiry into the Phenomenon of Sexual Inversion.* London: Spottiswoode.

Szasz, Thomas S. 1972. "The Product Conversion: From Heresy to Illness." In *The Homosexual Dialectic,* ed. Joseph A. McCaffrey, pp. 101–120. Englewood Cliffs, N.J.: Prentice-Hall.

Tauer, Carol A. 1989. "AIDS: Human Rights and Public Health." In *The AIDS Pandemic: A Global Emergency,* ed. Ralph Bolton, pp. 85–100. New York: Gordon and Breach.

Taylor, Clark L. 1978. *"El ambiente:* Male Homosexual Social Life in Mexico City." Ph.D. disseration, Anthropology Department, University of California, Berkeley.

Terry, Don. 1990. "In Harlem, Death Is an Old and Busy Neighor." *New York Times,* May 6:A1, 36.

Thomas, Anthony. 1989. "The House the Kids Built: The Gay Black Imprint on American Dance Music." *Outlook* 2 (1):24–33.

Thompson, Mark. 1987. *Gay Spirit: Myth and Meaning*. New York: St. Martin's Press.

Troiden, Richard R. 1979. "Becoming Homosexual: A Model for Gay Identity Acquisition." *Psychiatry* 42:362–373.

Turner, Charles F., Heather G. Miller, and Lincoln E. Moses, eds. 1989. *AIDS: Sexual Behavior and Intravenous Drug Use*. Washington, D.C.: National Academy Press.

Valentine, Bettylou. 1978. *Hustling and Other Hard Work: Life Styles in the Ghetto*. New York: Free Press.

Valentine, Charles A. 1968. *Culture and Poverty: Critique and Counter-Proposals*. Chicago: University of Chicago Press.

Vance, Carole S. 1989. "Social Construction Theory: Problems in the History of Sexuality." In *Homosexuality, Which Homosexuality?* ed. Dennis Altman, pp. 12–34. London: GMP Publishers.

Varenne, Hervé, ed. 1986. *Symbolizing America*. Lincoln: University of Nebraska Press.

Voelcker, John. 1990. "The Second Epidemic." *Outweek* 54:48–57.

Walls, Jeannette. 1990. "Word Up." *New York*, November 26:28.

Warren, Carol A. B. 1974. *Identity and Community in the Gay World*. New York: John Wiley.

Weeks, Jeffrey. 1977. *Coming Out: Homosexual Politics in Britain, from the Nineteenth Century to the Present*. London: Quartet Press.

———. 1985. *Sexuality and Its Discontents: Meanings, Myths and Modern Sexualities*. London: Routledge & Kegan Paul.

———. 1986. *Sexuality*. New York: Tavistock Publications.

Weinberg, Martin S., and Colin J. Williams. 1974. *Male Homosexuals: Their Problems and Adaptations*. New York: Oxford University Press.

Weinberg, Thomas S. 1983. *Gay Men, Gay Selves: The Social Construction of Homosexual Identities*. New York: Irvington Publishers.

Weltge, Ralph W., ed. 1969. *The Same Sex: An Appraisal of Homosexuality*. Philadelphia: Pilgrim Press.

Wepman, Dennis, Ronald B. Newman, and Murray B. Binderman. 1976. *The Life: The Lore and Folk Poetry of the Black Hustler*. Philadelphia: University of Pennsylvania Press.

Weston, Kath. 1991. *Families We Choose: Lesbians, Gays, Kinship*. New York: Columbia University Press.

Westwood, Gordon. 1953. *Society and the Homosexual*. New York: E. P. Dutton.

White, Marilyn M. 1987. "We Are Family! Kinship and Solidarity in the Black Community." In *Expressively Black: The Cultural Basis of Ethnic Identity*, ed. Geneva Gay and Willie L. Baber, pp. 17–34. New York: Praeger.

Wilkerson, Isabel. 1988. " 'Separate and Unequal': A View from the Bottom." *New York Times*, March 1:A12.

Wilkinson, Doris Y., and Ronald L. Taylor, eds. 1977. *The Black Male in*

*America: Perspectives on His Status in Contemporary Society.* Chicago: Nelson-Hall.

Williams, Leon, and June Hopps. 1988. "Acquired Immunodeficiency Syndrome and Minorities: Policy Perspective." *Journal of Social Work and Human Sexuality* 6(2):37–53.

Williams, Melvin D. 1974. *Community in a Black Pentecostal Church: An Anthropological Study.* Prospect Heights, Ill.: Waveland Press.

———. 1981. *On The Street Where I Lived.* New York: Holt, Rinehart and Winston.

Wilson, William Julius. 1980. *The Declining Significance of Race: Blacks and Changing American Institutions.* Chicago: University of Chicago Press.

Witomski, T. R. 1986. "Gay Bars, Gay Identities." In *Gay Life: Leisure, Love, Living for the Contemporary Gay Male,* ed. Eric E. Rofes, pp. 201–209. Garden City, N.Y.: Doubleday.

Wolf, Deborah Goleman. 1980. *The Lesbian Community.* Berkeley, Los Angeles, and London: University of California Press.

Woff, Charlotte. 1977. *Bisexuality: A Study.* New York: Quartet Books.

Wright, Jerome. 1988. "AIDS: Relationships and Attitudes." Paper delivered at the 87th Annual Meetings of the American Anthropological Association, Phoenix, November 19.

Wright, Richard. 1966a. *Native Son.* New York: Harper & Row.

———. 1966b. *Black Boy.* New York: Harper & Row.

Young, M., and P. Willmott. 1957. *Family and Kinship in East London.* London: Routledge and Kegan Paul.

Young, Virginia Heyer. 1970. "Family and Childhood in a Southern Negro Community." *American Anthropologist* 72:269–288.

Zehner, Matra A., and Joyce Lewis. 1983/84. "Homosexuality and Alcoholism: Social and Developmental Perspectives." *Journal of Social Work and Human Sexuality* 2(2/3):75–89.

Ziebold, Thomas O., and John E. Mongeon. 1982. "Alcoholism and Homosexuality." *Journal of Homosexuality* 7(4):3–8.

Zuckerman, Laurence. 1988. "Open Season on Gays." *Time,* March 7:24.

# Index

239